The Penobscot Dance of Resistance

Revisiting New England: The New Regionalism

SERIES EDITORS

Lisa MacFarlane   *University of New Hampshire*

Dona Brown   *University of Vermont*

Stephen Nissenbaum   *University of Massachusetts at Amherst*

David H. Watters   *University of New Hampshire*

This series presents fresh discussions of the distinctiveness of New England culture. The editors seek manuscripts examining the history of New England regionalism; the way its culture came to represent American national culture as a whole; the interaction between that "official" New England culture and the people who lived in the region; and local, subregional, or even biographical subjects as microcosms that explicitly open up and consider larger issues. The series welcomes new theoretical and historical perspectives and is designed to cross disciplinary boundaries and appeal to a wide audience.

Richard Archer, *Fissures in the Rock: New England in the Seventeenth Century*

Nancy L. Gallagher, *Breeding Better Vermonters: The Eugenics Project in Vermont*

Sidney V. James, *The Colonial Metamorphoses in Rhode Island: A Study of Institutions in Change*

Diana Muir, *Reflections in Bullough's Pond: Economy and Ecosystem in New England*

James C. O'Connell, *Becoming Cape Cod: Creating a Seaside Resort*

Christopher J. Lenney, *Sightseeking: Clues to the Landscape History of New England*

Priscilla Paton, *Abandoned New England: Landscape in the Works of Homer, Frost, Hopper, Wyeth, and Bishop*

Adam Sweeting, *Beneath the Second Sun: A Cultural History of Indian Summer*

Mark J. Sammons and Valerie Cunningham, *Black Portsmouth: Three Centuries of African-American Heritage*

Pauleena MacDougall, *The Penobscot Dance of Resistance: Tradition in the History of a People*

THE PENOBSCOT DANCE OF RESISTANCE

Tradition in the History of a People

Pauleena MacDougall

University of New Hampshire Press
Durham, New Hampshire

Published by University Press of New England
Hanover and London

University of New Hampshire Press
Published by University Press of New England,
One Court Street, Lebanon, NH 03766
www.upne.com
© 2004 by Pauleena MacDougall
Printed in the United States of America
5 4 3 2 1

All rights reserved. No part of this book may be reproduced in any form or by any electronic or mechanical means, including storage and retrieval systems, without permission in writing from the publisher, except by a reviewer, who may quote brief passages in a review. Members of educational institutions and organizations wishing to photocopy any of the work for classroom use, or authors and publishers who would like to obtain permission for any of the material in the work, should contact Permissions, University Press of New England, One Court Street, Lebanon, NH 03766.

Library of Congress Cataloging-in-Publication Data

MacDougall, Pauleena.
The Penobscot dance of resistance : tradition in the history of a people /
Pauleena MacDougall.
p. cm.—(Revisiting New England)
Includes bibliographical references and index.
ISBN 1-58465-381-7 (pbk. : alk. paper)
1. Penobscot Indians—History. 2. Penobscot Indians—Government relations.
3. Penobscot Indians—Social life and customs. I. Title. II. Series.
E99.P5M16 2004
974.004'9734—dc22   2004002178

Contents

List of Illustrations   vii
Acknowledgments   ix

Prologue   1

1. Dancing into View: Post–World War II Political Activism   16
2. Land, Power, and Reverence: Core Teachings That Sustain Resistance   36
3. Facing the Future: The Seventeenth Century   54
4. War Dance: Shifting Strategies in the Dance of Resistance   68
5. Liberties and Lands: Disappointment in the Promise of the New Nation   93
6. Dancing in Place: Retaining a Land Base   107
7. Bible, Primer, Hoe, and Plow: Resistance Through Religion, Education, and Subsistence   125
8. Spirit of a Nation: Retaining Political Sovereignty   150
9. Paddling Song: Traditional Skills as a Tool of Resistance   165
10. Birches and Baskets: Commodification of Culture and Economic Resistance   183

Epilogue: The Role of Tradition in the Story of a People   196

Notes   203
Bibliography   233
Index   245

Illustrations

Figures

1. Single-lane bridge across Penobscot River from Old Town to Indian Island   20
2. Selling Arms to the Indians   44
3. The chapel of Jesuit priest Sebastian Rasles at Norridgewock   61
4. Fort Shirley and Court House, 1761   86
5. Chief Joseph Orono's gunpowder flask   95
6. View of Penobscot Indian village. Sawdust trail across the frozen Penobscot River   121
7. Indian Island Church and Convent   131
8. Indian Landing and Indian Island in the log drive era   157
9. Athion Lewey, Indian guide, Grand Lake, Maine   177
10. Chief Blue Jay Warburban in front of Penobscot Indian workshop and store   189

Maps

1. Approximate location of Indian nations in Maine circa 1600   17
2. Maine in the eighteenth century, places mentioned in the text   76
3. Lands taken by the English, Massachusetts and Maine 1763–1818   108
4. Post-land claims Penobscot Indian Nation land holdings   200

Acknowledgments

First I would like to express my appreciation to the Penobscot people who offered me hospitality and provided me with work and an income from 1979 to 1988. I would especially like to honor some of the elders who taught me about Penobscot culture, including Madeline Tomer Shay, Theodore Mitchell, Fred Nicolar, and Roy Dana. There have been many in the younger generations who have helped me as well, including James Sappier, Timothy Love, Carol Dana, Paul Francis, Jr., Andrew Akins, Michael Sockalexis, and others too numerous to mention.

Second, I would like to thank some of my colleagues who have read and critiqued my work, including David C. Smith, Edward D. "Sandy" Ives, Marli Weiner, Colin Calloway, and Barry O'Connell. In addition, I have received suggestions and editorial comments from Pamela Dean and Elizabeth Hedler. David Sanger read one chapter and made helpful comments, as well.

To the American Philosophical Society, thank you for your support for my research through the Phillips Fund.

To the archivists, especially at the Maine State Archives in Augusta, the Maine Center for History in Portland, and the special collections librarians at the Raymond F. Fogler Library at the University of Maine in Orono, thank you for your very professional and considerate assistance.

I am especially indebted to my oldest and dearest friend, Heather H. Harris, for her support and professional editing skills, and to my family, especially my mother, son, and daughter, for their unfailing love and devotion.

The Penobscot Dance of Resistance

PROLOGUE

> It is obviously important that everyone learn as much as possible about American Indian *realities*, rather than the self-serving junk they usually teach in school.
> —WINONA LADUKE

Winona LaDuke's statement brings into focus a central problem for historians. How does one learn about American Indian realities? How can one understand the experiences of Native Americans in the present, and how can we best learn about their experiences in the past? Most of what we hear about Native realities in media reports reveals continual poverty, illness, and social problems. Yet Native Americans today are stronger, healthier, better educated, and more politically savvy than they have been in the last one hundred years or so. The 2000 Census reveals 2,416,410 people who identify themselves as Native Americans. While less than 1 percent of the total United States population, Native people showed a growth rate between 1990 and 2000 of 110 percent. These nearly 2.5 million people have a land base of about 39 million acres tribally held and 10 million acres individually held. Add to this 40 million acres received in land settlements, and you have about 90 million or so acres of land, about *3 percent* of Native American original holdings.[1]

Birthrates are up for Native Americans, in many cases higher than white and black birthrates, and most reservations have better health care than they did at the beginning of the twentieth century. Current efforts of tribal leaders foster better nutrition, support traditional religious practices (even for those who worship in other ways), and discourage the use of alcohol.[2]

Native Americans often take a political role in environmental protection, especially of sacred lands and of water. They hold to their traditional rights to water, fish, and other resources. They are actively involved in conserving culture—supporting arts, skills, folkways, dances, songs, and other living traditions. Spiritual beliefs are especially important; the repatriation of disturbed human remains is a primary issue.

However, the picture is not all positive. Those living on reservations continue to struggle with unemployment (the national average for Native Americans is 48 percent), education (26 percent still have less than an eighth-grade education), and poverty (41 percent live below the poverty level). Off-reservation Natives fare better but not greatly: Their national unemployment average is 39 percent, and the national average for off-reservation Natives living below the poverty level is 27.5 percent. The average life expectancy for all Native Americans is up considerably since 1940, when it was fifty-one for males and fifty-two for females. Now, men can expect to live sixty-seven years and women seventy-one. However, Natives' life expectancy still lags behind that of whites. Deaths from tuberculosis, auto accidents, alcohol, homicide, and suicide have all fallen dramatically in the last thirty years.[3] Twentieth-century efforts by tribal leaders to reclaim land and improve the lives of Native Americans have paid off, but the going is painfully slow. Native realities continue to include oppression and racism, poverty, serious illnesses, failed educational efforts, and fewer opportunities for economic improvement.

While Native Americans share the problems of racism, poverty, and lack of opportunity with other ethnic and racial minorities, in some fundamental ways their reality is different. Native Americans have national identities rooted in both place and tradition. The sense Natives have of themselves is of belonging to a particular Indian nation. They consider their communities to be nations for two reasons: They hold the "right of inherent sovereignty" because they have possessed their territory since time immemorial, and they have entered into treaty agreements with the United States—and treaties can be entered into only by nations.[4]

These treaty agreements are the central focus of Native peoples' political strength in the United States today. Treaties have become weapons used to resist "changing contours of hegemony," especially assimilation and termination[5] in the political economy of the United States. Historically, assimilation and termination have represented alterative hegemonic political solutions to the "Indian problem."

The "Indian problem" will never go away. Contrary to nineteenth- and early-twentieth-century predictions, Native Americans have not become extinct like the passenger pigeon and the great auk. The reasons Native people survive are complex and are not due solely to their own efforts, or to those of any single agent or group. Survival of Native American cultures results from a complex interaction between political, economic, and social forces in which historians and anthropologists have played a significant role.

At the turn of the century, American anthropologist Franz Boas and his students set out to preserve the cultures of the rapidly disappearing Native people of the United States. They began their work at the nadir of Native American existence. War, disease, and economic depression had reduced the population of Native Americans to a low of fewer than 250,000 in 1890. Turn-of-the-century anthropologists collected languages, mythology, religious practices, and other aspects of culture without regard to history. As anthropologist Marshall Sahlins so clearly points out, the idea of culture in the anthropological sense "emerged ... as an expression of that comparative backwardness, or of its nationalist demands, as against the hegemonic ambitions of Western Europe. ... At the same time, the term articulated a certain resistance to economic and political developments that threatened the people's past as well as their future."[6] That is, anthropologists defined culture as frozen and unchanging, therefore invalidating anything that did not fit the construct.

This notion of culture created a sense of unchanging boundedness and totality, a separate reality for Native Americans living on reservations. Anthropologists have described these enclaves of culture as if they were apart from the social, political, economic, and historical events experienced by the surrounding "greater" community. Eric Wolf aptly argues for a reapprehension of these "cultural billiard balls" as part of the "ongoing interactions of populations living in shifting political economies."[7]

Historians joined the dance as a result of political processes designed to solve the "Indian problem." In 1946 Congress established the United States Indian Claims Commission. The legislation required tribes to prove their cultural reality in order to be recognized by the federal government as a political entity and to claim territory. Anthropologists and historians took part on both sides of claims issues. The result of scholarly involvement included innovations in both disciplines. For example, Erminie Wheeler Voegelin established the Interdisciplinary Research Center, which created the Ohio Valley Great Lakes Ethnohistory Project archives. In 1951 the Newberry Library hosted the first Conference on Indian Affairs, at which time anthropologists and historians came together to collaborate on Indian research. Humanist and social science traditions merged as the group met with a goal "to illuminate not merely the Indian in terms of white society or the Indian in terms of his own society, but each in his own terms and in terms of the other."[8]

Ethnohistory emerged within anthropology as a discipline concerned with Indian-white relations in the colonial period in America. Societies focused on specific groups also formed about this time, such as the first Conference on Algonquian Studies, which has met annually ever since 1968. The marriage of two disciplines allowed both to grow beyond nineteenth-century tales of defeat and descriptions of racial inferiority. As Francis Jennings points out, "for historians who think in terms of culture, the contact between two societies with different cultures becomes something different from a war of conquest or annihilation. Conflict often does occur, but so do varieties of cooperation and accommodation."[9] William Roseberry also articulates the contemporary vision of placing culture in time, of unveiling the constant interplay between experience and meaning shaped by inequality and domination.[10]

The shift in ethnohistory scholarship began as students of Indian-white relations began to perceive the Indian as an actor in history. As Indians read these works, they fueled the growing Indian militancy of the 1960s and 1970s. "Culture" became a tool of resistance, and indigenous peoples successfully manipulated white guilt for wrongdoings of past centuries to gain political and economic power. Anthropologists and historians have assisted the struggle, but at a cost.

As Natives gained political visibility, radicals, or traditionalists as they call themselves, favored a separation from all and everything not Indian. Traditionalists grew their hair long. They wore Indian jewelry and began to construct a pan-Indian culture based on prehistoric spiritual traditions or borrowed traditions from other Indians. Academics assisted their struggles by defending the preservation of Native languages and the "cultural integrity" of Native cultures, endowing them with the "highest cultural values of Western societies, such as ecological wisdom."[11]

But not all Native Americans wanted a return to traditional lifeways. Internal struggles between the minority traditionalist and majority accommodationists have resulted in a great deal of change on reservations. Educated Indians negotiated financial settlements (rejected by traditionalists as a "sellout") for lands lost in violation of treaties, wrote grants, and obtained needed funding for better health care, housing, and services to the elderly. They often hired anthropologists and historians to assist their struggle with documentary research.

At the same time, some Natives became anthropologists and historians themselves. One especially significant contributor to Native studies theory was Vine Deloria, Jr., a Sioux Indian historian. In 1969, Deloria published *Custer Died for Your Sins: An Indian Manifesto*. Throughout the book, he scathingly critiqued anthropologists as self-serving intellectuals who had little concern for or interest in the needs of the people they studied, but often were called upon to speak for them.[12] Native people naturally resented this loss of control, particularly when anthropologists were represented as specialists in Native cultures rather than as students of Native cultural specialists.

Anthropologists took Deloria's critique seriously and developed guidelines for working with American Indians.[13] Some decided to stop working with Indians, but those who remained became much more critically self-conscious regarding their position in the dominant and oppressive colonial culture. Meanwhile, Native people continue to request scholarly work that orients itself toward indigenous issues rather than elite, hegemonic, national intellectual issues.[14]

Although trained in law, not in history, Deloria continues to be a force in American historiography, and his many writings, championing the cause of Indian sovereignty while upbraiding non-Indians for their roles in cultural imperialism, must be considered—especially by someone like myself, a non-Native writing about Native history.[15] Anyone who chooses to work professionally on topics relating to American Indian communities must be prepared for a political climate that includes at worst a deep antagonism toward non-Indians and at best a skepticism and mistrust of non-Indian scholarship. In addition, one will encounter numerous misunderstandings and misinterpretations of anthropology and history and the purpose of doing scholarly work.

Deloria's description of anthropology is itself outdated. Anthropologists and historians do not follow the old racist theory of cultural evolution that developed in the nineteenth century. Unfortunately, the literature of that time (and much of the twentieth century to about 1950) stands as a witness to earlier racist theories and continues to offend. In spite of its checkered past, however, it is to this same literature that many tribes go to locate information on indigenous traditions, tribe-to-government relations, Indian policy, relocation, termination, and many other things.[16] So in spite of Deloria's critique of scholarly research, this same research often is and continues to be of tremendous benefit to Native American communities. There is a relationship of mutual reward in Native American scholarship.

There are two issues raised by Deloria in his 1989 discussion of non-Native scholarship that I disagree with. First, he is wrong when he declares that scholars believe that tribal people represent an earlier stage of human accomplishment. No scholar worth her salt believes that. Second, he calls for anthropologists to study Anglo-Saxon prehistory. Certainly in the United States many anthropologists study Native American prehistory, history, and culture, but they also study the cultures and histories of Europe, Africa, Asia, and elsewhere. Furthermore, anthropologists and other scholars do not report back to their society about "quaint and romantic others."[17] Our goal is to understand all human behavior, and we recognize better than many nonscholars the similarity as well as the diversity of human cultures. Deloria does concede, however, in this same paper, "It seems to me that after two decades of reasonably constructive reforms in the relationship between anthropologists and Indians . . . we have an opportunity to leave the colonial mentality behind us and bring the accumulated knowledge and insights of anthropology to bear on the larger arena of human activities. And we have the responsibility to do so."[18]

Other Native scholars have written about Native communities' concerns with anthropology and history. Devon Mihesuah, an Oklahoma Choctaw, asserts, "A complete assessment of a tribe's history should take years of research in libraries and archives and communication with the tribal people in question."[19] She also emphasizes the importance of using oral histories as a way of gaining insight into American Indian experience of history. She suggests that all scholars strive for accuracy by scrutinizing available written data, incorporating the interpretation of participants and descendants, and holding their pro- or anti-Indian biases in check. A good scholar would follow her advice regarding the scrutinizing of documents, although it is true that not all see the value of oral history. I do not regard the present volume as a complete assessment of tribal history; it is only a beginning. I expect many more histories will be written, some of them by Native scholars. However, I have spent more than twenty years studying the documents, both primary and secondary, and talking with members of the community. I believe that the experiences that Penobscots have related to me, though taking place in the twentieth century, do help me understand the historical experiences of their people, and I value the contributions of oral history to our understanding of the written record.

The Penobscots have initiated research guidelines recently, as have many other tribes, but they do not wish to eradicate research on their history and culture. They do wish to ensure that such scholarship includes Penobscot voices and connects the past to the present. In the present volume, I have included Penobscot voices wherever I could find them, both in historical documents (such as petitions of the tribe to the government, letters written by individuals, and speeches recorded by non-Natives) and in interviews I conducted with several Penobscots about their experience of major historical events. At the same time, I have not sought personal, sensitive, or sacred information. The latter is especially offensive to Indians; as Native historian Donald Fixico writes, scholars should "avoid publication of sensitive Indian knowledge (especially ceremonials)." He also suggests that historians examine what it is they are writing and how one defines American Indian history. He continues, "The most important ethical concern is for American Indian history to be included in the scope of American experience."[20] It is my primary goal to make a contribution to that process. By examining the documents and experiences of Penobscots in relation to the dominant culture, I intend to illustrate how one American Indian tribe experienced and shaped American history in its region. I have done this with a sense of respect, have spent a great amount of time thinking about what Penobscots have told me, and have focused on how and why Penobscots participated in the American experience. There are a number of key points that Fixico makes in his article with which I agree. One is that a historian has the responsibility to understand the reality a tribe constructed throughout its history, including both physical and metaphysical experiences. Another is that Indians have been proactive in respect to historical events. The documentary record bears that out.

Also, I think it is important to emphasize a couple of key points made by Chippewa sociologist Duane Champagne. First, one should not exclude American Indian culture and history from the rest of human history and culture. Second, American Indians are part of the broad history of all humanity, and one does not have to be a member of a culture to interpret culture in a meaningful way.[21] Anthropologists have also written about this concept, especially the problem of academics' being pressured by Indian politics.

What is the cost to the disciplines when academics are pressured by modern Indian politics? Clearly, access to information is affected. Understandably, Natives want to control their own lives, but one unfortunate result of increasing sovereignty on reservations is the belief that information should be kept from non-Native people, and that only Native writers can write about Native history and culture. But this idea overlooks the fact that every historian deals with people she does not know—whether they are of a culture of the past or a contemporary culture. As Robin Fox argues, "I want to suggest that one cannot do good history, not even contemporary history, without regard for ideas, actions, and ontologies that are not and never were our own. Different cultures, different rationalities."[22]

A second problem for scholars is the misuse of information for political aims. James Axtell warns that scholars must take care not to bow to political pressures; they must preserve a self-conscious objectivity. "We can safely ignore any answers proffered by people or parties who have not mastered the documentary record."[23] I would say, in addition, that we must be careful not to give overmuch weight to the documentary record alone. Can we filter out all the ethnocentric bias of the observer? How well can we evaluate the materials fed to ethnographers by community consultants? I agree with Axtell that "evaluation is intrinsic to the historical process, not an option, because the moral connotations of the everyday words we use are part of their descriptive meaning. We hold not guilt, but responsibility and moral initiative"[24] to discover the truth about the past to the best of our ability. And I ally myself with Sahlins in guarding against "pseudo-politics of anthropological interpretation."[25] But it is not just documents that are the ingredients of historical work. It is also tradition, oral history, actions, and events in history. All Americans are a part of the Native American reality because of their participation in the political and economic workings in the world. "We have been involved with . . . Indians at every stage of our history and in every corner of the land."[26]

Although most Native Americans identify themselves with one or more of the many nations of Indian tribes, their sovereignty has actually been seriously eroded from the beginning of our combined history. The current struggle to retain as well as regain sovereignty is a constant battle fought by lobbyists and in the courts. Most Americans ignore the struggles; some sympathize, but few recognize this essential aspect of Native American reality.

Similarly, Americans generally see Native Americans through stereotypical lenses. As Thomas Parkhill has pointed out recently, even scholars are not exempt from viewing them in this way: "like other members of the dominant society, scholars are tangled in the web" of the "Indian" stereotype. The "generic Indian" holds timeless spiritual secrets, relates more intimately with nature, engages in collective production, shares commodities, and lives in an extended family. "Their religions are nature based; they believe in a living planet."[27]

This kind of invention, or definition, of "Indian" is oppressive to young people who define themselves as Penobscot, Shoshone, Iroquois, or Crow and whose worldview is complex and dynamic, not necessarily fitting into the stereotypical model. As Parkhill so aptly indicates, these stereotypes view "Indians" as people who have "lost their uniqueness and identity," rather than as "real people who, largely due to their own particular histories of conquest, cannot meet Americans' popular need for timeless secrets or for understanding their relationship to the earth."[28] As several Penobscots have expressed to me, "Why can't white people study their *own* traditions and learn about their *own* religions? Why do they need to copy ours?" The worst offenders are the "White Indians" and "New Agers" who appropriate sweat lodges and "Indian" ceremonies. These practices minimize and degrade the complexity of Native American lives and religious customs, making young Natives, especially, feel robbed and unappreciated.

For many years, Native people have felt invisible. They found themselves disappearing in history textbooks; they saw themselves defeated in "cowboys and Indians" movies and television series. The only good Indians were the dead ones or the friendly assimilated scouts who helped the white soldiers defeat the "wild Indians." One Wabanaki man, Jake Lolar, once remarked, "It really upset me because the Indians always lost. When I start wanting to be a cowboy there's something wrong... with the projection of who I am." And according to another, Dana Mitchell, "My struggle with my identity was to preserve that [Indian identity] because that is who I am."[29]

An examination of the history of one individual Indian nation tells a story of the complicated interaction of cultural systems overlooked by most Americans. Penobscots are real people whose lives advance along a meandering path from the past to the present. When we look closely at the history of the Penobscots, we find not just a people who lose and become invisible; rather, we find a people who, gradually adapting to changing circumstances, win at last both lands and visibility.

Few other Native nations in the eastern United States have longer histories of relations with Franco- and Anglo-Americans while maintaining some portion of their original land base. Although the Penobscots lost most of their territory by the nineteenth century, they tenaciously clung to their 146 islands in the Penobscot River. Late in the twentieth century, in the Maine Indian Land Claims settlement of 1980, they and their neighbors, the Passamaquoddies and Maliseets, at last obtained compensation for lands lost to Maine illegally.

After suing the Maine state government and negotiating an out-of-court settlement, the Penobscots greatly enhanced their economic condition. They currently pursue industries—building, for example, Olamon Industry, a company that manufactures cassette tapes on Indian Island and employs Penobscot workers. Penobscots manage their timberlands and wildlife, and employ a geologist to pursue mineral resources. They also continue to provide health services, K–8 education, and social services to the poor and elderly.

Among the Penobscots, interest in clean water is keen, as witnessed by a recent newspaper article on the topic. "Tribe Tests of Water Led to Fine," reads the front-page headline in the *Bangor Daily News* of July 24, 2000. Water-quality monitors hired by the Penobscot Nation to test the Penobscot River and its tributaries collected evidence that led to an $800,000 fine of Champion International Paper Company for falsifying records and not conducting water tests for up to eight years. The Bureau of Indian Affairs and the Environmental Protection Agency fund water-quality testing for the Penobscots.[30] The Penobscots have thus become key players in the state in protecting the environment, especially the Penobscot River, which has historically acquired chemicals through dumping from lumber, textile, and paper mills that have damaged the fish stocks and water quality upon which the Penobscots depend.

Penobscots insist upon sovereignty over their lands and their people and aboriginal rights to fishing, hunting, water, and other resources. Maine does not always agree, and often lengthy and contentious negotiations settle specific matters regarding fishing rights and other sovereignty issues. The state continues to insist that the Penobscots follow state laws, while the Penobscots insist that they are federally recognized and thus sovereign over their own territory. In fact, their sovereignty is limited by the state's rejection of the very concept of Native sovereignty.

Penobscots have made their own history by rejecting and resisting the controls placed upon them by their colonizers. Their experience of the sixteenth, seventeenth and eighteenth centuries differed greatly from any experience of the ten thousand previous years they had lived upon the land. However, Penobscots in the nineteenth century experienced the most radical changes in lifestyle. During this period, most became literate in English, tried their hands at many new occupations, including basket making for a commercial market, pursued educational opportunities, and began to learn how to "play the game." The seeds were planted during this very difficult time for twentieth-century activism, revival, and political action.

Here dances my story. In 1976 the Penobscots held a pageant on July 30 and August 1 (a Saturday and Sunday). Because of rain, the pageant took place in the gymnasium of the new community building on the island, rather than on the riverbank behind the rectory as had been planned. Several tables laden with home-cooked food and crafts and souvenir items bordered one side of the gym. Neat rows of folding chairs provided seating for the audience. Three young women, Norma Jean Pardilla, Delores Sappier Mitchell, and Julie Sockbeson sang for the dancing; they also used a shot horn rattle to accompany the songs. A young man played the drum; he did not sing.

One man told two legends while another acted them out to drumbeat accompaniment. Then an entrance round dance began the pageant, open to all participants, as the singers began to chant:

> Ye kwa no da Kwa no da no Kwa ye
> Kwa no da Kwa no da no Kwa ye
> Nwa no da no Kwa no da no Kwa ye
> Kwa no da Kwa no da no Kwan.[31]

Dance in Penobscot culture takes place in a number of different venues. The traditional greeting dance and songs such as the one above were used to greet visitors from other tribes. During the nineteenth century, the installation of democratically elected chiefs brought neighboring tribes to take part in the ceremonies, and the greeting dance was part of that ceremony. Tribal hall dances took place in the latter part of the nineteenth and early twentieth centuries. Each of the two political parties, the Old and the New Party, had a hall until they were united in 1931. Before that time, both tribal halls were used for dancing—both modern dancing (country dancing, fox-trots, and waltzes) accompanied by a small orchestra and traditional or "Indian" dancing accompanied by drum, rattle, and song.[32]

Traditional dancing took place at this time at two specific kinds of tribal hall dances: wedding dances and the inauguration or "governor's" balls. Usually during these occasions participants danced for about one and a half hours in the traditional manner, and then the older people would go home and the younger people would continue to dance the modern dances.[33] These fox-trots and waltzes were introduced as "record hops" by teenagers during the late 1930s and 1940s in the Old Party hall.

Penobscots performed dances and songs at social gatherings on occasions such as marriages, feasts, elections, formal greetings, games, war, trading, rejoicing after the hunt, and mourning. At least during the twentieth century, in the prerevival period (before 1970), dancing had a purely secular function. Anthropologist Frank G. Speck attributed the secular function of dance and music to the influence of the Christian church. "The change from sacred to strictly social dancing and singing may have transpired without coercion on the part of the priesthood, rather by free adoption of hymns through fondness for their soft melodies. The holy songs, I believe, have usurped the function of an original spiritual repertory, leaving the social dances to survive."[34] Several hundred years have passed since the church came to reside among the Penobscots, so it is not possible to determine at the present time what religiously oriented dances (except for death songs) might once have existed. At any rate, today traditional Penobscots consider all their music and dancing sacred, except for a few dances performed in public. Most dancing and singing takes place at exclusively Penobscot or Wabanaki gatherings, powwows, and other Native American events.

Dance seems an appropriate metaphor for this book because it is central to Penobscot culture. Dancing as a metaphor appeals to me personally, too, perhaps because of my own love for the art. My own experience of dance began as a very young child, witnessing the dances of my elders in Canada. These were the Scottish traditional step dances and Highland dances performed in kitchens and dance halls in the communities near my grandfather's home on Cape Breton Island, Nova Scotia. I loved the music and the dance, and my mother tells me that I used to march behind the piper, blowing with my cheeks puffed out in imitation of him, which often caused him to chuckle. Later, my mother, deciding that I was an awkward child who needed to learn some graces, enrolled me in dance classes. That began a love of dance that continues to the present day. Perhaps that is why my mind turned to dance when I searched for an appropriate metaphor for telling the story of Penobscot resistance. I thought of resistance to oppression as a type of dance. One side advances, another retreats, but just so far; then they pause, clutch one another and spin, break apart, then stop and swoop back, link hands in friendship, then break apart—one tries to catch the other but he turns once more, reversing direction. In the dance of resistance, the two lines of dancers do not know or trust one another. One side tries to control and change the other; the other sideslips out of their clutches in a cunning caper. The dance continues as time goes on and so do the dancers, "The one red leaf, the last of its clan, That dances as often as dance it can."[35]

I have danced with the Penobscots. For a brief time at a social occasion in the big community building on Indian Island, Lieutenant Governor Ann Pardilla pulled me into a snake dance and we wound round and round until the circle went so fast that people began to fall away. It was fun. I enjoyed the hospitality of the Penobscots on that occasion and many others during the time that I worked as a research assistant on the Penobscot Dictionary Project (1979–1988). During that time I came to know a few people on the island very well, those I worked with closely and the other assistants on the dictionary project. I came to know others less well, especially the members of the tribal administration. During that time, I listened a great deal and came to understand a little the depth of hurt that many felt from the racism prevalent in the local surrounding community.

Because the University of Maine is close to the Penobscot Nation, professors and students often conduct research relating to the Penobscot community. Often their papers do not make their way back to the community. Many Penobscots therefore feel invisible, or poked and prodded by anthropologists, like living relics of the Stone Age. Part of my work for the tribe included looking in historical documents for Penobscot words for the dictionary, and I began to realize how little recent history had been written about the Penobscots. I thought I might be able to make a small contribution to that history, in light of my training at the University of Maine and my familiarity with historical documents. When I left the dictionary project, I returned to the university to pursue a doctorate and wrote my dissertation on the nineteenth-century Penobscots.

The work begun in my dissertation, "Indian Island, Maine: 1780–1930," here extends back in time, placing the story of resistance in the context of history in the hope that we can learn more about the reality of the Native American experience. Native Americans live among us, and we live among them. Our history is their history, and their history is ours. Penobscots do not and have not lived an isolated existence; they have been buffeted and changed by historical events. However, I do believe that Penobscot experiences of those events differ to a great extent from the experiences of other Americans.

Significant secondary sources for this study include earlier works such as the writings of Penobscot scholar Joseph Nicolar,[36] the writings of Maine historian Fannie Hardy Eckstorm,[37] and the major ethnographic study by anthropologist Frank G. Speck.[38] Other earlier histories of Maine provided some context for the study. They include histories by Hubbard,[39] Sullivan,[40] and Williamson,[41] and more specific histories of the Catholic Church in Maine such as those of Lucey[42] and Lord.[43] More recent works that deal with related topics include the writings of Colin Calloway,[44] which focus more on the Western Abenaki of Vermont, New Hampshire, and Quebec; Kenneth Morrison's[45] study of colonial wars and alliances in Maine; Neal Salisbury's study of southern New England colonial history;[46] Steven F. Johnson's *Ninnuock*; and Frederick Wiseman's *Voice of the Dawn*.[47] The new history anthology of Maine, *Maine, the Pine Tree State*, provides additional context for much of Penobscot history, though it leaves them just after the French and Indian Wars.[48] Recent works that focus specifically on the Penobscots are rare; most notable is Bunny McBride's significant contribution of historical biographies of Penobscot women.[49]

Primary written sources are more numerous. Some are published in anthologies such as the works of Samuel de Champlain[50] and Baxter's *Documentary History of the State of Maine*,[51] but most are found in the state archives of Massachusetts and Maine, the special collections of the Raymond Fogler Library at the University of Maine, the Maine Center for History in Portland, various town historical societies, the Bangor Public Library, and numerous small libraries. The richest harvest was found among the uncatalogued papers of Maine's executive council and the legislative graveyard in the Maine State Archives in Augusta.

Unwritten sources include the invaluable testimony of Penobscot individuals in formal and informal interviews and videos.

While a number of recent books and articles have examined the land-claims case,[52] its pretext and its aftermath, what has not been recognized is the deep continuity of resistance discovered in the historical record, which I have brought forth in this book. Understanding this aspect of

Penobscot history will aid people in accepting the emergence of activism and the nature of the claims when they occurred. I hope that readers of this work will come to a greater understanding of Penobscot history and motives and that this will contribute to civil society in Maine today and in the future.

We begin the dance in the twentieth century with a description of the conditions and situation of the Penobscot Nation in recent years. The narrative then promenades back to describe the events that led to the making of today's modern Penobscot community. We will take a brief look at the events of the colonization period to set the stage for the story of the last two centuries, the nineteenth and early twentieth. During this time, Penobscots withstood the pressures to assimilate, to give up their separate identity and to meld with the dominant culture. They deftly hopped aside and trod a parallel but different path through history, sharing some elements of the dominant culture, rejecting others, and retaining those elements of traditional culture which they hold most dear.

Before beginning the narrative, I would like to offer some definitions to assist the reader in interpreting various terms. Generally, Native people refer to themselves as members of a particular village or tribal group. So, for example, most of the people who live on Indian Island near Old Town refer to themselves as Penobscots. The language they speak is also called Penobscot, although linguists often refer to it as a dialect of Eastern Abenaki. That is because formerly the language was spoken by a larger speech community that included the people who lived on the Kennebec River (Norridgwock, Caniba, Pigwacket) and in other communities in western Maine. All the people who once spoke Eastern Abenaki are often referred to as Abenaki in the historical literature. However, there are also people who speak a language known as Western Abenaki presently living at St. Francis, Quebec, who represent former residents of New Hampshire and Vermont and also refer to themselves as Abenaki. Throughout the narrative, I refer to Penobscots as people who live on the Penobscot River, and to Abenakis as related people from other communities. Other Native people represented in the text include the Passamaquoddies, Maliseets, and Micmacs. They often refer to themselves as Wabanaki, "People of the Dawn." The terms "Wabanaki" and "Abenaki" originate from the same word, meaning easterner. "Wabanaki" represents the Native pronunciation; the French used the term "Abenaki," and so that has come into the English language as well. The Passamaquoddy and Maliseet people speak the same language (although different from Penobscot); their territory ranged along the coast and the St. John River in eastern Maine and New Brunswick. The Micmacs speak a separate language; their territory includes Nova Scotia and the Gaspé

Peninsula of Quebec. Today in Maine there are one Penobscot, two Passamaquoddy, one Maliseet, and one Micmac reservations. While these are the cultural and political centers for the Native people of Maine, many of the Native people today choose to live off-reservation in Maine and elsewhere. The political border between the United States and Canada did not exist, of course, until after the American Revolution. Relationships between Native communities in Canada and in Maine were perhaps stronger before the borders were established, but some interaction continues due to kinship ties, and people continue to travel back and forth without difficulty.

Chapter 1

DANCING INTO VIEW
Post–World War II Political Activism

> Washington said, "Penobscots? Who are you guys? Where did you come from?"[1]
> —JAMES SAPPIER

The deep blue waters of the Penobscot River flow through the middle of an 8,592-square-mile watershed in the center of Maine. Numerous islands stand sentry as the currents swing around them. At one time these waters teemed with salmon, sturgeon, and other fishes. Mounds of fertile alluvium deposited over thousands of years created the islands upon which grow various colorful hardwoods: silver, rock, red, and white maples, gray oaks, yellow birches, stone-gray beeches, and majestic elms. Bald eagles soar from the tallest trees, plunging down to the water to catch fish. Spotted sandpipers caper along the denuded banks of the islands. Painted turtles warm themselves on sun-heated rocks. Occasionally a large, dark brown moose wades along the shorelines savoring the tender water plants. Long ago human life on the river depended upon the graceful glide of the birch-bark canoe in the summer, and the slower, more utilitarian snowshoes and toboggans in the snowy winter. On the islands in the Penobscot River above Bangor live the people of the same name, panawáhpskek, "at the place where the rocks widen out."

Early in the seventeenth century, the Penobscots formed a loosely organized political confederacy with neighboring riverine and coastal communities from the Saco River in western Maine to the Machias River in the east. The bands in this region spoke various dialects of the Eastern Abenaki language. West of the Saco River lived speakers of the Western Abenaki language, while the Passamaquoddy and Maliseet speakers lived east of the Machias River and beyond to the St. John. All these bands apparently lived in relative peace with one another but shared enmity against marauding Mohawks (at least in the early historic period). Today,

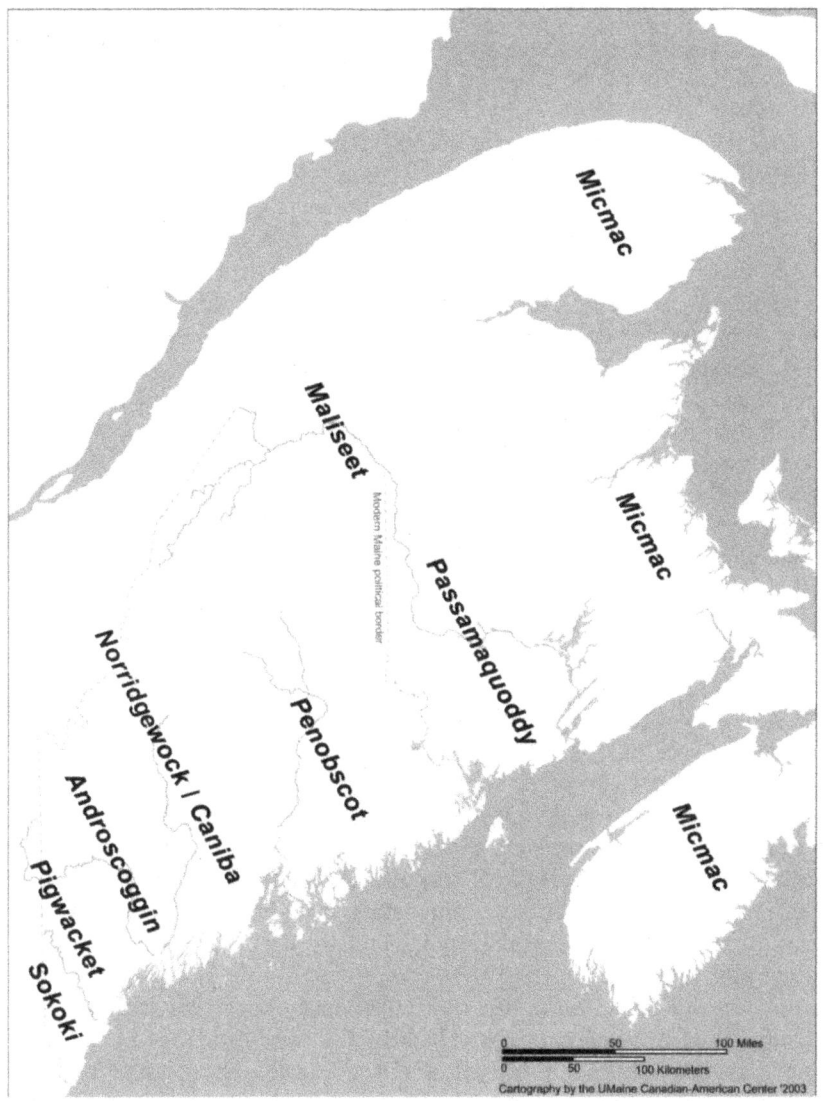

MAP 1. Approximate location of Indian nations in Maine circa 1600. *Cartography by Michael Hermann, Canadian American Center, University of Maine.*

all the other Eastern Abenaki communities are gone, lost to centuries of disease, warfare, and white settlement. The Penobscot community presently consists of the descendants of the original Penobscots together with members of the other Eastern Abenaki communities, some Passamaquoddies, Maliseets, and members of other Native American nations, and a few non-Indian spouses and children.

As Penobscot tribal leader James Sappier suggests, few Americans knew who the Penobscots were until they danced into view in the 1970s as a result of the Maine Indian Land Claims Case. The land settlement was the largest of its kind in American history. Maine Indians received $57.5 million for the purchase of land and another $27 million in trust for economic development. The Penobscots and Passamaquoddies received the great bulk of this settlement, while the much smaller band of Maliseets received $900,000 to buy land.[2] The story of how and why Penobscots emerged from near invisibility begins with the testimony of twentieth-century residents of Indian Island. James Sappier is typical of the baby boomer generation of Penobscots who obtained an education and worked off-reservation a good part of their lives. Most of their fathers were veterans of World War II or the Korean War who had returned to the reservation after serving their country only to find oppressive racism and denial of their voting rights.

Sappier graduated from Old Town High School in the 1950s, worked in shoe factories in the area, and then moved to Connecticut, where he worked for Pratt and Whitney Aircraft and later for Sikorsky Aircraft. He returned to the reservation after being laid off and became involved in tribal government. In a 1983 interview he said: "Men went to war, came back and had seen what was out there. 'Why should we live like this when we are treated half-way decent in another country?' So the out-migration started because, one, [there was] no housing on the reservation; two, no equal opportunity in employment on or near the reservation; and three, the [hostile] environment itself—the [attitudes] of local communities towards the Indians."[3] Although made full citizens by the United States Congress in 1924, Penobscots were turned away from the polls because Maine did not allow any nontaxpayers to vote. Veterans especially experienced a sense of despair, hopelessness, anger, and resentment. Many turned to self-destructive habits such as alcohol abuse.[4] However, some were determined to fight for their rights and began to lobby for change.

Early-twentieth-century conditions had been even worse. Those who lived through this "invisible time" had little hope of improvement or change. Ralph Proctor described this period of dormancy and depression on Indian Island in a report prepared for the Legislative Research Committee of the state of Maine in September 1942: "The houses are in bad repair, dirty, and no attempt has been made even to pull the three-foot weeds in the front yard. The whole impression one gets is of slackness, lack of pride or initiative."[5] Proctor's words exhibit little compassion for the deep depression and poverty experienced on Indian Island at that time. The per capita annual income was $875 on the reservation, and 42 percent of deaths were due to alcoholism.[6]

Government programs alleviated the depression to some degree. For example, Works Progress Administration workers paved roads, brought city water, electricity, a sewage system, and some sidewalks and streetlights. Of the sixty employable men living on Indian Island, half worked for the WPA, twenty-five worked in private employment in local canoe and moccasin factories for four to six months a year, and five had steady employment. However, in 1934 only nine men worked in the canoe factory for five months and three worked at the woolen mill for six months. Without the WPA, half of the men had no work, while the rest, save five, could expect only part-time employment. At the time of Proctor's report, 584 people lived on Indian Island and 64 lived off the reservation.[7]

The depressed economy sent many young men and women to war, while older men and women moved to Connecticut to work in wartime industries. The depression also stunted the market for women's baskets. As Proctor reports, "A very few baskets were on display at the stores on the reservations—only at Old Town were any evidences of this handiwork actually going on; three women were working there. Prior to this year a sizable number of Indians used to go to summer places to attempt to sell baskets."[8] Even during economically depressed times, some women continued the practice of making baskets to supplement their income. As one woman told me, while living in Connecticut she and her husband made and sold baskets to supplement factory earnings, as she put it, "to pay the electric bill."[9]

After World War II, veterans and their spouses found themselves leaving an independent life upon their return to the reservation, where they were considered wards of the state. Indian concerns fell under the jurisdiction of the state's Department of Health and Welfare until 1965, when the state set up a Department of Indian Affairs with an office on Indian Island. Veterans lobbied and received the right to vote in federal elections in Maine in 1954, but they could not vote for local representatives to the state until 1967.[10] In addition to the lack of political equality, veterans found little economic opportunity. Few Old Town employers hired Indian men.

Like most people, Penobscots take note of large events that mark significant moments in their lives. For one generation, it was the Great De-

FIG. 1. Single-lane bridge across Penobscot River from Old Town to Indian Island. *Courtesy Maine Folklife Center, University of Maine, photograph no. 8702.*

pression; for the next, World War II. For some Penobscots, it was the construction of the bridge from their island to the mainland in 1951; for others, it was the Maine Indian Land Settlement Act of 1980.[11] But of all these historic events, World War II was probably the catalyst for the greatest changes on Indian Island in the twentieth century, because men and women who fought in the war discovered a different world off the reservation. Upon returning, however, they learned that they were not treated respectfully as veterans of the United States but were denied jobs and marginalized on a reservation racked with poverty.

Most of the generation who experienced World War II are gone now. Clarence Francis is one of those who have passed on. But in 1983 he granted an interview to Pamela Wood and talked about his memories of life on Indian Island. Of his ancestors he declared, "They were river people—canoes . . . that's how they survived. They always lived on the river, surrounded by water. . . . The Indians were pretty good farmers . . . lumbermen, hunters, trappers and fishermen."[12] Francis remembered that a big change came in the 1940s. Penobscots who went to war came back having experienced being part of the mainstream culture. Some of them brought non-Indian spouses home. The taste of opportunity they had enjoyed elsewhere left them frustrated and dissatisfied with reservation life. Many moved away, while those who stayed found jobs hard to come by. Some veterans and their families traveled from factories in Maine to factories in Massachusetts and Connecticut, wherever there was work. Their frustration led some veterans to become politically active, seeking progress in reservation life. One of the first improvements they achieved was the construction of a bridge from the mainland to Indian Island. While the bridge made traveling from Indian Island to Old Town safer, especially in winter, not everyone saw it as a positive transformation.

Clarence's wife, Violet, remembered the building of the bridge as the pivotal twentieth-century moment. For her, the construction of the bridge in 1951 divided the past from the present. "I can remember back on this reservation when I was just a child. . . . We had a bateau to take the workers across the river to the canoe factory. . . . We used to be able to sleep in our homes without locking our doors. You can't do that now. . . . You don't know who's coming over. . . . We've taken on a lot of the white man's living."[13]

In 1950 the state began construction of a single-lane bridge that joined Indian Island to the mainland at Old Town, creating a firmer and safer connection between Indian Island and mainstream society. It was no longer necessary to cross the river by canoe or ferry to go to work or to school, and melting ice in the spring no longer claimed the lives of those returning along the sawdust trail. (Sawdust was put down on the ice to insulate it against thawing too quickly in the spring). The new bridge meant that children could safely cross over to attend school.

Beginning in 1888, most Penobscot children were taught by the Sisters of Mercy at the Indian Island School from kindergarten to sixth grade. After the sixth grade, some children were sent away to the Carlisle Indian School in Pennsylvania, and others went to Old Town schools, where they found it hard to remain, due to either homesickness or cultural dissonance.[14]

As the years progressed, more Penobscots endured the oppression and racism and graduated from Old Town High School. Some even went to college. In addition, perhaps due to the consciousness-raising of the civil rights movement in the 1950s and 1960s, young people began to have a better experience of school in Old Town. Junior Pehrson, born in 1961, reports that he actually enjoyed going to school:

Sometimes I wish I was still in school. I had a lot of fun. . . . As far as prejudice is concerned, between the kids I don't think there was any, but their parents would tell them not to hang around with this guy, because he was an Indian. . . . And after I got into sports, I started going over to these people's houses and they found out that I wasn't a bad Indian.[15]

Education and knowledge of the outside world brought by military service were two key factors that strengthened Penobscot resistance efforts in the twentieth century. Those efforts were supported by the civil rights struggles taking place around the country. Veterans such as Governor Nicholas Sapiel and James Sappier and college graduates such as Andrew Akins lent their experiences and skills to the movement to improve conditions on the reservation, which culminated in "An Act to Provide for the Settlement of Land Claims of Indians ... in the State of Maine" and increased self-determination. Initially there were four major players in creating progressive reform on Indian Island: Michael (Ranco) Sockalexis, Erlene Paul, Andrew Akins, and James Sappier.

Sockalexis, a student at the University of Maine in the 1970s, worked in an office on campus next to the office of the Students for a Democratic Society (SDS). He told me that he became a VISTA volunteer and along with Erlene Paul was the first VISTA volunteer to serve in his own community. Sockalexis, Paul, and Sappier set about writing grant proposals and trying to obtain funds for improvements on the Indian Island reservation, working closely with Passamaquoddies such as Wayne Newell and other reformers to get grants from the Department of Economic Development and the Department of Housing and Urban Development to replace old water and sewer lines and build housing. As non–federally recognized tribes, the Penobscots and Passamaquoddies could not obtain funds from the Bureau of Indian Affairs.[16]

Andrew Akins attended Arizona State College in the late 1960s and early 1970s. There, he joined other members of the Indian Club in political discussions and eventually became its leader. Various activists in Indian affairs spoke to the club, such as Lee Brightman of California. In January 1971, Akins and five other students piled into a van and traveled to Alcatraz, which was at that time occupied by protesters from the American Indian Movement. Akins was inspired by all these activities to return home and make improvements in the lives of his own people. Akins has said he does not hold present American leaders responsible for past injustices but he does hold them responsible for correcting past injustices. Most special programs for Indians are treaty related. Akins believes that if the United States could go to war and sacrifice fifty-five thousand men to fulfill a treaty with Vietnam, then it should also honor its treaties with the Indian people. He said, "I can't think of one treaty that hasn't been broken. Otherwise, the Sioux would still own the Black Hills."[17] Upon graduation from Arizona State, Akins returned to Indian Island with his wife, hoping to effect positive changes.[18] Jim Sappier was running the only government program on the island at that time, and he hired the two Akinses. They went to work first on housing and other infrastructure — buildings, sewer lines, water, and the treatment plant — but Akins had the preservation of Penobscot culture in his mind. He helped expand and open up new markets for the Passamaquoddy basket co-op in Calais, founded in the early 1970s. In 1978, Akins was hired as tribal administrator for the Penobscots. He, Governor Pehrson, and others[19] worked closely with the Passamaquoddies to obtain federal funds and federal recognition. Akins believes that the best leaders were those who had spent their lives living on Indian Island. These older veterans had seen the world but knew intimately the needs of the community. They were deeply committed to the tribe but also recognized that the younger, educated members needed to join their efforts. It was this combination of the old and the young working together that led to success. In March of 1976, the Bureau of Indian Affairs granted federal status to Penobscots and Passamaquoddies.

While the team of older, mature veterans and young, college-educated leaders busied themselves applying for grants and working with Passamaquoddies to develop a legal case to obtain additional rights and lands, a minority group of mostly young men and women formed a society. Labeling themselves "traditionalists," they began to practice shamanism as learned from Roland "Senabeh" Francis, who also taught them wood carving, traditional stories, woods lore, and ceremonial lore. Senabeh was known for his fine wood carving but also as a "medicine man." Senabeh spent time with his mother cooking up potions such as cherry cough syrup and sold them around the community. For many years prior to World War II, Senabeh lived all year long on Hemlock Island, eight miles north of Indian Island. Alone at his camp, he was satisfied to do his carvings and live close to nature. During World War II, Senabeh joined the Canadian army. For a time in the 1970s he taught language and culture in the Indian Island School as a volunteer through the state Comprehensive Employment Training Act program.[20] He was instrumental in founding the current cultural revival carried out largely by Barry Dana at the Indian Island School. Senabeh influenced several young artists, including Stanley Neptune, who today is well known for his wood-carving artistry.

Traditionalists soon formed a loose alliance with like-minded Passamaquoddies and Micmacs and called themselves the Wabanaki Federation. Groups of traditionalists gathered to sing and play the drum, but they also involved themselves in radical politics. Some helped the American Indian Movement and some went to protest at Wounded Knee. In April 1976, a group occupied Baxter State Park in Maine, claiming it was sacred land, and demanded that the state return the lands to them.[21]

Traditionalists traveled to other tribes, attending powwows and adopting pan-Indian ceremonies, customs, dances, and songs. They generally exhibited hostility toward whites and would not dance or sing in their presence. In the beginning of this movement, many traditionalists planned to move into the woods or upriver to uninhabited islands to live in the traditional manner without modern conveniences or other appurtenances of white people.

One scholar comments, "Traditionalists want everyone to know they are 'Indian' even if it means becoming the kind of 'Indian' idealized by white men on television and in the movies."[22] Traditionalists pursued crafts to a greater degree than other traditions, such as language and religion, but drumming, dancing, and singing were also a big part of the revival. According to Barry Dana, "For about twenty years people were not dancing. When I was hired by the school as the cultural teacher, I began teaching dancing. Dancing represents a real community celebration where we can have fun. It also represents a tradition passed on from our ancestors."[23]

Some Penobscots strongly opposed the traditionalists because their protests, these opponents felt, gave Penobscots a bad name. However, traditionalists have played an important and continuing role in political movements. Many view the land claims settlement of 1980 as a "sellout," because traditionalists believe that land should not be exchanged for money. In addition, they view the settlement as resulting in loss of sovereignty, because the agreement included language that specifically gave the state more powers over Penobscot affairs. The issue of sovereignty is ongoing, with the state refusing to accept the concept of nationhood within its borders and the tribe insisting upon federal recognition and independence from state authority.

The idea of sovereignty and self-determination for Indian people came to the forefront in Indian politics in the 1960s when Melvin Thom, a Paiute, founded the National Indian Youth Council. He understood that Indian sovereign rights must not be compromised in the struggle to solve the problems of reservation life. Thom described the federal termination policy of the 1950s as a "cold war" and called for resistance.[24] Additional resistance grew out of the larger civil rights struggles that began in the 1950s and reached a peak of consciousness-raising in the "Poor People's March" of 1968. Finally the threat of termination and the continuing loss of lands galvanized Indian resistance across the country in the 1970s, resulting in the dramatic takeover of Alcatraz from November 20, 1969, to June 11, 1971, and the founding of the American Indian (Red Power) Movement.[25]

These events rested upon a basketful of historical precedents. Many Native resistance movements in earlier centuries took the form of religious revivalism. For example, the Delaware Prophet (1760–1763), Shawnee Prophet (1805–1811), Winnebago Prophet (1830), and the Ghost Dance (1870–1890) offered spiritual solutions to oppression and to the painful circumstances of powerlessness under imperial control. Other, social revitalization movements such as the Handsome Lake Church (1799–present), Delaware Big House Religion (1760–1910), and Native American Church (1800–present) resulted from some tribal and some multitribal efforts to regain control over Native culture and resources.[26] But in the twentieth century, bolstered by the experiences of other civil rights movements, Natives began a number of political resistance activities.

Civil rights activities sent out waves of change that were not at first readily apparent. Such is the case with the occupation of Alcatraz. A series of fish-ins in the Pacific Northwest in the 1960s, the blocking of Cornwall Bridge between the United States and Canada by Mohawks, the Alaska Native Claims Movement, and other small tribal or multitribal protests preceded and fueled the Alcatraz event. But it was also part of a much larger movement for social change by a variety of racial, class, and gender groups.

Americans were inundated with television and radio news of sit-ins and protests from the days of Martin Luther King to the Poor People's March. The specific protests and struggles of Native Americans were less widely covered in the national media, but Native people avidly read about the struggles of other Natives in the newspaper *Akwesasne Notes*, founded at the end of the 1960s. Born in Mohawk country, the newspaper rapidly became pan-Indian with a circulation of about fifty thousand,[27] including readers living on Indian Island in Maine. *Akwesasne Notes* became the national Indian media voice for the Alcatraz occupation.

Alcatraz was occupied by a group of dissatisfied urban Indians from the San Francisco Bay area. Claiming the island by "right of discovery," the protesters informed the public in a press release that they planned to found a center for Native American studies, spirituality, and ecology, and a museum, "in the name of all Indians."[28] This bold move caught the attention of the whole country and catapulted Indian issues above the wall of American indifference. Vine Deloria refers to the occupation as "a master stroke of Indian activism."[29] For many Native Americans, the event changed their lives, providing them with an opportunity to join with other Natives in the fight for self-determination and national sovereignty.

Alcatraz was the springboard for other protests. For example, the American Indian Movement (AIM), born in Minneapolis in 1968, seized the *Mayflower* on Thanksgiving Day 1970 in Plymouth, Massachusetts, challenging the celebration of colonial expansion. Three years later the Oglala Lakota tribe, in a dispute that had originated from tribal factionalism, armed themselves in a standoff against the FBI. The dispute began with dissatisfaction by some members of the community with the leadership of tribal chairman Richard Wilson. Detractors viewed Wilson as a puppet of the Bureau of Indian Affairs. AIM supporters, led by Dennis Banks and Russell Means, joined the protest in February of 1973. In the end, two Indians and one FBI agent died in the fracas.

The last major Native American protest of this era took place in July 1978, in Washington, D.C. Called the "Longest Walk," it was a largely peaceful and uneventful demonstration in which several Penobscots took part. One Penobscot traditionalist, Aselema (Sammy) Sapiel, spoke to a reporter about his involvement in the Longest Walk. He said he was one of seventy people on Indian Island who considered themselves traditional, rejected Catholicism, and followed the old Indian religion. He reported that he was involved with AIM but wanted AIM to follow a spiritual rather than a militant path. He criticized his own tribal government for "favoritism," claiming that they would not give jobs or benefits to traditionalists. He hoped the protest would call attention to bills concerning Indian rights and claims currently in Congress.[30] By taking part in the national Indian movement, he and other traditionalists served a consciousness-raising role within their community, urging their leadership to stand firm on the side of Indian rights.

All these protests together achieved a great deal, especially contributing to a cultural renaissance and revival in Native communities. In the years following these initial protests, Native people began insisting upon the right to speak their own languages and to engage in indigenous cultural and religious practices, and began to seek legal remedy for lost territory. Additionally, more Americans today are aware of Native American issues because of these protests, although most of the gains realized by Native Americans in employment, land claims, and education were achieved by conventional means, through legislation and litigation.

Emboldened by other Indian resistance and hoping to achieve self-government, the Penobscots joined the Passamaquoddies to protest construction on Passamaquoddy lands. The Maine Indian Land Claims initiative began as a result of this protest and related events that took place at one of the Passamaquoddy reservations in eastern Maine, Pleasant Point.

Passamaquoddy resolve was strengthened when tribal elder Louise Sockabasin found, in a shoebox under a bed in her home, an original 1794 treaty with Massachusetts, along with official letters from General Washington to the Passamaquoddies. Sockabasin passed the treaty on to tribal governor and veteran John Stevens.[31] Stevens read these treaties and realized that the state had broken its promise to protect Passamaquoddy lands in perpetuity. Passamaquoddy territory had consistently been eroded over the years, and the state had not protected the Passamaquoddies from this loss. For instance, local people had begun building summer camps on Passamaquoddy reservation lands. As a result, Stevens led the 1964 protests against summer camp construction on Passamaquoddy lands. He traveled to Augusta and met with Maine's governor and attorney general to request funds to hire an attorney to help the Passamaquoddies get six or seven hundred acres of land returned to the tribe. This was actually a modest request, given that the tribe had lost ten times that much territory. The state officials refused to help, so the Passamaquoddies staged a protest by occupying the land. Penobscots joined them in their protests.[32] At that point, an anonymous donor from Connecticut gave the Passamaquoddies money to hire a lawyer, Donald Gellers, who began to prepare their case.[33]

In 1968, as Gellers prepared a case intending to sue the state of Maine to return the Indians' lands, he was arrested for possession of marijuana and was tried, convicted, and sentenced to a prison term. Thomas Tureen, a recent law school graduate who worked for Gellers, took over the Indians' case. In his own account of the land claims case, Tureen called the arrest "fortuitous."[34] Gellers had based his argument on the concept that the 1794 treaty was valid but that Massachusetts had never negotiated a release from the Passamaquoddy and therefore should have protected the land rights agreed to in 1794, despite the Nonintercourse Act of 1790.[35] Tureen thought Gellers's arrest "fortuitous" because Tureen's own argument was different and ultimately successful. He changed the tribe's approach and argued that the Nonintercourse Act of 1790 made all consequent agreements between the state and the tribes illegal. Maine became a separate state from Massachusetts in 1820, and at that time agreed to honor all treaties between Massachusetts and resident Indian tribes. Gellers had also been trying to force Massachusetts to sue the state of Maine for mismanagement of the Passamaquoddy Trust Fund and to make compensation of $150 million to the Passamaquoddy for the six thousand acres lost to the state.[36] In contrast, Tureen based his case on the idea that the Nonintercourse Act applied to the Penobscots, Passamaquoddies, and all other Indian tribes in the eastern part of the country, as well as the West, which made the 1794 treaty invalid.

Tureen could make this argument because of a promise made by the state of Massachusetts during the American Revolution. At that time, Massachusetts was anxious to curry favor with the Penobscots in exchange for support, so it prepared a treaty recognizing the Penobscots' right to a six-mile-wide corridor along the Penobscot River from head of tide (now Bangor) to the Penobscot headwaters. In return, George Washington approached the Maine tribes to request their aid with the war effort, and they complied in the belief that their lands would be protected. Then after the war, in 1786, Massachusetts sent negotiators to the

Penobscots in order to obtain more lands for settlers. The Penobscots rejected the offer. Since the treaty of 1786 was never ratified, Tureen believed that the Nonintercourse Act of 1790, which declared that Congress must approve all treaties with tribes, should be legally binding.[37]

Then, in 1796, another treaty between Massachusetts and the Penobscots was ratified by which Penobscots gave up all their lands except the islands in the river, but since the treaty was signed after the Nonintercourse Act went into effect, Tureen argued, it was an illegal treaty. General Henry Knox, who settled at Thomaston, Maine, and served in George Washington's administration as secretary of war, wrote the Nonintercourse Act. In practice, it applied to the West and was never enforced in the eastern states, but it was the cornerstone of Maine Indian claims because it essentially declared illegal all treaties and negotiations that took place after 1790 between Massachusetts and the Maine tribes.

Not all Penobscots were convinced that their claim had a chance in the courts. Some members of the Penobscot community initially feared to pursue the case at all, lest they lose the little bit of state aid they had at the time. Also, many feared violence, partly due to the actions of Maine governor James Longley, who traveled the state stirring up fear and resentment—predicting a "nation within a nation,"[38] with two governments within the state.

By 1971 the claims case was well on its way, but Tureen discovered by chance that a federal statute of limitations on filing Indian lawsuits would expire in July 1972. "The clock was ticking," according to Tureen.[39] Maine's political leaders—Governor Kenneth Curtis, Senators Margaret Chase Smith and Edmund S. Muskie, and Representatives William Hathaway and Peter Kyros—all called on President Nixon to hurry the lawsuit to a hearing because the suit was causing the state numerous legal problems. On July 17, 1972, the claim was filed.[40] The next day, Congress extended the statute of limitations. In 1975, the federal district court held that a trust responsibility existed and that the Nonintercourse Act applied, even to tribes not federally recognized.[41] This meant that the Maine tribes had a case.

The two tribes' suit called for two-thirds of the land in the state to be returned to the tribes, plus damages. This was so astounding to everyone concerned and had such far-reaching implications to the landowners of Maine that the Maine congressional delegation reacted by asking Congress to extinguish the claims. Congress refused.[42] Anti-Indian reactions in newspaper editorials and letters expressed fear of loss of land titles. Tureen blamed Governor Longley for anti-Indian propaganda, citing "the demagogic power that he had . . . to use the media."[43] Tureen enlisted the aid of Harvard Law School lawyer Archibald Cox, who had been fired by Nixon. Cox agreed to meet Tureen and gave him helpful suggestions on how to proceed with the case. The prominent law firm of Hogan and Hartson donated time to the case. Still, times were uncertain, and Tureen feared that "Congress might well have wiped us out but for Jimmy Carter coming into office." In July 1977, retired judge William B. Gunter, at President Carter's request, suggested a take-it-or-leave-it offer of one hundred thousand acres, but the tribe rejected that solution.

By the fall of 1977, a White House task force had produced a joint memorandum of understanding, announcing that the claims would be settled on behalf of the tribes. Large non-Native landholders were outraged at the five-dollars-per-acre figure based on tax valuation: "There was a howl of protest [from landowners]," Tureen said.[44]

There was tremendous uncertainty among tribal members as to the ultimate resolution of the case, and some feared that the U.S. Congress would extinguish the Indians' claim. A significant question came from a surprise corner when Francis C. "Bobcat" Sapiel of Indian Island, attending the president's "town meeting" in Bangor, asked Carter if he would uphold the Indians' right to bring their claim by vetoing legislation to end the claims. The president said yes, he would veto any such legislation.

Another turning point involved *State of Maine v. Dana*, in which Allen J. Sockabasin and Albert C. Dana of Indian Township challenged the state's right to prosecute them for arson. They claimed they resided in Indian territory and therefore were not subject to state law. "I was scared to death of it," Tureen said about the case because if the state won, it would show state rather than federal jurisdiction on tribal lands and undermine federal recognition of the Nonintercourse Act.[45] But the Maine Supreme Judicial Court ruled that Sockabasin and Dana were indeed on Indian territory and subject to federal, not state, criminal law. If the decision had gone the other way, Tureen feared that the land claims could have been a lost cause. The result of this case created an impetus for serious negotiations. Tureen said, "Negotiations occur when the stakes are high, and when neither side is sure of the outcome."[46]

Tureen and the other negotiators feared that public sentiment against President Carter and the subsequent election of President Reagan might work against them. Therefore the negotiated $81.5-million joint tribal settlement was hustled through referendum votes on the three reservations, votes in both chambers of the state legislature, and in the United States House and Senate. President Carter signed it into law on October 10, 1980. It provided for the purchase of three hundred thousand acres of land at fair market value. The Houlton Band of Maliseets received one-tenth of the settlement; the remaining nine-tenths was split evenly between the Passamaquoddies and Penobscots. The Department of the

Interior set up a $27-million trust fund for economic development to be invested with the interest distributed to the tribes.[47] Penobscots received about $800,000 in interest. At a general meeting, they voted to distribute about 70 percent of that amount to tribal members and to allow the federal government to invest the remaining 30 percent. A million dollars was sent aside for senior citizens.[48] As one tribal leader observed, "there was no dancing in the street."[49] In spite of the tremendous opportunity for economic growth made possible by the settlement, many members of the community criticized the settlement as a sellout. A number of members said they would refuse to sign forms making them eligible for per capita funds as a protest against the settlement.

In spite such dissatisfaction among some members, the tribes accepted the settlement. The Justice Department described the case as "potentially the most complex litigation ever brought in the federal courts with social costs and economic impacts without precedent and incredible litigation costs to all parties."[50] At the time, the settlement represented "the greatest Indian victory of its kind in the history of the United States. Never before has so much land been returned to Indian control after so long a time"—while most other Indians in the country had never even heard of the Penobscots or the Passamaquoddies![51] Most significantly, however, the claims established a precedent for other Native American cases in the East.

The Maine Indian Tribal–State Commission, established by the federal government just after the land claims settlement, was charged with dealing with all the gray areas emanating from it.[52] The commission consists of four members from the state government and four Maine Native Americans. Currently, the commission promulgates fishing rules for three bodies of water under its jurisdiction in Penobscot Territory, sponsors workshops for state and tribal biologists and wardens to discuss fishing regulation and enforcement issues, and publishes a pamphlet on fish and wildlife provisions under the settlement. The commission made recommendations to the state legislature to support the addition of several pieces of land to Passamaquoddy and Penobscot territory and has presented testimony and information concerning a number of issues, including land use regulation, environmental protection, and court jurisdiction. In 1995, the commission produced an educational video titled *Wabanaki: A New Dawn*, portraying the Maine Natives' quest for cultural survival.[53]

Many Penobscots and Passamaquoddies believe that the negotiators gave up too much and that too many issues were left unsettled. Some of these issues deal with hunting, fishing, and trapping rights, and with legal and judicial jurisdiction. In addition, tribes have limited jurisdiction over criminal activity in their territories. The major concerns of the protests had involved the issues of sovereignty, negotiating lands, and accepting money for lands. Today the reservations are recognized by the settlement as municipalities, with all the federal and state responsibilities and entitlements thus implied. The Penobscots' position is that they are a federally recognized tribe and thus a sovereign political entity with jurisdiction over all their internal affairs. The issue has never been adequately settled in a way that both parties have been able to agree upon. As the twenty-first century begins, many issues are still unsettled, with numerous matters continuing to be negotiated in and out of court.

It may be a bit more difficult to answer the question of whether the health and welfare of the Penobscots, Passamaquoddies, and Maliseets are better today as a result of the Maine Indian Land Claims Act. Current statistics tell part of the story. Today, the total population of Indian Island remains relatively unchanged at 464 persons. While the tribal roll includes more than 2,000 persons, the number living on Indian Island has not increased considerably. Fifty-one percent are female; 85 percent are Native American. The number of persons living on the Island who are not Native has grown somewhat as younger generations increasingly marry outside their race. Such interracial marriages are much more acceptable today, but also the number of eligible partners among Maine's Native people is quite small. More and more young people are attending college. Among those surveyed by the 1990 Census, 3 percent of Indian Island residents hold professional or graduate degrees, 12 percent hold bachelor's degrees, 6 percent have associate's degrees, 18 percent have attended college, 40 percent have graduated from high school, and 22 percent have less than a high school education. These educational attainments compare very favorably with the population of Maine as a whole.[54] The population on the island is quite young; 143 currently attend school, 177 are employed (53 percent of those over sixteen years old), and only 5 percent are unemployed, but 41 percent are not in the labor force.

Education has improved the financial condition of most members of the community. In 1990 the average family income was $21,155, but 26 percent earned between $15,000 and $35,000, and 23 percent earned more than $35,000 annually.[55] While these income levels are somewhat below the average for the state, they represent a significant improvement over the earnings of Penobscots in the first half of the twentieth century. Many Penobscots work on Indian Island for government services; others work for private and public institutions off-reservation. Ten percent work in clerical positions, 13 percent in managerial, 4 percent in forest and fisheries, 14 percent as laborers, and 7 percent in precision production or crafts. Eleven percent are in professional jobs, 7 percent in protective services, 5 percent in sales, 24 percent in other services, and 5 percent in technical and related support.[56]

In terms of education, employment and income, Penobscots are greatly better off than they were between 1940 and 1970. To some extent, this may simply be a result of the greatly enhanced economic opportunity experienced by all Americans in the post–World War II era. However, the political activism of the 1970s created many improvements in reservation life. Federal recognition brought federal aid in the form of grants that greatly improved social services, health care, and housing on the reservation. The land claims did lead to some industry and jobs on the reservation, and put cash in the pockets of families. While the land claims settlement alone did not create the overall improvements in education and health, winning the land claims case in court did give the people a sense of accomplishment. No longer must they see their history as a series of loss after loss. The psychological benefit of winning can be seen in the increasing health and welfare of the community as a whole. So while the land claims settlement itself may not have effected great positive changes in the community, the totality of political activism of the 1970s that culminated in the claims gave Penobscots more political clout than they had ever had in the past. Empowered by their newfound political strength, Penobscots continue to move to improve the quality of life of their community.

At the beginning of the new century, there are several contended issues of political resistance, including clean water and fishing rights, the use of the term "squaw" in Maine place names, and the state's refusal to recognize the tribe's federal status. The Penobscots have taken an increasingly stronger stand against the pollution and damming of the Penobscot River. Much of the work along these lines rests on the shoulders of John Banks, a Penobscot who is trained as a forester. Banks has directed the Penobscot Department of Natural Resources since 1980. His department oversees 4,887 acres in reservation islands and 123,000 mainland acres in trust and fee lands. His staff includes twenty-four biologists and fieldworkers who monitor the wildlife and water quality for the Penobscot Indian Nation's environment. They have led the fight for cleaner water by appealing to the federal government to suspend the licensing of offending industries, including hydropower and pulp and paper mills. Banks points to the eagles along the Penobscot that are dying from dioxin poisoning (dioxin is an effluent from the paper-bleaching process), while elsewhere in the country eagles are experiencing a strong rebound in numbers. Signs are posted all around Indian Island warning people not to eat locally caught fish because of possible dioxin poisoning. The Penobscots identify with the river, and want it cleaned up. As John Banks explained, "We say that the river gives us life, and we mean that in a spiritual sense, we are the river. If we destroyed any of it—the islands, the animals on them, and the water around them—we would weaken that connection. We would lose a part of who we are."[57] Therefore, to clean up the river is to improve the health and welfare of the Penobscots who live on the islands within it.

If the court settlement itself did not directly improve the quality of life for all Penobscots, it did give their government the opportunity to collect assets and gain political leverage. Recently, Penobscots used that political leverage in the Maine legislature to request and win legislative changes that removed offensive terminology from Maine's place names. The move was based on the idea that the term "squaw" is an offensive term to Native women. The word "squaw," originally from the Algonquian languages, meaning only "female," came to have a more universal usage as adapted by English-speaking fur traders and was applied in a pejorative sense to any Native woman. The word became a cultural expression in English of historical antagonism toward Native Americans, especially Native American women, who were naturally offended by such usage.[58] Young Penobscot girls going on the school bus to Old Town were subject to taunts of "squaw, squaw," mostly by young boys.[59] At first Maine legislators did not understand the nature of this kind of emotional abuse, but after several Penobscot and Passamaquoddy women testified about the pain this usage caused them, the lawmakers voted to remove the offensive term from Maine's place names.

Cultural changes in the latter part of the twentieth century, largely brought about by the efforts of traditionalists, have created a great social impact on the Penobscot and Passamaquoddy communities. Barry Dana, Dana Mitchell, Stanley Neptune, Carol Dana, Theresa Secord, Michael Sockalexis, and others have taken upon themselves the task of educating the young people about the language, crafts, and musical traditions of the tribe. Their efforts have paid off handsomely in increased self-esteem and have helped instill in the children a sense of pride in their heritage. The importance of revival of pride as a survival mechanism is evident even in the newer practices, such as the 100-mile run up Mount Katahdin—a place sacred to the Penobscots, where the earth mother reaches the sky—instituted by Barry Dana in the 1980s. Dana began his run as a personal spiritual quest but has been joined by a number of other young men in the run from Indian Island to Katahdin. As he tells it, "Every step and every stroke is a connectedness to the earth."[60]

Others go to the mountain for an annual spiritual renewal. In these newer and revived traditions, Penobscots say they have found a new sense of hope.[61] Generally, they, with their Passamaquoddy neighbors, seek a spiritual unity that allows them to be themselves, not someone defined by outsiders. As Wayne Newell explains, "There was a time when survival meant not being you." But today, the singing, dancing and spiritual rituals these people hold dear create a sense of strength and unity that allows them to transcend individual weaknesses. Penobscots talk about the power of the song, prayer drum, and dancing to the centrality of their spirit. According to Barry Dana, "The drum is very powerful. It brings people together, it gets them to sing, and it gets them to dance."[62]

While many of the young people have learned to dance in school, their elders at community celebrations frequently join them. Often they are invited to dance at basket-selling events organized by the Maine Indian Basketmakers Alliance. The alliance is the brainchild of Theresa Secord, a trained geologist who held the post of tribal geologist for a number of years. Secord learned to make baskets in 1988 from Madeline Tomer Shay, a renowned basket maker and one of the last fluent speakers of the Penobscot language. Secord has been executive director of the Maine Indian Basketmakers Alliance since 1993. She organized the basket makers of all four of Maine's Indian tribes into a cooperative, which promotes basket making by protecting brown ash resources, publicizing basket making, and holding basket-selling events at several venues around the state. During the 1990s, and largely due to the support of the National Endowment for the Arts Apprenticeship Program, many of Maine's Indian basket makers have been honored and supported in their work. They have taken on apprentices, and currently the craft is experiencing a renaissance.

Stanley Neptune and his family have worked to renew the craft of wood carving, particularly the wooden war club and walking sticks. Neptune learned his craft initially at the age of twenty-one from Senabeh. When he had successfully carved about twelve walking sticks, Senabeh taught him to carve a war club. Neptune actively pursues his craft, selling his clubs and canes throughout the eastern United States. He promotes his art as distinctly Penobscot in form and design.[63]

While traditionalists promote their crafts, traditional song and dance, and ceremonial practices, not all Penobscots follow these ways. The Roman Catholic Church has been active in the area for several hundred years, and many Penobscots remain Catholic. As James Sappier has said, "Three hundred years is a lot of tradition." Others follow various Protestant religions and some traditionalist practices. The church and the community have worked to incorporate Penobscot traditions into Roman Catholic worship, but with the loss of the language in the last century no one can sing the traditional Penobscot hymns, and most follow the same worship practices of other American Catholics.

Even those who worship in the Christian traditions retain various aspects of their Native culture. Whether it is the enjoyment of traditional Penobscot legends of Gluskabe or stories about "little people," Penobscots in the twenty-first century have regained a sense of pride in who they are, as a separate and distinct ethnic group. Yet many Indian people feel they still bear the scars of the oppression of the last five hundred years. Michael Sockalexis and other Native people call these feelings "historical trauma."[64]

Cultural revival is for many Penobscots a key ingredient to survival. It is part of the dance of resistance. In one rendition of the "creation dance," two children dance forward, one carrying a pipe, the other a flag. They wear fringed buckskin clothing beaded with double-curve designs. One little girl dances while paddling an invisible canoe. A young boy, dancing in four directions, represents Gluskabe. As the children dance, the story emerges of Gluskabe's origins. He begins to move and feels the heartbeat of the earth. The children once again create themselves. After the dance, the young boy representing Gluskabe tells his audience that he was honored to represent Gluskabe. He relates that dancing "is special for me because my father has always encouraged it, and my grandfather was a very skilled dancer."[65] The children prove that a dance of resistance can be a peaceful dance. The story of the twentieth-century Penobscots' struggle to renew themselves is a peaceful story. As we begin the twenty-first century, it seems at last to be a story with a happy ending. Although early-nineteenth-century historians such as Williamson predicted the demise of the Penobscot tribe, at the dawn of the twenty-first, the Penobscots are thriving.[66] Historians are often wrong. But if one looks at the events of the past, it is not surprising that many believed the Penobscots would disappear. They did not know that the dance of resistance began long ago. It began at first contact, approximately four hundred years ago.

Chapter 2

LAND, POWER, AND REVERENCE
Core Teachings That Sustain Resistance

> Three things of Klose-kur-beh's teaching are held more sacred than all others. The first was the power of the Great Spirit, second, the land the Great Spirit gave them they must never leave, and third, they must never forget their first mother, but must always show the love they have for her, and all work must cease during the observances of her honor.[1]
>
> —JOSEPH NICOLAR

Four hundred years of resistance and adaptation to cultural hegemony requires a certain solidarity. For the Penobscots, that solidarity grows out of basic beliefs about spiritual power, the land, and reverence. These concepts form the traditional beliefs and customs of the culture. The writings of anthropologist Frank G. Speck, collected in the Penobscot language as well as in English from numerous cultural specialists, and Penobscot writer Joseph Nicolar, present the traditional beliefs of the Penobscots in tales about Gluskabe. "The world was all spiritual, . . . there was a living spirit in all things, and the spirit of all things has power over all and as the spirit of all things center in the Great Spirit."[2] That Great Spirit created Gluskabe. Gluskabe is the cultural hero of the Penobscots, and he teaches them all the important traditional beliefs about the world and about how humans should behave. Studying this tradition assists historians' interpretation of the past, for, as folklorist Henry Glassie writes, "historians need tradition" because "it helps historians handle the massive matter of continuity, perhaps guiding them to discriminations among the disparate occurrences jumbled under the rubric of change."[3] The study of Penobscot traditional views elucidates our understanding of the meeting of two very different traditions and how they danced together or apart, or stood firm in hostility. Therefore we must turn to traditions to understand Penobscot history, especially those beliefs and customs illuminated by legendary and mythological tales.

Gluskabe represents both a cultural hero and a quintessential Penobscot man. He is the man by whom other Penobscot men measure themselves and, as such, is a symbol of the Penobscot male self-image. His traits are the ideal traits: skilled hunter, clever and tricky, able to outwit others, physically strong. He is a man who is capable of magical acts because of his spiritual power. The name Gluskabe (Kəlóskɑpe) derives from the word kəlósko, meaning, "he lies, tells falsehood, deceives," referring to his ability to outwit his enemies through deception. Anthropologist Frank Speck, who collected a large body of Gluskabe tales from Penobscots in the early twentieth century, defined him as "the major transformer personage . . . the chief of shamans."[4] Both Speck and Nicolar's collections of Gluskabe stories embody the cultural wisdom of the community, passed down from past generations to the present.

The mythological age in which Gluskabe lived was one in which animals and humans shared similar characteristics.[5] His grandmother, Woodchuck (monímk̓ehso), symbolizes important traits of womanhood and of the community. Wise and thoughtful, she held the knowledge of the past and future, and used it to teach Gluskabe the skills and values necessary to the survival of future generations of Penobscots.

Grandmother taught Gluskabe to share resources and protect the community: "Kətačəwıtákık alálohke təč wəlıhálakohotıt kóhsənawa. 'You must do whatever will benefit our descendants (the Penobscot Indian people).' "[6] Grandmother Woodchuck also taught Gluskabe to hunt, fish, make a living, and construct a canoe and hunting tools, such as a bow and arrows. Gluskabe began to learn how to be a man by hunting rabbits and catching fish; then he graduated to deer. When he killed a bear, Grandmother Woodchuck rejoiced: "Wənıhk̓ɑp, koláwınena məsela pəmí-kolıč. 'Now we shall live well with abundant fat. You did well.' "[7] Then Gluskabe learned other important skills such as how to hunt ducks. While he learned all these skills, he also learned to act in ways that would benefit his people.

Grandmother Woodchuck repeatedly reminded Gluskabe to conserve game resources for future generations. For example, once when he gathered up all the game in bags, Grandmother Woodchuck admonished: "Kʷask̓alɑmólətəwač nıhkɑ́ni kowənawa. 'Our descendants will starve to death!' " Again, when he collected all the fish above a weir he had constructed in the river she scolded him: "Nək̓enəss, áhtɑmɑ kəlálohkewo məskekátahat námehsak. 'Grandson you have not done well annihilating all the fish! Our descendants will have no fish, Turn them loose!' "[8]

Explanations of the natural world—the physical appearance of animals or their behavior, or the origins of formations of land and water—form the basis of a large body of Penobscot oral literature. One story serves as an example. "Gluskabe and the Moose" tells the story of how Gluskabe created the moose by stomping him out of the ground in response to the cries of hunger from his people. (Chimney Pond on the side of Mount Katahdin currently fills the hole left when the moose emerged from its northern slope.) As Gluskabe ran, his snowshoes left great piles of sand, today known as the ridge or esker called the Enfield Horseback. The story tells of Gluskabe chasing the moose toward the village where his people lived. When he reached Castine, he leaped across Penobscot Bay to Cape Rosier, leaving a large snowshoe track, called in Penobscot Mátɑkəməssək, "at the Old Irregular Snowshoe." Then, when he slew the moose, he created Cape Rosier, known in Penobscot as Móslhkəčl, "moose rump."[9]

The moose story is not just a quaint story about how the land came into being. It is a story that reminds Penobscot listeners that they are bonded to places in the natural landscape through cultural symbols. The story reminds them of Nicolar's admonition,

"The land the Great Spirit gave them they must never leave," of their great depth of history, and of their spiritual connection to this place. Place-names are more than references to a place. Each place-name is a poetic reminder of activity, function, and cultural description. While Native American place-names have not received much attention recently, several anthropologists have derived important cultural information from their study. Franz Boas suggested as early as 1900 that geographical nomenclature could be studied as a way to explore a people's mental life. Yet little work has been done other than J. P. Harrington's study of Tewa place-names and Floyd Lounsbury's Iroquois place-names paper. However, Keith Basso revisited the idea in the 1980s, making important connections between Western Apache everyday narrative, place-names, and moral narratives.[10]

Basso realized that Western Apache place-names thoroughly described the physical details of a place. He wondered why Western Apaches were so fond of saying them; that led him to investigate the matter in detail. He discovered that place-names performed an important stylistic function in Western Apache storytelling. A listener needed to hear only the name of the place to receive important cultural messages.[11]

Among the Penobscots, place-names also fulfill important cultural functions—tying the people to the land and to specific places on the land. The Penobscot language has many terms associated with the natural world that strengthen one's sense of place. Since the prevalent means of

Table 1.
Geographical Elements in the Penobscot Language

Shape	Direction	Position	Material	Color	Water Form	Landform
-ɑn, sphere	-ɑsəw-, diagonal	nɑwɑ-, middle	-ɑm-, gravel	wɑp-, white	-təḵ, stream	-atən, mountain
-sekat-, flat	sɑk-, coming out	mos-, bottom	-kı-, dirt, land	wısɑw-, yellow	-ɑkame-, lake	-ahsəḵ, ledge
nıkətaw-, fork	sesk-, steep	sıp-, edge	alɑnəsḵ-, clay	meḵ-, red	-əpeḵ, body	nɑlɑ-, crevice, channel
wɑl-, concave	nal-, downstream	asəp-, beside	məsk-, grassy		-ıčəwan, current	nemahkı-, marsh
apıḵ-, hollow	amıl-, off from shore				-ahsən, small body of water	
wɑk-, bent	ehsənočı-, approaching shore					
		neḵı-, between				

travel was by water, it is not surprising that aspects of water, currents, and subtle geographical formations from the point of view of being on the water and looking shoreward figure largely in Penobscot descriptions of their own world.[12] Geographical elements in the Penobscot language are combined in numerous ways to form words that are used to describe places. The terms can be classified into categories such as shape, direction, material, landform, and water form as illustrated in table 1. These elements combine to connect people with place through meaning.

Thus we have place-names like mskìhtəḵ, "grassy stream," pskèhtəḵ, "branching stream, tributary," and kəsɑwehsıke, "pointed ledge." Each place-name describes in detail the physical appearance of a place. Other place-names point to important cultural resources, for example, masḵesísıpo, "Birch stream," and wəlamánəssək, "Olamon" (a town) or "red paint place." The Penobscots used birch bark in the manufacture of canoes, bowls, and other vessels, and red paint (red ocher clay) in ceremonial and burial rites. A few places are named for persons, such as Orson Island (Orson is the Penobscot word for John, and the person so honored was the Revolutionary War–era chief of that name). Penobscot place-names cluster along the Penobscot River, but Passamaquoddy, Maliseet, and Micmac peoples tell stories about Gluskabe that celebrate local places. For the Maliseets, Gluskabe created landforms along the St. John River, for example. In that way, Gluskabe tales bind each community to its place on the landscape.

As transformer, Gluskabe practiced the additional responsibility of creating certain attributes in animals. For example, Gluskabe took tobacco away from Grasshopper so that his descendants would have some. In the process, he split the back of Grasshopper; that is why the grasshopper now has wings. The story relates that Grasshopper had a mouthful of tobacco that he chewed and spit all the time.[13] Penobscots observed this chewing and spitting behavior in grasshoppers in nature, and the tobacco story provides a logical explanation. Another story tells of how the river dried up and all the people were dying of thirst. Gluskabe discovered that a giant bullfrog was holding the water back in its mouth. Gluskabe felled a yellow birch tree on the bullfrog's back. The story provides an explanation for why bullfrogs look broken-backed.[14] Other stories explain attributes of various mammals, birds, fishes, whales, and shellfish. For a people traditionally relying upon hunting, these stories teach the young about animal appearance and behavior, making an additional cultural connection between the natural landscape and belief.

Aboriginal, pre-Christian belief among Penobscots rested upon the idea that spiritual power could be acquired by some individuals known as sorcerers, or mətəwəlɪnəwak. The word has ancient origins in the Algonquian language family. Proto-Algonquian *mete:w-, "member of the Mystic Cult," a practitioner of the Midewiwin religion, is followed by the *-ɪlenyɪw- "person." Powers of the mətəwəlɪnəwak included being able to transform themselves into animals, cast a spell or curse an enemy, violate the laws of nature (such as sinking into the ground while walking, or flying), and communicating telepathically. In addition to the spiritual power of mətəwəlɪnəwak, the world was imbued with spirits that could have a benevolent, neutral, or malevolent disposition. A word such as mácəhɑneto, "evil power, devil," is derived from the Proto-Algonquian *-naʔt(o), "sing," because singing is a central feature of Algonquian spirituality and medicine.[15]

The mətəwəlɪno was a person who possessed supernatural power. "His chief activity was to overcome rivals and demonstrate wherever he could the superiority of his own strength."[16] This strength was, of course, supernatural. Men and women could possess this power, and there was some indication that whole families might be mətəwəlɪnəwak. The power was either acquired by birth or grew within a person. Certain members of the tribe became quite famous for their magic powers.[17] Mətə́wəlɪnəwak called upon this power by drumming and singing. Both human and mythological Mətə́wəlɪnəwak had animal helpers called páwəhɪkan (instrument of mystery), "token, talisman, fetish, object used for magical purposes by shamans."[18] If such a helper were slain, the mətə́wəlɪno would also expire. Mətə́wəlɪnəwak figure largely in Penobscot stories, as do cultural heroes who often exhibit superhuman, if not supernatural, abilities.

Cultural heroes in Penobscot mythology provide insight into the important attributes of Penobscot leadership. Major political leaders in Penobscot history were often mətə́wəlɪnəwak. But not all had magical powers; some had superhuman but secular qualities. One such Penobscot hero was Kʷə́nawɑs, "Long Hair." Like all the major male heroes in Penobscot lore, he was very similar to Gluskabe except for being human. He, like Gluskabe, was raised by his grandmother, Woodchuck. His upbringing was the same as that of Gluskabe. He too learned to hunt and fish and make canoes. There are several stories about Kʷə́nawɑs as a hero. He rescued villages from bad people who had conquered them. He was also responsible for choosing the dog from among all the animals to be a human companion, because the dog was the only animal that was willing to share the poverty of human life. Other male heroes resembled Gluskabe, in that they provided some service to the Penobscot people. For example, Kìwahk̓e, "Forest Giant," heard a voice while hunting. He went on a quest to find a new village for his people. Kèsɪhlɑt, "Fast runner," outwitted his in-laws through sorcery. Pìhtes, "Froth," resided in water and in his story impregnated a young girl while she swam. The girl gave birth to a son who became a true hero and a great magician. She named him Bubble Froth. Bubble Froth killed a great white bear, the greatest magician in the world.[19]

In addition to the human sorcerers and heroes, tales about other supernatural beings abound. One such being, the personification of Mount Katahdin, took a Penobscot woman for his wife. She bore him a son who became a great magician. Other supernatural beings included Kʷèləphot, "Turned Over," responsible for introducing herbal medicines to people, and Kʷàk̓e, "Cannibal Giant." Another well-known sprite was Pə̀mole, "He Whizzes By," a strange-looking malevolent creature who lived at Mount Katahdin. Penobscots feared that Pə̀mole would kill or devour them. Their legends told of an encounter with a hunter who became trapped unexpectedly by snowfall without his snowshoes. In the story, the hunter offered a sacrifice of oil and fat to Pə̀mole, who spared his life. Pə̀mole took the hunter to the interior of Katahdin. Within the mountain, Pə̀mole had a spacious wigwam, well provided with venison. He lived there with his wife and daughter. The hunter married the daughter, who conceived him a child. As with all other supernatural marriages in Penobscot lore, the child had magical powers.[20]

Understanding the nature of Penobscot beliefs, especially regarding spiritual power and attachment to place, helps clarify and explain the Penobscots' choice of leaders, historical decisions, resistance to assimilation, and adaptation to historical processes. Throughout the historic period, Penobscots confronted numerous new situations such as epidemic diseases, warfare, new technology, an influx of settlers, loss of game and other natural resources, and assaults on their lands, persons, and culture. In spite of the many challenges to their way of life, they found within their own belief system ways to resist and adapt. It was not just the men who had to cope with new challenges; women also needed to find meaning and explanation in their lives.

Women and girls appear in Penobscot literature, as well. Women, too, can be mətəwȧlınewak. In some stories, they are simply mentioned as the wife or daughter of the protagonist. However, many stories have heroines and sorceresses. The most prevalent positive female heroine is the grandmother, usually named Woodchuck, purveyor of wisdom. Her role was to raise the male hero (both Gluskabe and Kʷə́nawɑs), to whom she taught life skills and social responsibility. She was quite self-sufficient and able to survive without a male protector. The tales about grandmothers promote the great respect held for elders in Penobscot culture.

Some old women lived alone in the woods. Some of them were malevolent. For example Máskık̓əsı, "Toad Woman," stole children from their parents, while the female version of the cannibal, Kíwahk̓esk̓e, fattened up a boy to eat, and Pohkəčınsk̓ehso, "Jug Woman," is an old misshapen hag with magic powers. Numerous stories about Jug Woman exist, including a standoff with Gluskabe. Her baby was the skunk cabbage. Sk̓éwtəmohs, "Swamp Woman," a benevolent old woman dressed in moss, saved hunters or others lost in the woods.[21] Sometimes the old woman could change herself into a beautiful young woman and entice a lost hunter into her arms.

Several stories tell about women both young and old who were abandoned by their husbands or family members and left to die. In every case the woman was able to stay alive by using such survival skills as snaring rabbits to obtain food. Penobscot legendary females might be good or bad, but they are usually powerful and often magical. One such story has the ring of historical truth. In it, Mohawk raiders kidnapped a young woman and took her south. She had numerous adventures during her captivity. The Mohawk tortured her, burning her fingernails, which became deformed by the torture, resulting in her name, "Arrowhead Fingernails." She eventually escaped and returned alone to her village with great difficulty. The Penobscots have many stories about war with the Mohawks.[22] This particular version is important because it centers on a female protagonist. In these stories, we find traditional wisdom about Penobscot women and their role in Penobscot society. The courage and survival skills necessary to a Penobscot woman shaped real Penobscot women like Pidianske, Molly Ockett, Molly Mollasses, and Molly Spotted Elk, who experienced colonialism in different ways, finding themselves married to Europeans and having to send their children away to Catholic school, or being captured and held prisoner by Europeans, losing their families in warfare, or experiencing the humiliation of the rape of a daughter, poverty, and illness. They met these challenges with courage, with the knowledge that their traditional beliefs were sound, with creativity, and with an understanding of their own worth as Penobscot women.[23]

Historical narrative, morality tales, Gluskabe tales, and other types make up the rich body of Penobscot oral tradition. One story in particular gathers together a number of elements we find in other stories. A woman literally becomes part of the land in her death, her sacrifice brings survival to the community, and her memory is invoked with reverence. She is Green Corn Mother, honored by the Penobscots in song and dance.

> Yaw ni go we yaw no go weh yaw- ni- go weh[24]

The green corn dance begins with an older woman, representing the first mother, dancing while the death song is sung. As the legend relates, she is sad because there is no food for her children. She instructs her husband to kill her, drag her body over a large, open field until all the flesh is worn off her bones, and then bury her bones in the middle of the field. When seven months have passed, he is to return and gather what he finds on the land, and to eat all but enough to plant the next year. He may not eat her bones but may burn them, and they will bring peace to him and his children. The husband consults with others in the community and reluctantly follows her orders.

> Lo la da gair kwe ya hy ya weh hu lo la da gair kweya hy ya weh hu

In the second part of the dance, all the other dancers join in the dancing. They form two lines, facing one another and dance toward each other and back several times. They then go down the center and pass through to form a circle. Near the end of the dance, Corn Mother appears in silence, passing out corn. Then, all the dancers dance fast and hard until the end. Corn Mother's flesh transforms into tall, yellow maize plants, skàhmonal. Also, tobacco plants sprout where her bones lie. The dance ceremony honors and reveres the first mother, who represents the gifts of

FIG. 2. Selling Arms to the Indians. *Courtesy Deering Collection, Raymond F. Fogler Library Special Collections, University of Maine.*

food and tobacco from the Creator, through her sacrifice. It also serves to cement culture to the land, through the media of story, song, dance, and ceremony.

The values, morals, and beliefs of the Penobscots, though often scorned by outsiders as superstitions, "devil-worship," or evidence of ignorance, assisted the survival of the community in the face of many overwhelming changes in the course of their history. Cultural traditions became foundations of resistance. The mortar of this foundation—resiliency to retain their lands, concern for the future of their descendants, respect and compassion for elders, and reverence for the spirituality in all things—holds the community fast against the many events and circumstances that threaten it.

These threats came with Europeans, who brought diseases, settlers, firearms, and other new technology that changed the world of the Penobscots. While Penobscots had experienced change before Europeans arrived in their territory, the changes tended to be gradual, and thus more easily absorbed. Frederick Hoxie notes that "gradual change and a remarkable aversion to centralization" marked the history of all indigenous communities in North America. The introduction of maize horticulture, and the invention of the bow and arrow, or the birch-bark canoe, clearly affected vast areas of the country in a profound way, but "their impact seems to have been diffuse and gradual rather than direct and abrupt." North America did not see the kind of concentration of authority in large political, economic, or religious institutions that existed in Europe at the time of contact, while at that time in Europe, urbanization and higher population density were also more familiar. Thus the two worlds did not understand one another very well.[25]

The meeting of the people of Europe and North America resulted from a series of cultural, religious, economic, and political forces in Europe driving an exploding population to find new land. Crowded European countries, ravaged by warfare as each of the major countries' monarchies hoarded wealth, concentrated on building large armies and competing for diminishing resources. The British, French, and Spanish sought a western route to the resource-rich Indies because the Portuguese controlled the eastern route. Mariners were able to cross the Atlantic Ocean only because rapid changes in the technology of boats and navigational aids allowed for longer sea voyages.

The situation was very different in the Western Hemisphere. Various scholars have estimated the pre-European-contact North American population at between three to five million people, with about seven hundred thousand living on the Atlantic coastal plain and piedmont.[26] While many of the North American communities practiced agriculture, little animal husbandry took place, and the population had not experienced the enormous population growth of Europe and therefore had not strained natural resources. Most people in the Northern Hemisphere lived in relatively small villages or bands that moved in response to the availability of natural resources. There were no large cities or centralized powers such as in European monarchies and therefore no large armies.

The two worlds were very different in appearance, but they were even more different in worldview. Europeans had the confidence, based upon their religious beliefs and the scientific revolution, that they could comprehend and eventually control everything around them. They were not of the natural world, but distinct from it. The belief that faith in God raised humans to a higher level, separate from nature, spawned the idea of nature as a wilderness. A wilderness could be defined as an area of uninhabited land provided by God to Christians for cultivation and building civilization. Much of this belief flowed out of the Protestant Reformation, which gave every Christian a mission to serve God and to be intolerant of anyone who did not.[27] When the Christians met the residents of the Western Hemisphere and began calling them Indians, they knew the Indians were human. However, they saw Indians as humans who lived apart from the mission of God and within nature. Europeans believed very strongly that their mission was to change the nature of the Native people and turn Natives into Christians.

Native people did not at first understand the new visitors. Not so much overawed by European technology as puzzled by European behavior, Native Americans rapidly became resentful of the kinds of controls Europeans exerted over Native people's lives and resisted those controls at every turn.

When Europeans arrived, the Penobscots belonged to a loose political alliance that included a number of small but related villages that shared language, social traditions, and a commitment to assist one another to resist outside threats from foreign tribes, for example. Leaders of such alliances led only because of their personal standing in the community and their reputation in warfare and hunting. They did not acquire much personal wealth and remained in place only as long as their people saw that the leader placed the community's welfare above his own. Often such leaders belonged to prominent families with spiritual as well as secular powers, and leadership passed down to other male members of the same family (not necessarily sons). The political system in place allowed for dissent, and often disgruntled families would collect their belongings and move up- or downriver to begin a new village when they were unhappy with the decisions of the majority. This system worked very well, since all neighboring villages were related by language, kinship, and culture.

Penobscots lived a life based upon hunting and gathering. They built homes with wood frames covered with birch bark, other plant materials, or hides. They had temporary, seasonal villages and larger, more permanent villages located near water, which was essential for both subsistence and travel. The Penobscots practiced some agriculture, with the usual cultivation of a combination of squash, maize, beans, and various roots. Other cultural practices are less well known, and they varied in time and space. These included various burial rituals, personal adornments, clothing types, and religious beliefs. We know that many cultural and spiritual beliefs had to be hidden or changed after Europeans arrived in Penobscot country. Much of what we know about this early period of Penobscot history comes from the writings of Europeans who first encountered Native peoples in Maine. These Europeans have provided small glimpses of aboriginal life, but explorers and settlers often misunderstood and misinterpreted the culture. Therefore what we know about the Penobscots in the early centuries of our written history, we know from carefully reading the documents of Europeans' first encounters with Penobscots.

Estevan Gomez, an experienced Portuguese pilot hired by Charles V of Spain, first brought the Penobscot River to the attention of Europe through his map drawn after a journey up the river to Kenduskeag in 1525.[28] He met some quite friendly Penobscots at Mount Desert who were fishing, captured fifty-eight individuals, and shipped them to Lisbon.[29] No evidence has come to light of the ultimate fate of the victims. David Quinn has pointed out that the Penobscot River subsequently appeared on maps that were sent to other European countries, notably France and England. Some of these maps depicted the Penobscot River as a channel to the St. Lawrence, creating much interest in Europe in the Penobscot as a possible passageway to Asia.[30]

These early, mostly unfriendly encounters with Europeans required a response from the Penobscots. Their first strategy of resistance, to dance away to a safe distance, may be evident as early as 1580, when English explorer John Walker traveled up the Penobscot River and stole three hundred hides from the deserted Indian village he found there. The Penobscots undoubtedly knew the visitors were coming long before Walker's party arrived and, fearing additional kidnapping, hid from them. Penobscots suffered losses in these early encounters, but such experiences were not new. That is, neighboring bands had stolen people and goods from them, so their world was not turned upside down by these sporadic encounters with Europeans. Staying away from the newcomers as a strategy of resistance worked very well when Europeans came only occasionally and for a short time. Once Europeans began to settle in New England, bringing unknown pathogens and warfare, Penobscots would frame more elaborate strategies for survival and resistance.

The French first arrived in the person of Samuel de Champlain. His encounter with Penobscots was undoubtedly aided by the presence of Native guides who interpreted for him and smoothed the way for a meeting with Penobscot leadership. Champlain first met Penobscots at Mount Desert Island (which he named) in August of 1604. Two canoes of Natives brought Champlain some fish, which they traded for some biscuits and other items. The Natives then guided Champlain to a village on the Penobscot River (Pentagoet) to meet their chief, Bessabez (Bashabes). Champlain went as far inland as Kenduskeag (presently Bangor, Maine), but the chief came a few days later from a northern village. Champlain left detailed accounts of the inhabitants of villages he visited along the Maine coast, including their political alliances in a confederation led by Bashabes.[31]

English accounts similarly describe the Natives and their political alliances in the early seventeenth century. James Rosier described the events that took place in May 1605 during the expedition of George Weymouth.[32] The English landed at Allen's Island (near St. George's River) and saw three canoes land at an adjoining island. The English signaled for the Abenakis to approach, and the Natives cautiously sent just one canoe of men across the water. Rosier described these men as wearing beaver and deerskin clothing, with a cloak hanging to their knees. Some had sleeves and some did not. They also wore beaver-skin loincloths. Men wore their hair long; if married, they tied it in back of their neck in a knot. Rosier says that the men were very civil and merry. The English exchanged some trinkets and knives, glasses, and combs for skins. The Natives told them about their leader, Bessabez, and encouraged the Englishmen to come to visit him so that more extensive trading could take place.

The next day, more Abenakis arrived, their faces painted black or red, striped with blue over their lips, nose, and chin. One man had a coronet of stiff red fur; others wore white-feathered skins of some fowl. They also wore jewels in their ears and bracelets of wampum on a leather string. The Abenakis entreated the English to come visit Bessabez, but the English refused. Instead, the English kidnapped five of the men in two canoes with their bows and arrows. They ended the confrontation by sailing away with Tahanedo, Amoret, Skicowaros, Maneddo, and Sassacomoit.

The English account confirms the French reports that the Abenakis in central Maine were allied under the chief of the Penobscot River, Bessabez. In 1606, another English voyager, Martin Pring, returned Tahanedo to his home. Two of the other kidnapped men were later returned with yet another English voyager, Sir John Popham.[33] While the accounts of these expeditions brought information and maps back to Europe, fueling additional expeditions, they also serve today as useful documents for understanding the location of communities, the political alliances, and the economic impact of the early fur trade on the Penobscots. In all these things, Bessabez played a significant role.

We know from both French and English sources that Bessabez resided on the Penobscot River somewhat upriver from Kenduskeag. Champlain describes meeting Bessabez and another chief, Cabahis, whose village was on a smaller river (perhaps the St. George). Bessabez (Pósɑpehs) means "old complete or real man," suggesting that his people venerated him. This great chief arrived to meet Champlain at Kenduskeag with thirty followers in six canoes. Champlain tells us that the people sang and danced in greeting when Bessabez arrived. When he landed, they all sat in a circle on the ground. Cabahis also came with twenty to thirty companions. Bessabez greeted Champlain and asked him to sit down, offering him venison and other game. Champlain told him that the French wanted to settle there to teach them cultivation and wanted them to reconcile with their enemies, the Micmacs and Montagnais. Bessabez welcomed the idea, indicating that his people desired peace and wanted to hunt beaver and trade the fur for European goods. Bessabez was primarily interested in French weapons, for the Micmac and Montagnais already had guns. The Penobscots did not, and were at a disadvantage as a result.[34] Champlain knew of the enmity between the Abenakis and the Micmacs, Maliseets, and Montagnais. However, it is not clear whether hostility grew from the European visitors' making alliances and supplying arms and other goods to allies or whether it preceded European contact.

Several incidents recorded by visiting Europeans provide a glimpse into the complicated relationships among the various native communities living around the Gulf of Maine between 1604 and 1625. Lescarbot tells us that the Micmac interaction with Basque fishermen resulted in the Micmacs' acquiring the shallop, a wooden boat somewhat sturdier and more seaworthy than the birch canoe.[35] The Micmacs used these shallops to travel great distances. Most of the Basques were traveling to Newfoundland, though some may have gone as far west as Nova Scotia. There is no evidence for Basques on the Maine coast. This early alliance may already have affected Micmac-Abenaki relations. In one instance a Micmac named Oagimou retrieved the body of another Micmac, Panounias, from a village on the Penobscot River and returned it to Port Royal, Nova Scotia. If the Micmacs spoke Basque (as Lescarbot reports), one must infer that the two peoples had extensive contact and at least a trading relationship. In any case, Basque-Micmac trade provided Micmacs with European goods including shallops, possibly firearms, and other technological innovations that gave them an advantage over the Penobscots.

Champlain also wrote that the Abenakis of the Androscoggin and Kennebec River regions no longer grew corn along the coast because of their wars, since their enemies came and took their crops. This observation indicates that the war had been going on for some time prior to 1607. It is impossible to say for certain, however, whether the presence of Europeans in Acadia caused the war by providing a trade advantage and introducing shallops and new weapons to the Micmacs, or whether the presence of Europeans simply gave the Micmacs a technological advantage in a long-standing argument. Either way, the war did take place and created the necessity for an alliance of Abenakis in central and western Maine to combat the eastern threat posed by marauding Micmacs. Such an alliance could be made only under the direction of a powerful political and spiritual leader—Bessabez.

It appears that Bessabez may have been neutral at the start of the war, but events drew him into the conflict. When Champlain visited the Penobscots in 1604, his guides (Maliseet and/or Micmac) were able to converse and visit with the chiefs there. When Champlain continued to the Kennebec, however, his guides left him because they were great enemies of the people of the Kennebec. Bessabez's people hunted and fished at least as far east as Mount Desert Island and as far west as Merrymeeting Bay, according to Champlain's observations. Other, lesser chiefs lived in each village. On the Kennebec lived a chief called Sasinou or Sasanoa, who, as this story began, was a great enemy of the Micmacs. A leader from the Androscoggin was Marchin, and at Saco Bay, Honemechin (Olnemechin) was a chief whose language was unintelligible to Champlain's Micmac and Maliseet guides. Of Marchin, Champlain wrote, "He had a reputation of being one of the valiant ones of his people. He had a fine appearance and moved with dignity."[36] Champlain reported that Marchin returned an Etechemin (Maliseet) boy. The return of a captive took place as a gesture of peace, but indicated earlier conflicts. Of Olnemechin, we learn only of his different language and the fact that he lived in a village fortified against enemies with a palisade of logs. Farther east, the Maliseet-Passamaquoddy people lived mostly along the St. John River but hunted and fished in territory that overlapped with Penobscots at Mount Desert Island.

Chief Secoudon (Chkoudon) led the St. John people. Panounias, a Maliseet who had married an Abenaki woman, was a friend of the French. Together with his wife, he served as guide to Sieur de Monts on his 1605 voyage to Cape Cod. Membertou (Mabretou) was the Micmac chief at Port Royal. He and his wife lived in the home of a French trader. Membertou led a war party of Micmacs against Sasanoa, Olnemechin, and Marchin. Membertou was also the grand chief of the Micmacs, according to Lescarbot. These chiefs were the major political leaders who took part in the Micmac-Abenaki War that occurred between 1607 and 1615. Its origins are only partly understood, but its outcome resulted in the death of Bessabez and many of his followers.

The events of the war are sketchy, but they are important because they illustrate how the presence of the French and consequently the uneven distribution of technological resources such as firearms placed the easternmost tribes in a position of political power over those who did not have access to these weapons. Penobscot leaders quickly developed strategies of resistance to respond to the new threat. We know from Champlain's account that the people of the Saco and Kennebec Rivers held Micmac and Maliseet prisoners. Therefore the hostilities must have begun before Champlain and company arrived. In September of 1606, the French engaged Messamoet (Port de LaHave) and Secoudon (St. John) as guides and as negotiators with the Abenakis of the Androscoggin and Saco Rivers. The French hoped to make peace and to trade with the Abenakis.

The two guides brought their shallop filled with French goods and presented them to Olnemechin. But when Olnemechin did not reciprocate, Messamoet decided to make war on him.[37]

Then, in November of that same year, some of Secoudon's people told him that Iouaniscou and his followers had killed some people from the Penobscot and Kennebec River communities near Mount Desert Island and carried off their women as prisoners.[38] While we do not know who Iouaniscou was, Champlain tells us that Panounias (from St. John) was killed in revenge for what Iouaniscou did.[39] Therefore, Iouaniscou was probably a renegade or overzealous Maliseet who perhaps had a family feud with some of the Penobscot or Kennebec people.

These events led to an alliance of Micmacs and Maliseets against the people from the region between the Penobscot and Saco Rivers. As grand chief of the Micmacs, Membertou took leadership of his war party. When Oagimou retrieved the body of Panounias and returned it to Port Royal, Membertou urged all to take revenge and make war on their enemies in the spring.[40] Between June 1 and June 20, Champlain reports that Membertou assembled thirty or forty people (Lescarbot reported two or three hundred and said that many of them were from the Gaspé). The war party left for Saco on June 29 and returned August 10.[41] Membertou reported that he had killed twenty and wounded ten or twelve and that the chiefs, Olnemechin and Marchin, had both been killed. Curiously, Champlain claims that Sasinou killed the Abenaki chiefs and was himself killed. This seems unlikely, because Sasinou was chief of the Kennebec and reportedly held Micmac or Maliseet prisoners and thus would be allied with the Abenakis. An English account confirms the French account of the war between the Abenakis and the Micmacs and Maliseets. Martin Pring returned to the Maine coast in 1607 or 1608. When his crew reached present-day Nova Scotia, they met Micmacs who could speak French.[42] He also reported that the Micmacs were at war with chief Sasinou (of the Kennebec) and that they had killed Sasinou's son that summer.[43] Lescarbot tells us that Bessabez was appointed grand chief over all the Abenakis upon the deaths of Olnemechin and Marchin and that the English later killed him.[44] Williamson, however, reports that someone from the Micmac-Maliseet alliance killed Bessabez in 1617.[45]

These early-seventeenth-century conflicts illustrate the complexities of political alliances among the Natives of Maine. It also appears that the presence of Basque, French, and English fishermen, explorers, and traders exacerbated whatever conflicts were already in place. The introduction of firearms into one area created a necessity for firearms in other communities; this, in turn, fueled competition, conflict, and the beginning of the fur trade in this region. However, Penobscots had yet another challenge to confront beyond the introduction of new weapons.

After the death of Bessabez, a severe outbreak of smallpox that traveled from Maine to Rhode Island killed thousands of Native people. Some tribes disappeared altogether.[46] Thus, war and disease left Natives weakened and vulnerable to an increasing number of European settlers who began to build homes along the coast—primarily in southern Maine.

The loss of Bessabez and the loss of population from the smallpox epidemic weakened the Penobscots' military capability and therefore their negotiating strength with neighboring tribes and the Europeans. Most of the Abenakis could trade with the French to the north in Quebec, or with other middlemen between themselves and the French, but warfare with the Micmacs posed some problems. Therefore, they were seeking direct trade with the English who entered the Gulf of Maine.

Though the Penobscots were eager to trade and enjoyed the technology of Europeans, several encounters convinced them of the inferiority of the Europeans' social skills. Traditionally, meetings between different communities followed a certain protocol. An exchange of persons would be made as a sign of trust. In one encounter, both sides offered to exchange men to sleep in each other's camps at night, but the Europeans broke the basic rules of hospitality by kidnapping some of the Native men. The Penobscots soon learned to be mistrustful and to resist the Europeans' control. These early encounters established an economic relationship based on trade for furs in exchange for European goods. The introduction of firearms in this trade facilitated hunting for furs but had the less desirable effect of causing the Natives to become more dependent upon European trade. Not surprisingly, bows and arrows disappeared in a relatively short period of time. Firearms became the weapons of choice for all the Native people in the Northeast, who used the new weapons to obtain furs for the newly expanded fur market.

The need for guns, powder, and shot, and especially for gun parts and repairs, increased the dependence of Native people on European traders. Their world began to change as European settlers increasingly seized aboriginal lands and as missionaries and strange new illnesses called traditional spiritual beliefs into question. Tradition, though silenced, could not be eradicated. Lewis Spence writes, "When a religious system is suppressed and another takes its place and official status, the customs associated with the older faith are not easily discarded by the folk. The sanction of tradition keeps them alive." They wish to take no risk of offending the older gods.[47] Henrie Glassie defines tradition as both static and fluid: "It can whirl in place, revolving through kaleidoscopic transformations, or it can strike helical, progressive or retrograde tracks through time."[48] Tradition, as Glassie defines it, is "the means for deriving the future from the past."[49]

When the Penobscots encountered new challenges brought by Europeans, they were able to turn to their traditions for responses. The traditional hunting skills of men assisted in the hunting of fur-bearing animals for trade with Europeans to obtain firearms that made hunting easier. Traditional alliance making through trade and kinship ties was extended to the French. That led the English to mistrust Natives. Penobscots attempted to develop trade with both nations, but found relations with the English more problematic. The consequence of new alliances with Europeans redrew Native political alliances and shifted the center of Native power away from southern to central Maine. The introduction of firearms also altered the waging of warfare, giving advantage to those who had them and weakening those who did not.

Initial contacts with Europeans taught Natives that their advantage lay in their knowledge of the interior waterways and their ability to move away from coastal threats. Their traditional knowledge assisted them in establishing both a fur trade and later military alliances with the French in Quebec. Penobscots' reactions to first contacts that led to such decision making shaped their future.

In the following narrative I will show that, as Europeans who came to North America brought their own traditions and marked the landscape with place-names like New England, Cape Elizabeth, Mount Desert, and Acadia, the Penobscots countered the redefining of their world and followed their traditions as a means of coping, resisting, and adjusting to the new realities in their lives, ensuring a future by bringing forth traditions from the past.

Chapter 3

FACING THE FUTURE
The Seventeenth Century

> If tradition is a people's creation out of their own past, its character is not stasis but continuity; its opposite is not change but oppression, the intrusion of a power that thwarts the course of development. Oppressed people are made to do what others will them to do.... Acting traditionally, by contrast, they use their own resources—their own tradition, one might say—to create their own future, to do what they will themselves to do.[1]
>
> —HENRY GLASSIE

The presence of Europeans brought both difficulties and opportunities to the Penobscots. Hostile acts and diseases characterized the difficulties, while trade, new technology, and other previously unknown cultural and political practices provided opportunities. As we saw in the last chapter, Natives and Europeans initially forged their relationships in mutual suspicion, reinforced with instruments of war. As trading began in earnest, this mutual suspicion continued. Nevertheless, both sides adapted technology and lifeways from each other. Penobscots reacted to the newcomers in their territory by collocating new ideas as well as new technology into their own cultural traditions. They began to create a future based on their own needs, relying on negotiation, war, and alliances to resist control. Economically, they adapted their traditional hunting skills in the shift from trade with neighboring tribes to fur trading with Europeans. They also began, under the influence of Jesuit priests, to adopt some European methods and crops into their agricultural practices. Penobscots incorporated some Roman Catholic beliefs into indigenous religious beliefs, while new clothing, new weapons, and tools also found their way into the Penobscot lifestyle.

Lack of recognition by European nations of Penobscots' rights to land brought new challenges in the seventeenth century. As the English and

French began to make claims on their territory, the Penobscots soon realized they were dealing with two nations—and that they could trade with either. However, kinship ties through marriage cemented Penobscot relationships with the French. In addition, the English preference to move into southern Maine, out of Penobscot territory, further strengthened French-Penobscot alliances. While some English traders, Isaac Allerton at Machias, for example, tried to gain a foothold in Penobscot territory, the French traders, with the backing of the French military, had better success. The English alliance with traditional Penobscot enemies—the Mohawks—created further instability for English-Penobscot relations.

But who were the Penobscots in the seventeenth century? The historical and archaeological record suggests rapid population loss and consequent coalescing of villages. Epidemic diseases made their way to the Northeast at least as early as the seventeenth century. The paralyzing effect of lethal epidemics explains why Native Americans were unable to restrain the colonization of America to any extent. Like European populations during the Black Death of the fourteenth century, Native American populations dwindled from such new pathogens as smallpox, tetanus, and influenza. High mortality profoundly influenced Native American mental health, which in turn affected the energy and success with which people engaged in subsistence activities. High mortality also undermined the faith of many Native Americans. According to Dobyns, the loss of core confidence left them peculiarly vulnerable to the transculturation promoted by invading Europeans.[2]

Native American encounters with disease before Columbus did not significantly reduce population numbers. McNeill suggests that domestic animals were largely responsible for carrying diseases to humans in Europe, and the lack of large herds of such animals in Native America before Europeans arrived probably prevented such epidemics from spreading across the continent.[3] But the abrupt confrontation with infections from European and African populations took a great toll.

We do not know to what extent the northeastern region was affected by epidemics before 1615. We do know that an epidemic of uncertain type swept through the Massachusetts Bay area between 1616 and 1617. Smallpox arrived in 1633, followed by influenza in 1636, scarlet fever in 1637, and smallpox again in 1639. McNeill writes that the smaller and more isolated populations of North and South America were just as vulnerable to European infections as the denser populations of Mexico and Peru, even though the numbers in less densely populated areas were insufficient to maintain a chain of infection on the spot for very long at a time. McNeill postulates ratios of 20 to 1 or even 25 to 1 between pre-Columbian populations and the nadir of Native American population curves (in 1900).[4] Very cold temperatures between 1600 and 1700 may also have had an effect on populations in the North, resulting in poor agricultural crops. Scarcity of food led to greater susceptibility to illness, and famine aided in the spread of diseases.[5]

Ramenofsky explored evidence of pre-seventeenth-century epidemics in the Northeast using the archaeological record of population change independently from historical records. Her method involves analyses of settlement data to determine if a period of stability existed until the period of historic documentation. She notes that in the absence of medical assistance, initial introductions of infectious parasites typically result in large-scale epidemics with mortality ranging from 30 to 100 percent. The archaeological record from central New York suggests that population continued to increase through the sixteenth century, refuting Dobyn's hypothesis that epidemics devastated the Northeast prior to 1613, twenty years before recorded epidemics for that area. However, the archaeological analysis shows that the Iroquois population drastically diminished during the seventeenth century.[6]

Interactions between northeastern populations of Iroquois and Algonquian peoples suggest that using a corollary between her data for the Iroquois and that of the rest of the Northeast is reasonable. Dobyns reports that epidemics in New England took place in 1568, 1574, 1586, and 1592.[7] However, the twenty-four epidemics occurring between 1613 and 1690 in the Northeast may have been more overwhelming in terms of population decrease. In the winter of 1633–1634, an epidemic originating in New England spread north and west. From 1668 to 1670 another epidemic originated in New France and diffused east, south, and west. Once again in 1678 diseases in New England moved west. Infected survivors of decimated villages moved to other villages, resulting in the catastrophic decline visible regionally by the seventeenth century.[8]

The results of Ramenofsky's investigation of aboriginal population loss in eastern North America do not entirely refute Dobyn's hypothesis that aboriginal population decline tended to precede written documentation and was catastrophic in nature. Central New York populations appear to have increased in the sixteenth century. However, there is the enigmatic disappearance of St. Lawrence Iroquoians to consider. These communities may have experienced consequences of disease earlier than the New York Iroquois due to accidents of proximity. Remnant populations from St. Lawrence may have moved to New York villages, creating the record of apparent population increase in the New York area. However, the situation is more complex than Dobyn's model suggests. Because local or regional catastrophic population loss began early and occurred in less than a hundred years, survivors may have already adapted to that loss by coalescing in remaining villages at the time of the initial descriptions of communities by early explorers. Processes of village fusion and fission, or abandonment of whole regions, are evidences of those adaptations.[9]

Those groups that were located farther inland and those that were mobile did not suffer high mortality from disease as quickly as those in close proximity to European settlements. One hundred years of relative health followed preliminary sixteenth-century disease experience, during which time populations adjusted to the catastrophe and recovered somewhat, demographically.

Some additional evidence from Maine archaeological data may help illuminate the problem of population loss due to diseases. Current archaeological research supports anthropologist Frank G. Speck's description of the Penobscot community as a "social or dialectic unit" rather than a historically homogeneous group.[10] By this he means that the Indian Island village represents the surviving population of a number of other communities that no longer exist. Archaeologists hypothesize two pehistoric populations for Maine—one that subsisted on coastal resources and another that lived year-round at interior sites. Sanger's research in Passamaquoddy and Penobscot Bay refutes the hypothesis, indicating winter occupation in coastal sites.[11] Boothbay Harbor also shows evidence of year-round occupation. For the past 3,500 years or so (dubbed the Ceramic Period by archaeologists), coastal populations moved around the marine area. Interior sites along lakes and rivers in Maine suggest summer to fall occupancy. Sanger believes that winter hunting sites may be in different, as yet unfound, locations. Archaeology challenges the assumptions made by historians that Native Americans regularly traveled from coast to interior as part of a seasonal round. It may be that they altered the course of their movement in response to the European initiation of trade in furs. Bourque postulated as early as 1973 that the fur trade brought interior hunting people to the coast in the summer in order to take advantage of European summer sailing itineraries.[12] Jesuit priest Pierre Biard first documented this movement for the Micmacs, and most scholars have applied this concept to other Maine–Maritime Provinces populations.[13]

Sanger reports many archaeological sites along the coast and approximately two hundred discovered along the Penobscot River. But when Champlain and other explorers arrived in the early 1600s, he reports few people living on the coast. In addition, Champlain noted that communities along the Kennebec had ceased growing corn at coastal sites due to marauding neighbors. The local people told him he would have to go far inland to find Indians who cultivated corn.[14] The failure of agricultural crops during the "Little Ice Age"[15] may have been a factor in bringing Micmacs into coastal Maine to raid for corn and other crops.

But what of population loss and the spread of epidemics? If the coastal population represented in the archaeological record disappeared rapidly just prior to the seventeenth century, it may have been in large part due to epidemics introduced by earlier traders and fishermen visiting the St. Lawrence and the Gulf of Maine during the sixteenth century. Historical documents provide supportive evidence. Biard reported that the chief of the Port of St. John was ill and that about sixty others had died during the year at Cape de la Heve (Lunenburg, Nova Scotia), although none of the French had been sick. He also noted the sparse population of the region at the time of his visit. Micmac chief Membertou reported that in his youth his people were "planted thickly as the hairs on his head."[16] The death of sixty in a single community in a single year must have been devastating. In addition, the epidemics that followed throughout the seventeenth century continued to devastate the populations of the Northeast such that much of coastal Maine became unpopulated during this time.

Similarly, Biard reported in 1612 that the people in Penobscot (about three hundred) had a fever and had been sick for four months. He also reported that the people living along and between the St. John and Kennebec Rivers numbered about one thousand and the Micmacs numbered about two thousand. These figures seem very low, but they may represent populations already much reduced by diseases. Two generations later, in 1646, Jesuit priest Father Druillettes sojourned at the Norridgewock village on the Kennebec, staying for three seasons, then returned to Quebec. He visited Norridgewock again in 1651 and reported that many had died in the community while he was away. He called upon twelve to thirteen villages along the Kennebec and the coast of Acadia. Most of the Kennebec villages had disappeared by the end of the seventeenth century.

Once an epidemic passes, some population recovery takes place as resistant survivors pass their immunities along to their offspring. However, smallpox and influenza and childhood diseases that created a high infant mortality rate continued to keep numbers low in the Penobscot River communities until the twentieth century. Coping with such severe loss required some adaptation of traditions. At first, Native Americans turned to their healers for assistance. In most cases, they could not help. Instead, healers ordered the most practical solution: hasten the death of the terminally ill. Biard reported that sick persons ceased eating and that native physicians customarily threw water on them or buried them while still living.[17] Biard also reported that the Natives believed in two sources of disease, the first the mind of the patient, which desires something, and the second sorcery, "which can only be repelled by sweats and other ceremonies."[18] Sorcerers performed religious incantations, ceremonies, and dances to heal the sick. If a healer declared that a person would die, the community abandoned him.[19]

Catholic priests challenged these practices, taking up abandoned ill people and nursing them in their homes. So many died in spite of the best efforts of Indian healers that people began to doubt their own beliefs and turned to the priests for comfort. According to Trigger, the Hurons believed that the Jesuits were responsible for the epidemics. Like Native healers, Jesuits appeared to have great supernatural power, and the baptisms they performed were feared as charms that caused death.[20] However, the Penobscots had a different experience. Biard reported that the Natives perceived that the French were protected from the epidemics as chosen people of God. They accepted baptism as a sort of sacred pledge of friendship and alliance with the French, though they had little understanding of Christian teachings at this time.[21] Biard, biased as a Catholic and French missionary, may not have reported accurately about this, but perhaps priestly kindness and care for the sick and prayerful manners influenced Penobscot respect for the French missionaries. Penobscot spiritual leaders continued to have influence in Penobscot communities, even with the priest present, and most people embraced those elements of Christian belief that made sense to their own belief system as one way of coping with the presence of missionaries and the terrible epidemics.

Population decline from disease clearly weakened the Penobscots' military strength and prevented them from stopping the movement of settlers onto lands adjacent to their villages. It also destroyed the elderly and children more than any other group. An important result of destruction of the elderly is the loss of traditional knowledge such as languages, prayers, and skills. The loss is even more significant when the variation of traditions between villages declines; the traditions become more homogeneous when numerous villages disappear and the remaining communities become refugee communities.

Penobscot response to the new economic reality brought by the fur trade also instituted much social change. Europeans needed Penobscot cooperation, while Penobscots viewed trade with the Europeans as a useful means of improving their way of life. But Europeans pressured Natives to change, especially to become Christian, and this created strife. Native people sought to enhance and change, not to eradicate, their culture, in spite of European beliefs that their own way of life represented a "higher" civilization. In addition, private traders caused Native communities social problems by using alcohol to get Natives drunk and cheat them. In response to complaints about trading abuses, Massachusetts attempted to regulate all Indian trade. Natives sometimes found English goods scarce and traded with the French. When Penobscots could not obtain French goods, they traded with the English. While much fur trade took place between the Penobscots and the French, the English of Massachusetts initiated trade with Maine's Natives.

Hubbard reports that the New Englanders raised a substantial crop of corn in 1625 and the Massachusetts Bay Colony sent boats laden with corn to the Kennebec and returned with seven hundred pounds of beaver and other furs.[22] A year later New England's traders went to Monhegan Island and purchased all the goods they could from some Englishmen who were breaking up their plantation there. The Puritans also purchased goods from the French. They then exchanged these goods for furs with the Indians. The Puritans needed this trade in order to survive as a colony. Because they were out of favor with the English government, they had to survive on their own, since few English goods found their way to Massachusetts at this time. The fur trade supported them for a number of years.

The Puritans demonstrated some awareness of Penobscot needs by responding to their demand for wampum. Within just a few years, the Pilgrims discovered a great demand for wampum among the Indians in Maine.[23] Boston traders purchased wampum from the Long Island Indians; it gave the Boston traders an advantage over the fishermen and other individual traders on the Maine coast. Wampum consisted of circular beads made of white and blue clamshells. The Natives used the shells to make beads to decorate their clothing. They also wove the beads into belts used in marriage contracts and to send messages from one community to another. Puritans had extended their trade to the Penobscots by 1629, reaching into territory previously dominated by the French. Maine's Natives successfully hunted animals and prepared pelts for this new market. Maine became the greatest source of beaver pelts for the Plymouth colony. Between 1631 and 1636, the Pilgrims sent twelve thousand pounds of beaver pelts to England.[24] But their exclusive channel to the pelts of Maine soon closed as French fur traders once again moved into the region.

For a time, the Puritans became embroiled in the conflict that arose between two French trading rivals, La Tour on the St. John River and D'Aulnay at Pentagoet. Perhaps because D'Aulnay took the Puritans' Penobscot outpost from them in 1640, the Puritans preferred to trade with La Tour. La Tour approached Boston in November of 1641 asking to trade with the colony but also asking for aid against D'Aulnay. Boston merchants began trading with La Tour but declined to become involved in the traders' disputes. The Boston government allowed La Tour to land and train his soldiers in Boston, however. Hubbard indicates

FIG. 3. The chapel of Jesuit priest Sebastian Rasles at Norridgewock. *Courtesy Deering Collection, Raymond F. Fogler Library Special Collections, University of Maine.*

that although La Tour was implicated in the death of two Englishmen at Machias, the fact that he was a Protestant, and an enemy of their Catholic enemy at Penobscot, allowed Massachusetts leaders to forgive his transgressions. D'Aulnay sent a letter to the colony charging the Puritan traders with breach of covenant in entertaining La Tour and his wife. Fearing a war with France, the Massachusetts Bay Colony sent D'Aulnay a small present as payment for damages. However, when Puritan captain Dobson sailed his trading ship from Boston to Cape Sable and traded with the Indians there, D'Aulnay captured him and sent the men home in two old shallops.[25] This event forced the Puritans out of the fur trade. However, other traders took their place among the Penobscots.

Penobscots altered their tradition of conservation of game for future generations during the fur trade.[26] However, some traditions, such as the sharing of resources with other members of the community, especially families with no hunters, and reverence for their land continued. Since Penobscot territory teemed with animals whose pelts provided a means to obtain trade goods, hunters soon began to collect pelts in greater numbers than their previous needs for clothing and bedding had warranted. With these furs they could easily purchase European agricultural items such as flour and other grains and salt pork. These items alleviated some of the hunger of winter famine. But the increasing decimation of furbearers created additional food shortages. Jesuit Sebastian Rasle, living at Norridgewock, reported that the hunters had "so destroyed the game of their county that for ten years they have no longer found elks or deer. They go to the seashore twice a year to obtain food."[27] While elk and deer are not furbearers, Rasles reported that Penobscots sold dressed elk skins to the French and English in exchange for coats, blankets, large kettles, guns, hatchets, and knives.[28] Elk skins were valued for clothing, and their flesh supported hunters and their families. The lack of elk and deer represent diminishing hunting resources in the region. The fur trade reduced natural food resources, forcing increasing dependence on trade for subsistence.

Economic competition among all people involved in the fur trade resulted in conflict. The D'Aulnay–La Tour rivalry is a good example. La Tour's wife died when her husband's rival destroyed their trading post. However, when D'Aulnay died, La Tour married D'Aulnay's widow and consolidated most of the Acadian fur trade for a time.[29] Although the French retained the post at Penobscot until 1654, the District of Maine came under the jurisdiction of Massachusetts beginning in 1652. Well-documented territorial disputes between New England and Acadia centered on the region between the Penobscot and Kennebec Rivers.[30] The New Englanders captured trading posts at the St. John River and Port Royal, Nova Scotia, as well as on the Penobscot River. Consequently, the Massachusetts government began granting fur trade patents to individuals in 1657. However, after the early period of coastal trade, New England rarely profited, but in order to keep colonists safe and to foster good relations, Massachusetts maintained a system of truckhouses to supply Indians with goods.[31] Good relations eluded the parties, however, since the English insisted upon dominating the Native American people and moving settlers onto their lands.

Penobscots became accustomed to trading with both the English and the French during this early period of colonization. The pattern of French-English tug-of-war over trading posts continued for more than a century, and the Penobscots did their best to try to keep the peace, although with little success.

Barter and trade were not new to Penobscot culture. The Penobscots played a game that illustrated the importance of barter in their culture. Called nolǝmahǝméwɑkan, "barter dance game and ceremony,"[32] it consisted of two groups of players who would exchange articles. These might be as modest as a spoon or more valuable items such as snowshoes, moose skin garments, or an ax. After completing the exchange, dancing continued throughout the night.

Meanwhile, as Penobscots came to know both European nationalities, they began to adapt new ideas and materials into their culture. The Penobscots borrowed words from Latin, French, and English to describe new items. They adopted many French words for religious terms and English words to describe domestic animals. Some examples are alámeske (animate intransitive verb), "he offers mass," from French *á la messe*; Saláwəyı, "salt" (French *sel*); áhahso (English horse); pìksı (English pig). Curiously, the days of the week show a kind of blending of elements of all three cultures. For example, Monday through Thursday are called αmskawashsalóhkemək, nısalóhkemək, nehsalóhkemək, yewalókemək, "first workday, second workday, third workday, fourth workday." The concept of "workdays" reflects European ideas, not a hunter-gatherer society. The word for Friday reflects the Catholic religious idea of the Crucifixion, eskéwahtəḱek, "day of the cross." The weekend days, ketáwsαnətek and éhsαnətek, "Saturday and Sunday," derive from the English "Sunday." Penobscots borrowed words for garden vegetables such as turnips, cabbages, and so on, from the English, while their words for soup (lasòp), beer (lappìel), and ragout (làko) come from the French. A bit of Latin can be found in pàhtələyαs, the Penobscot term for prayer, priest, or nun, from Latin *pater*.[33] Of course, the same process took place in American English with the adaptation of many Native words.

With the French appeared the associated influence of the Roman Catholic faith represented mostly by Jesuit priests. In addition to the fur trade and the introduction of European items that the Penobscots accepted into their culture, the presence of Jesuit priest Louis P. Thury, sent to the Penobscots in the autumn of 1688, initiated significant innovations. In 1696, Thury began building a new church for the Penobscots upriver from St. Castin's fort. In addition to building the church and promoting his religion, Thury also promoted new agricultural products and methods in hopes of "improving" Penobscot health. Thury described a scene of all the men, women, and children working in their fields and expressed the hope that they would harvest enough grain to feed themselves year-round. He reported that the men agonized over cultivation, since it was women's work—men's work was hunting.[34] This is a significant remark, because it reinforces the idea that men did not take part in agriculture prior to 1696. It may be that women did not, either. We know from Champlain's accounts that Native people from eastern Maine traded with the people at Saco for agricultural produce.[35] Also, none of the early explorers mentioned seeing gardens on the Penobscot. Apparently agriculture was not very important on the Penobscot River in the seventeenth century, until the French Jesuits encouraged farming. Penobscots began to grow crops to supplement hunted and gathered foods, but they also began to eat other European foods they acquired through trade.

Some of these foods included white flour for biscuits and fry bread, salt pork, and a mixture of new vegetables and grains cultivated by settlers. New items of material culture included woven cloth for clothes and bedding, metal pots, cups, spoons and knives, firearms, jewelry, and so on. Soon Penobscots sifted through European religion, languages, stories, music, and other aspects of European culture. They retained the most attractive and re-created these into the newly defined Penobscot tradition for the current generation. The core values regarding the importance of land, spiritual power, and reverence remained, even as European actions assaulted those values.

Treaties developed in Europe between France and England ignored Native claims to the land. For example, the English returned the entire region of Acadia to France, including the coast of Maine as far west as Penobscot Bay, as a result of a 1633 treaty.[36] As a result, the law prohibited any Englishman from trading with the French. Charles D'Aulnay, the French governor of Acadia, seized the English fort at Pentagoet (present-day Castine) on the Penobscot River in 1635. Governor Bradford of Massachusetts sent an expedition to resecure the fort, but it failed. The Massachusetts colony needed to trade with the French but in doing so had to break English law.

To reinforce their claims to the land, the English forged an alliance with the Mohawks that increasingly distanced Massachusetts's authorities from Maine's Native people. Massachusetts's officials ensured enmity with the Eastern Algonquians when they allied themselves with the Mohawks in 1677. Hubbard says, "Fear thereof was the only thing that awed the Indians about Pemaquid into a . . . more ready compliance with the English."[37] The Mohawks obliged the English by arming themselves and traveling into the territories of the Eastern Abenaki, killing Blind Will, a chief of Piscataqua villages and enemy of the English. Maine's Natives turned to the French for assistance, and marriage between the Penobscot chief's daughter and a Frenchman strengthened the bond.

Madockawando was chief at this time. We know he was a powerful shaman from his name, which means "supernatural tree shaker." Madockawando permitted his daughter to marry the Baron de St. Castin, who accompanied the new French governor of Acadia, Hector Andigné de Grandfontaine, to Pentagoet in 1667.[38] With this marriage, Madockawando forged an important kinship alliance with the French, hoping to provide his people with a source of trade goods. We know more about the baron than we do of the sagamore.

Castin was only eighteen when he arrived at Penobscot, but he already had five years experience in the military. He lived among the Penobscots and developed a thriving fur trade business from which he gained substantial wealth. He became the recognized leader of the French at Penobscot and married about 1678 when he was twenty-six years old. He had already spent about nine years among the Penobscots when he was married, so this was not a decision made in youthful haste. He took pains to have his marriage approved by the church in 1681 or 1682, but even that action did not provide him with approval from either the French or the English. The English accused him of having several wives. (He may have actually had two as a war chief, according to Native custom, but there is no record of a second Catholic marriage or death of a first wife.) The French governor of Acadia (Perrot) arrested him at Port Royal in 1687, on the charge of libertinism and debauchery. However, the governor was a fierce fur trade rival and hated Castin, so little weight can be placed on the charges.

Castin responded to the charges, dismissing them as being "on pretence of a little weakness I had for some women."[39] Perrot's successor, M. De Menneval, was instructed to coerce Castin from his "vagabond life and trade with the Indians, &c., and his illicit trade with the English," to pursue a line of conduct more becoming to a nobleman. In spite of the lack of support Castin received from the French in Acadia, he seems to have remained politically loyal. He asked for thirty soldiers to keep the English at bay—claiming he could assemble an army of four hundred Abenakis who had his confidence.

Madockawando is reported to have been the adopted son of Essemonosque (Assiminasqua), the Kennebec sagamore who signed deeds in 1653. If so, it is difficult to determine exactly how he became the Penobscot chief, though the two communities were closely allied. Williamson reported that John Attean was a descendant of the Baron de Castine. If this is true (Williamson knew Attean, lending some credence to the tale), then the baron's descendants reside at Indian Island to this day. We do know that Madockawando and his war chief Mogg fought alongside the French throughout the King Philip's and King William's Wars. He led his people until disease took him in 1698.

Castin, meanwhile, as a result of his successful marriage alliance, carried on a very profitable fur trade with the Indians. Castin remained among the Penobscots until after King William's War, when he returned to France in 1701 to take charge of his estates. He died in France in 1703. At least two of his sons, Anselm and Joseph Dabadis, remained in Maine to take leadership roles in Penobscot affairs. They continued to live in two worlds as their father had, traveling to France but also living among the Penobscots.[40]

Anselm was a military leader who took a contingent of French and Indian warriors to battle against the English in 1707, at Port Royal. He was under the command of the French governor of Acadia. At least six of his men were Penobscots, though we do not know their names. Anselm was often called the Baron de St. Castin and married a French woman at Port Royal. He and his brother Dabadis lived with their mother's people on the Penobscot at least until 1727.[41]

Kinship ties strengthened the bonds Penobscots had with the French, through Castin, but did not lead them to become true French allies. While Native people would fight in wars for most of a century (1676–1763), they fought alongside the French mostly for protection from the English and because of their need for trade goods, not because of any interest in European political maneuvering. They did, however, adopt Catholic Christianity, for the most part welcoming the aid given by the French Jesuit priests in their villages.

The presence of Jesuits resident in Native communities brought about both political and cultural changes. Anselm Castin reestablished a fort on the St. John River where additional fur trading could take place. Thus the French had allies and fur trade partners among Native people from the Kennebec to Port Royal in Nova Scotia. They encouraged all the eastern tribes to be friendly with each other, and there is no evidence of further wars among any of Maine and Maritime tribes after the Micmac-Abenaki War of 1608–1615.

However, there was fighting between Maine's Natives and the Iroquois. According to oral tradition, the Penobscots never feared the Europeans nearly as much as they feared an Iroquoian tribe allied with the English known as the Mohawks. There are several stories among both Penobscots and Passamaquoddies of Mohawk wars and one notable tale of a Penobscot woman who escaped capture and torture by the dreaded Iroquoian enemy.[42] Druillettes indicated, during his mission to Boston before 1650, that the Maine Indians regarded the Mohawk with dread. Mohawks, allied with the English, continuously fought the Maine Indians and their French allies. The Penobscots desired trade with the English for guns and ammunition, tools, and food. They undoubtedly would have promoted peaceful relations with the English if it were not for the European wars fought in North America. Additionally, numerous small and scattered incidents that developed between settlers and Penobscots enhanced hostility. Druillettes reported in 1651, for example, that Mohawks intended by a general massacre to assist the English in destroying the Kennebec Natives because the Abenakis had been for many years allied with the Canadian Algonquians.[43] Penobscots feared that the English preferred to destroy them rather than to negotiate peace.[44]

As the seventeenth century drew to a close, conflicts and disagreements between the European settlers and the Native people of New England led to serious armed warfare and dreadful consequences for the Native populations. Natives hoped to remove the settlers from their lands—while the English and French fought with each other over dominance of North America in general and the area known as the Province of Maine or Acadia in particular.

No one could predict that such arguments would lead to a century of war, the displacement of many of the Native people, and the coalescence of refugees from many villages to a few villages located on interior riverine sites. Many Natives from southern and western Maine had permanently moved to Canada by the end of the century of conflict. Those who remained clung to smaller and smaller pieces of territory and found larger and larger populations of European settlers powerfully intruding in the lives of the Penobscots.

Chapter 4

WAR DANCE

Shifting Strategies in the Dance of Resistance

Kwa ha hi-a
Kwa nu kwa nu de he no
Kwa nu de kwa nu de he no[1]

Each man shaves his head, reserving a little lock on the top, decorated with bird feathers and porcelain beads. He paints his head and face with red, white, green, yellow, and black colors, methodically applied by the aid of a little tallow. The warrior wears a ring in his nose; his ears are elongated by the weight of rings that swing and touch his shoulders when he moves. He smears his shirt with vermilion; he dons porcelain necklaces, silver bracelets, a large knife hanging over his breast, a girdle of variegated colors, and shoes of elk skin. War captains wear a gorget; chiefs fittingly sport a medallion that exhibits on one side the portrait of the King of France and, on the other, Mars and Bellona, who are joining hands with this device: *virtus et honor*.[2]

All the men are arranged in rows; in their midst stand large kettles of cooked meat cut into pieces. Designated captains begin to chant in order to bring the party to order. Once the group quiets, an orator solemnly addresses the guests. "The speaker addresses the panegyric of the king, eulogizes the French nation, argues in favor of war, and eloquently presents motives of glory and religion. At the end of his oration he names the captains who will lead the war party. The first Captain seizes the head of one of the animals whose flesh forms the feast, raises it high and cries 'Behold the head of the enemy!'"[3] Shouts of joy and applause greet his performance. The captain then sings his war song while dancing through the line of warriors carrying the beast's head. As he sings, he extols his war exploits and the audience answers his chants. During the song, he introduces an occasional grotesque joke. As he finishes his performance, he throws the animal head down disdainfully, as if his enemy could witness his actions. Other captains follow the first warrior; when all dances are completed, the distribution and consumption of the food ends the feast. While Penobscot dancers used their "welcoming dance" to greet visitors to Penobscot shores during the first part of the sixteenth century, the following hundred years saw dancing to a more frenzied drum. Through the war feast and dances, warriors gained courage and spiritual strength for battles. For a hundred years, Penobscots frequently performed war dances to prepare for battles throughout the Northeast.

Each generation must rechoreograph the dance of resistance for different reasons. Previous generations of Penobscots had experienced the numbing consequences of deadly, seemingly unrelenting illnesses. But survivors recovered, and their children carried more resistant antibodies. The uncertainty of the fur trade created cycles of lean times, but more difficulties awaited eighteenth-century Penobscots as political changes in Europe brought unwelcome conflict to their shores. The global trade problems and imperial visions that brought war to Europe during the last quarter of the seventeenth century and much of the eighteenth century fueled local antagonism.[4]

Political machinations of the French and English created complex problems for the Penobscots and their other Abenaki allies.[5] When involved in war, the Abenakis became dependent upon the French for supplies and thereby more easily influenced by them. In peacetime, however, it was the Jesuits who had to cope with the complications of English-Abenaki relations. The Abenakis became disillusioned with the French in Quebec, who urged them to fight New England (against the Jesuit protests) but supplied them with very few necessities. Those Abenakis who had gone to Canada gradually trickled back to their homes in Maine. The Jesuits, especially Rasles, favored the migration home because of the deleterious influence of French taverns near the mission in Quebec.[6] The Abenakis began returning in hope of finding peace with the English, refusing to join forces with the French military but holding firm to their Jesuit priests. Temporary migration was acceptable, but reverence for homeland prevailed.

Penobscots resisted taking sides in the battles of European nations, but English settlers marched upstream along major Maine rivers with their cattle, which grazed on Native Americans' corn. These settlers showed little regard for indigenous land rights. In addition, Penobscot kinship ties and alliances with the Norridgewock Abenakis and with the French, the need for supplies to sustain a hunting and fur-trading lifestyle, and revenge for attacks, kidnappings, and destruction of their property spurred Penobscots into the European quarrels, most often as allies of the French. Colonial historians generally name the wars of this period as King Philip's War (1675–1678), King William's War (1688–1699), Queen Anne's War (1703–1713), Dummer's War (1721–1726), and the French and Indian Wars (1745–1763; known as the Seven Years' War in Europe and Canada). All the wars had local manifestations involving Penobscots for reasons that had little to do with events in Europe. These provincial hostilities endangered the Penobscots' reverent relationship to the land, removed vital political and spiritual leaders, and disrupted subsistence activities and kinship ties.

King Philip's War in southern New England brought an end to peaceful relations between the Pilgrims of Massachusetts and the Indians throughout New England. Colin Calloway writes that the war "constituted an ecological disaster for the Abenakis" in Vermont, because it disrupted trade, agriculture, and seasonal mobility.[7] Unlike the Native people of Vermont, the Penobscots did not take part in the fighting at first, but a breakdown in negotiations with Massachusetts later brought them into battle.

Richard Walderne, a fur trader and influential member of the General Court of Massachusetts, was appointed by that distinguished assembly as sergeant major of the militia forces in Yorkshire. The General Court sent Walderne with Nicholas Shapleigh to negotiate a treaty with the Penobscots, threatening to sell all the Penobscot prisoners being held in Boston into slavery in the West Indies if the Penobscots in Maine refused to comply. The Penobscot chief Madockawando responded, "We were driven from our lands by the English about Kennebec and many of us died. We had no corn, powder or shot to kill venison and other fowl. The English pretend they are our friends, yet they did nothing to help us."[8] Madockawando's words reflected the troubled nature of Penobscot-English relations. Madockawando rejected the terms of the treaty on the grounds that it favored only the English and helped his people not at all.

Walderne asked Madockawando to bring Androscoggin villages into the treaty negotiations; the eminent chief agreed to organize a meeting of all parties at Taconic (on the Kennebec River). However, Walderne rudely interrupted Madockawando's venerable father's speech and refused to guarantee necessary supplies for hunting, so the talks were suspended. Madockawando's men joined other Abenakis in skirmishes against English settlers in southern Maine.

During February 1677, the Massachusetts councillors prepared an expedition against the Kennebec Abenakis. Headed by Major Walderne, the soldiers traveled to Black Point, where they met Abenakis who requested peace. Leaving some men at Arrowsick to build a fort, Walderne next went to Pemaquid. The village chief, Mattahando, said he wanted to make peace and would deliver English captives. Not satisfied with the three captives produced by Mattahando the next day, Walderne's soldiers killed the chief and twelve others and captured four, including Madockawando's sister. They also ransacked the village, removing a thousand pounds of dry beef and a large amount of corn.[9]

This attack on Madockawando's kinsmen and -women sealed the Penobscots' alliance with other Abenaki nations against the English. The men who had been leading the villages on the Kennebec, St. George, and Penobscot Rivers were related to one another and closely allied. Mattahando, the slain chief at Pemaquid, oversaw a village in which the captured sister of Madockawando lived. A Penobscot had adopted Madockawando from his birth home at Norridgewock and raised him to be chief at Penobscot. The chief who later replaced Madockawando was his cousin Wenongonet. Therefore, when Madockawando said "we" were driven by the English from our lands at Kennebec, he spoke as a member of an extended kin network, as well as a political confederacy.[10] Kinship ties between villages strengthened the loose confederacy of Maine tribes during periods of warfare. But it was economic necessity, not kinship ties, that drove Penobscots to attempt trade with the English when French traders were unavailable.

By bringing furs and skins to the trading post, Penobscots could obtain various necessities including firearms and ammunition. They relied entirely on guns for hunting, as the art of bow and arrow making quickly declined with the introduction of firearms. In order to keep their guns in working order, Penobscots needed parts as well as powder and shot. So any disruption in trade threatened their traditional hunting and gathering livelihood. Trade was threatened by each of the wars that took place between the Penobscots and English or the French and English. The first English threat to Penobscot subsistence came during King Philip's War.

When news of the hostilities in Massachusetts reached York, Maine, on July 11, 1675, the General Court of Massachusetts was informed and decided to disarm local Natives. This, of course, led to great fear and resentment among Native Americans, who needed their guns and ammunition to make their living. Initially, the Penobscots did not get involved, but when officials banned the sale of ammunition to all northern tribes, they, too, joined the other Abenakis in assisting the southern New England tribes, for they could not live without these essential items.[11] Trade abuse, especially the use of alcohol to cheat Abenakis, also plagued them.

The abuses of the fur trade motivated the Jesuits to assist the Abenakis. There was a Jesuit priest stationed at Kennebec and at Penobscot from time to time. The Jesuits complained to Boston about English fur traders who sold the eastern Indians rum and other strong liquors.[12]

English settlements were located in southern Maine near the coast, but the English feared that the Jesuits would encourage the Abenakis to attack the English villages in support of the French government. However, France provided unequal protection and provisions to its missions, and French traders engaged in the same unethical practices as English traders. So in order to encourage their charges to embrace Christianity and to protect them from war and unscrupulous traders, the Jesuits often had agendas different from those of the government of France.

Even more disturbing to Penobscots was the loss of the area of defense between the English leaders in Boston and New York and the Natives of Maine. After King Philip's War, southern and central New England Indians could not present any military resistance to English oppressors. By eliminating this "frontier" in southern New England—lands inhabited and held by Native Americans—the war destroyed the buffer zone between the colony of Massachusetts and the tribes of Maine. Calloway suggests that the "Indians are 'the frontier'; once their armed resistance is overcome, once the frontier has passed them by, they no longer seem to count to the English."[13] Thus the English sought to remove Native people from their lands, rather than accommodating themselves to Native societies. Without a threat from southern New England Indians, the English were free to colonize ever farther north, where they faced the great Abenaki-French alliance.

The war captains' feast in preparation for war illustrates the strength of the Maine tribes' allegiance to the French, in the oration eulogizing the nation and king of France and the medallions the chiefs wore. For the Penobscots, the allegiance represented more than a political alliance, because of the marriage of the Baron de St. Castin to Madockawando's daughter. Kinship alliances are stronger than all others in Native culture. According to Raymond J. DeMallie, marriage is viewed from the perspective of alliance in a relationship of exchange and thus is fundamental to political organization in Native culture. The oldest functioning male in a family is the leader and has authority that rests on his status and reputation as a good hunter and head of family.[14] Thus, after the English military destroyed Castin's trading post and a New Hampshire sailing vessel kidnapped fifteen Penobscots at Machias, chief Madockawando, as head of a large extended family, led his warriors on raids against the English in 1677.[15]

As war spread to Maine, many Kennebec River Abenakis moved farther away from the English and closer to the Penobscot River, because they could get food and hunting supplies from Castin's trading post. This brought the Penobscots and Kennebec Abenakis closer politically as well. One year later, apparently in response to English settlers' fears of the

Baron de St. Castin, Captain Benjamin Church led an expedition to seize Castin's trading post and fort at Pentagoet. The Baron de St. Castin fled with his family into the woods, leaving all his possessions behind.[16]

Castin was outraged at the unprovoked plundering of his home. The Penobscots suffered tremendously at the loss of all of Castin's supplies. Chief Madockawando, with several of his followers and an interpreter, traveled to Boston to try to fix the problems ill-formed policies had caused. They told Massachusetts leaders about Castin's loss, and Massachusetts leaders treated the chief with courtesy and provided him with presents, transportation home, and promises of protection, peace, and amnesty.[17]

At the end of King Philip's War, the Penobscots still held all their territory along the Penobscot, but they had lost control of Pemaquid. They did not recognize any subservience to France or England. They did not seek to make war on the colonists; however, they did understand that English settlers in Massachusetts and other English immigrants coveted Maine's rich resources and threatened their very existence. Therefore, they stood ready to defend themselves.

The first assault on Penobscot landholdings began at the end of King Philip's War with the building of an English fort at Pemaquid in 1678, ordered by New York governor Edmund Andros. A member of an English faction opposed to the Pilgrims, Andros hoped to monopolize trade and fishing and block the influence of Massachusetts in Maine.[18] Walderne's killing of Mattahando and destruction of the Pemaquid village had paved the way for Andros to construct a fort on the site, which gained a piece of Penobscot territory for the English. At this time, few Europeans had settled along the coast between the Penobscot and St. Croix Rivers, leaving the Penobscots generally unmolested. To counter Andros, and to retain some control over the Penobscots, the Massachusetts Council directed two men, John Palmer and John West, to lay claim to the lands eastward from the Penobscot to the St. Croix River, inhabited by Penobscots and Passamaquoddies. The council's actions brought more English settlers into contact with Penobscots, threatening their subsistence from hunting and the fur trade.[19]

A ten-year period of peace followed King Philip's War. Nonetheless, when King William's War began in Europe, the English once again invaded Penobscot territory. When some aggrieved Androscoggin Abenakis in mid-August 1688 killed cattle in North Yarmouth, King William's War came to Maine. Most of the fighting took place in southern coastal Maine, but the Penobscots stood by their French allies, with Castin supplying Penobscot warriors with food guns and ammunition.[20]

Although Madockawando favored negotiating peace, reconciliation remained elusive. Then, in September of 1689, Captain Benjamin Church led a contingent of English and southern New England Indians against the Abenakis of Maine.[21] Church routed the Abenaki forces in the southern Maine regions and then proceeded to the Kennebec. He attacked the Pejepscot fort on the Androscoggin River and retrieved English captives. He also killed a significant number of men and women but was unable to break the French-Abenaki alliance.[22]

The English had barely tolerated the presence of French Jesuit priests in Maine when it was still part of French Acadia. When the Jesuit Sebastian Rasles arrived at the Kennebec, the center of disputed territory in 1694, the English viewed the mission even more gravely. Massachusetts had consistently attempted to convince the Abenakis that they should oust the Catholic missionaries and, just prior to the outbreak of war, had attempted to assure Abenaki neutrality. According to Rasles, Governor Dudley pleaded with him not to "influence your Indians to make war upon us." Rasles replied, "My religion and my office of Priest are a security that I would give them only exhortations to peace." Soon after this exchange of letters, the Abenakis became actively engaged in war. Rasles said that he "exhorted them to observe strictly the laws of war, to practice no cruelty, to kill no person except in the heat of combat, to treat humanely those who surrender themselves as prisoners, etc."[23] While the English accused Rasles of fomenting Abenaki aggression against them, the priest's writings suggest a reluctant agreement to the necessity of war, rather than an exhortation to war.

In 1696, the Baron de St. Castin gathered some two hundred Penobscot warriors and an additional fifty Micmacs and, with the aid of two companies of French soldiers, set out to capture Fort William Henry at Pemaquid.[24] They successfully seized the fort on July 15. In retaliation, Captain Benjamin Church again led an expedition eastward. He arrived at the Penobscot River in August 1696 and made his way north, destroying the principal habitat of the Penobscots at present-day Old Town.[25]

With their main village in shambles, the Penobscots had to rebuild their homes. They faced a long, hungry winter, as it was too late to replant crops. Fortunately, before any further actions could take place, England and France concluded a peace at Tyswick on September 11, 1697, effectively bringing hostilities to an end in North America within a few months.[26] Just a few months later, the Penobscots lost their influential war chief, Madockawando.

War chiefs had to be strong fighters who could lead a company of warriors. However, the best of these also needed extraordinary spiritual power to draw upon for wisdom and strength. A spiritually powerful war chief could attract allies from several villages to present a formidable force to their mutual enemies. Not since Bessabez had such a powerful leader as Madockawando led the confederation of tribes throughout Maine. His name, Matáhk'əhanəto, "Supernatural Mover of Trees," indicates that he was not just a political leader but a great spiritual man as well. Forging an alliance with the French by allowing his daughter Pidiaske to marry Castin, he assured that the supply of food and other necessities for his people's survival would be nearby at Castin's trading post.[27] Madockawando's alliance included not just the other Abenaki villages in Maine but Passamaquoddy and Maliseet villages as well. Together with Castin, he led the eastern tribes, joining Pierre le Moyne d'Iberville in destroying the Pemaquid fort.[28] His strategy of making alliances with all the eastern tribes allowed him to lead his people successfully until his death from smallpox in 1698.

Madockawando signed two deeds during his lifetime, one in 1693 at Fort Pemaquid to Governor William Phipps for lands on both sides of the St. George, and the other in 1694 to Captain Sylvanus Davis for lands east of Muscongus from Madomock upriver to the falls.[29] We will never know exactly what Madockawando's intentions were in signing these deeds. He also signed a truce with the English at the Fort Pemaquid meeting in 1693.[30] Madockawando based his political decisions on his kinship with Castin and others, on his desire to have a trading post close to his village, and on his strategy of extending his alliance eastward. He, more than other Penobscot chiefs, can be characterized as a warrior with a strong alliance to the French. Later, after the death of their chief, Penobscot leaders complained that the St. George territory should still be theirs. There was a hearing, depositions were taken, and of course the English prevailed.[31]

Only a brief, uneasy, four-year peace would occur before the next outbreak of war between France and England, known as Queen Anne's War in Europe, in 1703. To the Penobscots and their Abenaki allies, peace between France and England meant a loss of French support in their campaign to drive the English from their lands. The previous wars had jeopardized their relationship to the lands, as village after village fell to English aggression. The death of Madockawando and several other important eastern leaders from an epidemic in 1698, together with the loss of French military support, also weakened the Penobscots' ability to wage war against the New England settlers. In addition the Baron de St. Castin, their old ally and kinsman, left two years after the epidemic and did not return. Fortunately, the short period of peace provided the Penobscots time to find a new leader.

Wenongonet (Wə̀nakənet, "Lifter") followed Madockawando, leading the Penobscots for about twenty-five years. We know little about him

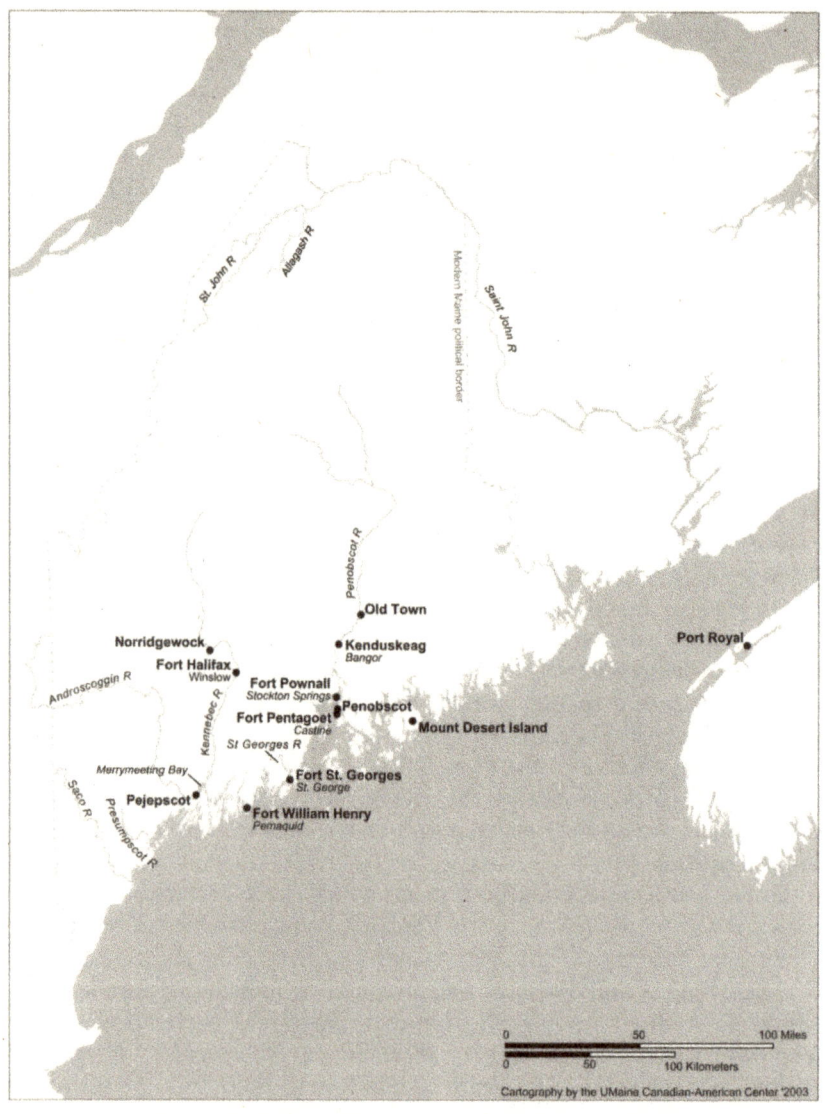

MAP 2. Maine in the eighteenth century, places mentioned in the text. *Cartography by Michael Hermann, Canadian American Center, University of Maine.*

other than that he had an assistant chief named Squadock. The two men sent messengers to Boston in 1701 and signed a peace treaty in 1702.[32] We know that the Penobscots respected Wenongonet, because the next chief changed his name to Wenongonet to honor his memory.[33] Wenongonet died during Dummer's War in 1724. During Wenongonet's rule, Castin's son Anselme d'Abbadie left school at Quebec and went to the Penobscot village at Pentagoet in 1704 to rally the tribe to the French side. The French military gave him the rank of ensign in 1707, and he always served more as a French officer than as trader or chief. He became a privateer in 1709 and sank thirty-five English ships. Between 1711 and 1714, he lived at Pentagoet (presently Castine) and Kenduskeag (presently Bangor) and then withdrew, first to the St. John River and then to France, where he died.[34] The presence of Castin's sons strengthened the Penobscot-French alliance, but the destruction of the Abenakis on the Kennebec River and westward weakened the Penobscots' ability to defend themselves.

During the next several years, Jesuit priests played a role in trying to preserve tribal lands and the people on them. It appears from letters they wrote that the French missionaries' concerns often focused more on the Abenakis' welfare than on advancing the interests of France. At the dawn of the eighteenth century, Anthony Gaulin was the Jesuit at Penobscot, Joseph Aubery was at St. Francis (Quebec), and Sebastian Rasles served at Norridgewock on the Kennebec River.

When the Jesuits acted independently from French politics, the Acadian governor Brouillan became deeply disturbed. The governor criticized all the priests in Maine for urging the Abenakis to take a neutral stance and to continue to trade peacefully with the English. The Jesuits encouraged trade between the Abenakis and English to protect the Natives from French traders like Sieur de Villieu of the Acadian Fishery Company, who sold them liquor and tried to cheat them.[35]

The Jesuits were motivated at least partly by a desire to improve the lives of their charges, according to their definition of improvement. They hoped to bring all the small, scattered villages into one large community with a central church and a settled, agricultural town. Like the English, the French Jesuits sought to settle and "civilize" the Indians by creating self-sufficient agricultural villages. The French and English visions of assimilation were not that different. However, the French were not bringing large numbers of settlers into Maine, so their influence was restricted to a few priests and fur traders. Meanwhile, the English came in larger numbers and assaulted Native lands. The French battered Native culture (religion especially), though perhaps, in the case of the Jesuits, with benevolent intent.

Two of the Jesuits, Gaulin and Aubery, hoped to save the Indians from English abuse by proposing that they move to Canada. The priests believed that the Indians could not live on territory controlled by the English, because the Natives were dependent upon the French for food and ammunition. They could not remain, the Jesuits warned, without dying of hunger. Sebastian Rasles took part directly in the planned move, proving that he had the interests of the Abenakis in mind. He knew that it would be impossible for the Abenakis to continue living in peace near the English.[36]

Rasles insisted that the Abenakis were closely bonded to the French only because of their firm attachment to the Catholic faith and not due to a military alliance. He did not accept war right away. He tried to take a neutral position on English-Abenaki relations in 1702. As a result, his position as a French missionary was in jeopardy. The French governor even accused Rasles of encouraging the Abenakis to make peace and trade with the English. The governor of Acadia wrote to the head of the Jesuits complaining about Rasles. He said he would much prefer someone who knew better how to manage the interests of religion and those of the king. He viewed those interests as inseparable. Sebastian Rasles and his superior obviously disagreed, but Rasles remained at his mission in spite of his disagreements with French political leaders.[37]

For the Penobscots and their neighbors the Norridgewocks and Androscoggins, fighting in Maine resumed in 1703. Unruly English settlers in Maine created the local manifestation of Queen Anne's War. Local settlers mistrusted both the Indians and the intractable government in Boston. They often held different political views from those held by leaders of their government, and they often ignored laws written in Boston to protect Native American settlements, allowing their cattle to consume Indian corn and building dams in streams, blocking migrating fish.

One way Natives resisted engaging in hostilities with English settlers was simply by moving away from them. During the war, some of the Penobscots and Norridgewocks went to Canada for a time. In 1705, Captain Church's expedition to the Penobscot River made a diligent search in the region of their main village at Kenduskeag but could not find anyone.[38] This does not mean that the Penobscots were *all* in Canada—often they moved to interior villages to stay out of harm's way. But they never stayed away for long; their attachment to their sacred homeland called them back.

Hoping to improve relations with the Maine tribes, Massachusetts governor Dudley established a series of truckhouses with goods priced below those at French trading posts. But factions in the Massachusetts legislature feared giving the governor too much control over trade and impeded his efforts. As a result, truckhouses continued to operate without government oversight, and unscrupulous traders continuously supplied the Abenakis with rum and then cheated them when they became drunk. Tribal leadership did not stand by idly, but resisted these abuses by taking political action.

Five Abenaki sagamores went to the Massachusetts Council in Boston in 1714 to ask for regulation of the truckhouses.[39] Dudley could not respond adequately until the General Court met in February. He told the sagamores to ignore orders from the French governor. He also told them to call the Abenakis who had gone to Canada back to Maine to settle on English ground. Since the Massachusetts authorities ignored Abenaki requests for fair trading practices, the Abenakis returned home to Maine. Rasles wrote a blistering letter to Boston. He deplored the disorders and outrages committed among the eastern Indians by interloping traders selling them rum and other strong liquors.[40] Apparently, Massachusetts authority did not effectively reach the frontier. Petty politicians in the Massachusetts legislature had sabotaged any hope for a planned, effective trading policy with Maine's Natives.

After the Treaty of Utrecht terminated Queen Anne's War in 1713, tension between the English settlers and the Abenakis grew unabated. The French agreed to let go of their whole southern coastline in Acadia. With the English firmly entrenched to the south of the Abenaki villages, life for the Norridgewocks and Penobscots became far more difficult. Disagreements arose primarily because settlers continued to move onto Native lands and started farming and cutting timber without regard to the effect it would have on the original inhabitants. The people of the Kennebec and Penobscot Rivers opposed these activities in different ways. On the Kennebec, where English settlers were in close proximity to the Norridgewock village, protest included some acts of violence. The Penobscots, however, put their efforts into keeping English settlers at a respectable distance. Resident missionaries in both communities assisted their efforts. One of these was Etienne Lauverjat, sent to the Penobscot village in 1717 by the bishop of Quebec.

Lauverjat spent a long time at Penobscot after having been trained at the St. Francis mission, under Joseph Aubery. He assisted the Penobscots in their attempts to keep peace with both the English and the French. The Penobscots asked Lauverjat to write a letter to the Massachusetts government for them because they were hoping to make peace with the English, breaking with their brothers from the Norridgewock community on the Kennebec. Governor Vaudreuil of Canada criticized Lauverjat for complying. Lauverjat wrote to assure the governor that the Abenakis who wished to befriend the English had died. He claimed that all the

Penobscots were "wholly devoted to the French, or if there are some still pro-English, they have but little authority."[41] Later that year, Lauverjat wrote another letter to Massachusetts, telling the English not to settle any farther north than Pemaquid and reminding the English of the terms of their peace treaty, which promised that the Penobscots' lands would be kept free of white settlements.[42] Here was a case of a priest walking the thin line between the two major political interests, while seemingly attempting to promote the interests of the Penobscots.

The Indian policy of Massachusetts had been and continued to be inept in terms of keeping the peace, but ultimately served English interests in obtaining land for settlements. Unlike the Jesuits, the Boston authorities did not try to understand the Abenakis' wishes or respond genuinely to their complaints. The governor ratified Native treaties but depended upon the General Court for their execution, and Massachusetts was prey to the usual feuding between the governor and rural politicians. The legislators of the Bay Colony displayed their lack of compassion for Native Americans by subjecting Indian policies to the fortunes of partisan politics.

After the Treaty of Utrecht was signed in Europe, a conference was held at Portsmouth (in present-day New Hampshire) to prepare a peace treaty between the English in Massachusetts and the Abenakis. Negotiations faltered from the start. Mediators told the Abenakis that the king of France had surrendered all their lands to Great Britain. This was incomprehensible to the Abenakis. They remarked that the French had never said anything to them about it and wondered how the French could have given their lands away without asking them. In their view, God had first placed the Abenakis in this region. The Abenakis agreed that the English might settle the Maine lands without molestation or adverse claims by themselves or by any other Indians. The Massachusetts government told them that, as British subjects, they could have no relations with the French.[43] The Abenakis learned that the English interest in treaties arose from their belief that the all the lands that the Natives held could be negotiated away from their owners. Only the English benefited from the terms of the treaties.

The English claimed lands "by right of Conquest and driving out the natives . . . or by treaties."[44] Unlike the Spanish, who based their claims on the right of discovery, English treaties created dividing lines between the land in English possession and the land that remained in the possession of the various Indian nations. The Penobscots recognized land ownership in a different sense, with heads of families assigning areas to nuclear families for hunting. They did not consider the land something to be exchanged, nor could they understand the Europeans' political claims to the land. This process of land encroachment by settlers gradually placed the Natives under the political and economic jurisdiction of the English, against their will.

The French, too, showed little understanding of Native reverence for their land and its inhabitants. In Quebec, the French thought they should move all the Abenakis to Cape Breton Island. The Jesuits, however, including Father LaChasse, the missionary on the Penobscot River, told the French officials that the Indians had an extreme attachment to their own country. They suggested that the two European countries settle their boundaries with the Natives instead of trying to move people to new lands. The Jesuits apparently understood better than French officials the importance of homeland to the Abenakis. If the Jesuits had not stood by the Abenakis, the Abenakis might have abandoned the French at this juncture.[45] Or perhaps they chose the lesser of two evils.

Meanwhile, settlers were flooding into southern Maine. Germans and Ulster Scots arrived in Boston in 1718. Investors brought some to the Kennebec area of Maine, and the non-Native population of the countryside increased fivefold in just a few years.[46] The presence of so many new yeoman farmers, who typically paid little heed to laws, caused much consternation among the Penobscots. These farmers needed game to survive and began hunting, cutting trees, and clearing land, placing ever more pressure on local resources.

Between 1717 and 1718, the English persistently moved into the Kennebec Valley, bringing a Protestant missionary, Joseph Baxter, with them. They did not come in a conciliatory frame of mind, and the Kennebec Abenaki remained united in opposition to the settlers. Samuel Shute, the new governor of Massachusetts, did not sympathize with the Abenakis. At a conference at Georgetown on Arrowsick Island, he insisted that the Penobscots and Norridgewocks avoid all contact with the French and that they behave as subjects of King George, follow the Bible, and worship as the English did. He introduced Baxter and warned them to accept him with all affection and respect. When Wiwurna, orator for the Kennebec Abenakis, rose to speak, Governor Shute rudely interrupted him. Wiwurna refused the minister, refused to accept King George as sovereign, and tried to limit English claims to Native lands. Shute haughtily answered Wiwurna, at which juncture the Abenakis became very angry and walked out of the conference.[47]

Other Abenakis came in the evening and agreed to the English terms but found it impossible to communicate with Governor Shute. The Massachusetts government's inability or reluctance to restrain the actions of settlers against Native people eventually led to war once again.[48] Massachusetts repeatedly ignored requests from the Norridgewocks and Penobscots to set a reasonable boundary and respect their homeland. The Jesuit at Norridgewock, Sebastian Rasles, wrote several letters on behalf of the Norridgewocks to try to settle disputes.

One New England leader described Rasles as "a constant and Notorious Fomenter & Incendiary to the Indians to kill, burn, and destroy."[49] Rasles's letters to the Massachusetts government indicate that he encouraged the Indians' resistance. His spirited defense of his and the Abenakis' interests infuriated Boston leadership. In their view, nothing could be more malicious.

The Penobscots actively joined Dummer's War in 1721, when Massachusetts captured their kinsman Joseph D'Abbadie de St. Castin (son of the Baron de St. Castin and Pidiaske, the daughter of Madockawando) and accused him of rebellion.[50] Penobscots joined Abenakis in attacks against English settlers on the lower Kennebec and at Damariscotta. These actions precipitated a declaration of war by Massachusetts against the Penobscots.[51] Someone intercepted letters linking Rasles to the governor of Quebec, and Massachusetts used the letters as evidence to fuel the enmity of New England toward the Jesuit. Massachusetts captain Westbrook set out to capture Rasles, but the priest escaped. Although the larger powers tried to keep the matter from becoming a full-fledged war, local settlers and Abenakis from the Kennebec were killing each other. On March 9, 1723, Massachusetts forces once again burned to the ground the village at Indian Island on the Penobscot River. The following August, four companies of English soldiers left Fort Richmond on the lower Kennebec and marched for two and one half days to Norridgewock. There, the Englishmen shot and killed numerous villagers and their priest. Since the French military did not send support and both St. Castin and the Jesuits were gone, the Abenakis' hope of support from the French ended, and local settlers no longer needed to fear that the presence of a Jesuit would bring the French military against them.[52]

New England happily learned of Norridgewock's destruction. The surviving Abenakis of Norridgewock fled to Canada or to the Penobscot for a time. At least twenty-seven leading Norridgewock men survived the attack to later attend negotiations.

Meanwhile Wenemouet (Wɪnɪ-mɑwəwet, "Weak War Chief") had become chief at the death of Wenongonet.[53] Wenemouet served as a member of the tribal council, as attested by his signing of a peace treaty at Marepoint, in January 1699. He signed another treaty at Portsmouth in July 1714. Wenemouet led forty others to Quebec to meet with Governor Calliere, hoping to obtain trade goods.[54] He started a break with other Abenaki tribes in 1725 when he sent a wampum belt to the English, seeking peace. He succeeded in convincing Governor Dummer to agree to a cease fire east of the Kennebec, and Dummer ordered an end to hostilities against the Penobscots.[55] Wenemouet became ill; his second in command, Loron Saguarum, spoke on his behalf at conferences with the English.

Loron Saguarum (*Laurence Sákəwet*, "One Who Speaks with Intent to Injure") took the lead in negotiating peace with Massachusetts colony leaders at Boston. Ten delegates from the Penobscot community went first to Quebec to try to persuade other Abenakis to keep the peace, as set forth in Dummer's Treaty (July 1727). They were not successful. The Penobscots then negotiated with Massachusetts governor Dummer, assuming they represented their own interests and had fulfilled Dummer's request to assist negotiations with the Canadian Abenakis. Loron (as he is referred to in the historical documents) tried to educate Dummer about the important issues that created conflict, but the governor could not or would not address the critical problems.

Factions of the Penobscot tribe continued to try to negotiate for peace.[56] One faction, led by Loron and other delegates, went to Boston for that purpose. When the Penobscots' Jesuit missionary Lauverjat read the treaty to them when they returned, Loron protested that the priest's reading was different from his understanding of the terms. Loron asked the priest to write a letter to the governor and requested that he reply in French, "that it may be understood by many, and that the interpreter may not be taxed with interpreting in another sense."[57] If many understood French, then one must infer that the Penobscots spoke at least two languages at this time. If the English and Penobscots were negotiating through interpreters in three languages, it is easy to understand how misunderstandings could arise. Apparently, the Penobscots did not speak English. As a result, it was easy for Massachusetts leaders to dupe them into signing a treaty that did not reflect accurately the verbal agreements made at the peace conference. Apparently, Massachusetts leaders did not negotiate in good faith, taking advantage of persons who did not speak English and misrepresenting their intentions.

Nonetheless, Wenemouet devoted himself to achieving a lasting peace. In April 1726, he sent messengers to all the Abenakis, Maliseets, and Micmacs, asking them to attend a Penobscot meeting to discuss framing a peace.[58] Norridgewocks returned from Canada; other Abenakis and Iroquois camped at Taconic.[59]

In the summer of 1727, all the tribes ratified Dummer's Treaty.[60] After the treaty was signed, the Penobscots realized that it did not represent what the English negotiators had told them, so they began looking for new ways to resist English dominance, while enduring the presence of English settlements. They could not remove the settlers, but they hoped at least to keep them at bay, away from their hunting lands and their small, vulnerable villages. Without the Jesuits and French support, the Abenakis would never again be able to unite a force large enough to oppose the English and remove them from Native lands. At the peace conference with the English in July 1729 at Falmouth, Wenemouet protested tree cutting and settlers' moving onto lands. He insisted upon the St. George River as a boundary between English settlers and Penobscot hunting territories.[61] Unlike Madockawando, Wenemouet did not lead the whole Abenaki nation.[62] He began to lead the Penobscots away from agreements that were made by the larger confederacy. He did not have the spiritual power of a great chief, but he did lead his people toward greater accommodation and interaction with the English. His leadership signaled an important change in political strategy for the Penobscots, one in which they would seek peace with the English in order to remain on their own lands. They needed peace with the English to do this, and they needed to be able to trade with the English rather than rely on the French for goods. But it would take a long time for these policies to take hold, and it would not be in Wenemouet's lifetime. He died in 1730, still hoping to achieve an amicable accommodation with the English.

Dummer's War particularly devastated the once powerful confederation of Abenaki villages in Maine. The Androscoggins, Pigwackets, Kennebecs, and Penobscots suffered major defeat and loss of life and territory.[63] The Androscoggins inhabited the Pejepscot River, while the Pigwackets lived on the Saco and Presumpscot Rivers in western Maine. They spoke the same language as the Norridgewocks and Penobscots and enjoyed political as well as kinship alliances with those other central Maine communities. But no large Native villages existed in western Maine at this time.

After Dummer's War, there appeared to be about twenty-five warriors at Presumpscot, four at Saco, seven at Pigwacket, and twenty-seven at Norridgewock. In addition, the Pejepscot River inhabitants made up three villages with several hundred residents in 1755.[64] The numbers suggest a population of about 450 Abenakis remaining in Maine in addition to the 400–500 Penobscots, and 1,000 or so Passamaquoddies and Maliseets. The western Maine groups tended to live in small bands rather than large villages, occasionally visiting kinsmen at St. Francis and on the Penobscot.[65] If we compare these numbers to those related by members of the Weymouth expedition in 1605, a calculation of 90 percent loss of population seems likely. However, these earlier estimates remain problematical, as already suggested.[66]

While Dummer's War effectively destroyed the former great Wabanaki alliance, the French and Indian Wars brought the English more permanently into Penobscot territory, especially between Penobscot Bay and

Kenduskeag (present Bangor). The combination of weakened alliances and the proximity of the enemy to Penobscot territory created a need for strong and experienced leadership. Loron Saguarum led the Penobscots following Wenemouet's death. His name suggests spiritual power and the ability to cause injury with his voice. Saguarum had extensive diplomatic experience, having led a delegation consisting of himself and three other leading Penobscots to discuss peace with the English in November 1725.[67] Two months later, he wrote a letter to the leadership in Boston requesting a meeting at Pemaquid to discuss peace.[68] Six months later, he wrote, through the interpreter Gyles, that he was sending three delegates to Boston—Alexis, Captain Lewy, and Edgeremet—to meet with Governor Dummer.[69] Loron's oratorical skills ensured that he would be the principal speaker at most conferences in 1740 and 1742. His efforts at peace negotiations were thwarted by events in Europe.

The French and the English went to war again in March 1744. Called King George's War in New England, it again created fear among colonists that the French would turn their Native allies against their English enemies. Massachusetts approached the Maine tribes requesting military support against the Canadian Natives who were fighting alongside the French, but the Maine natives refused.[70] In October, the situation deteriorated when a party of Englishmen killed one Penobscot and wounded several others. Although Massachusetts sent condolences to the tribe, government leaders continued to insist that Maine's Natives provide military support to the English. Maliseet and St. Francis warriors attacked Fort St. George in July 1745. A few days later, the Kennebec and Penobscot men attacked Pemaquid.[71] Massachusetts then declared war on the Penobscots and Kennebecs in August 1745. But the French-Abenaki alliance had been fatally weakened by France's inability to supply its Native allies. They could not muster a conquering force.

France lost many of its Native allies midcentury because Canada was unable to receive trade goods from France due to the English blockade at Louisbourg. One French captain observed, "Our Indians, disgusted and dissatisfied, are taking their furs to the English, are becoming attached to them to the prejudice of our interests and to the detriment of the trade."[72]

In a last effort to engage the French to aid them, the Abenakis reported to French officers that the English had established a fort below Norridgewock. The Chevalier De Raymond reported that "the first Abenakis who had come from that direction said that [the English] had built a fort in the village of Naransonac [Norridgewock] itself and another on the Naransonac River 4 leagues above and that they had gone up this river as far as the source of the Pentagouet [Penobscot] River which is the height

FIG. 4. Fort Shirley and Court House, 1761. *Courtesy Deering Collection, Raymond F. Fogler Library Special Collections, University of Maine.*

of land where there is a lake [Moosehead] and a portage of 4 leagues [Northeast Carry].[73] The Chevalier continued his report by calling for France to pay forty or fifty pounds for each English scalp the Abenakis could bring, thus hoping to use the English fear of Natives against them and rid Maine of the English settlements.

Chief Loron tried to accommodate the English by bringing the Norridgewocks into the peace agreement, saying, "We were all one nation before." He sent an emissary, Squadok, to Canada. When the envoy returned he told his chief that the Norridgewocks wished to return safely to their homes. Of his own role in the peace process, Loron declared, "I have been the man that has been the first in all treaties—I have been the man that has quelled all the rest [of the allies]."[74] Loron had inherited the situation created during Wenongonet's leadership of a broken alliance with other Abenakis and the French. Though the French tried to reestablish it, the English were so geographically close to the Penobscots by now and the Penobscots needed their trade so much that the French were unsuccessful. The breakdown in spiritual matters also concerned Loron. In his report upon returning from Canada, Squadok related, "Brother, once more, we don't like a great deal of Rum it hinders our Praiers. One kegg and one bottle is enough for one man the women must have none." He explained that the women bought and sold rum to the men and "are debauched thereby."[75]

After the war ended, Massachusetts dominated trade with the Abenakis at government truckhouses. Often corrupt and greedy individuals dominated this trade. The Penobscots protested, but in vain. Chief Loron Saguarum wrote to the governor of Massachusetts that, "if [the price of] any goods rise [the price of] our furs are to rise with them," as specified in Dummer's Treaty. He also declared that the manager of the truckhouse understood nothing of the Abenaki language or trading practices and that the Penobscots had been a long time without provisions and necessities. The letter reveals the Penobscots' desperation brought on by the long wars, the increasing number of settlers, and the consequent lack of food. The Abenakis began to kill domestic animals in order to feed their families. Loron informed the governor that his hunters had killed what they thought were three wild horses for food, but later six Englishmen with guns accosted his party. Loron promised to pay for the horses; he and his men gave up their guns as a pledge.[76] The letter makes clear the extent of Penobscot hunger. Giving up their guns left them entirely dependent on trade for food, as they hunted large game only with guns.

In addition to having fewer goods to supply, the French also took part in shady practices such as withholding and making a profit from gifts sent from France and meant for Native chiefs. The Natives viewed any sign of stinginess and greed by traders as reason for suspicion and mistrust. Furthermore, Native traders knew "by tradition the agreements that their forefathers made."[77] They needed no written contracts or records and complained bitterly when either English or French traders cheated them.

The parties continued to negotiate regarding trade and peace. The English terms of an agreement with the Penobscots included a restriction on trade. The governor ordered Penobscots to trade only at English truckhouses. Furthermore, three members of each tribe had to reside at Fort Frederick as hostages. Penobscots worried anxiously about their safety, especially as one of the Penobscots had been killed at St. George the previous year. They also complained about the scarcity and measure of English trade goods. They said, "we used to have our corn at Georges measured in half a bushel. It is now measured in a gallon pot by which we lose 3 quarts in half a bushel."[78] The Penobscots' need for trade goods led them to agree reluctantly to the peace.

While the Penobscots wanted to be able to trade with the English, they did not welcome English settlers moving into their territory, and they did not trust that they would be treated well at the truckhouses. They declared, "We would be glad to have no English houses as far as we can see down the river."[79] They also resented having to come near the English fort to trade and asked for a truckhouse upriver near the falls at Kenduskeag, hoping to avoid the trouble that frequently arose between their people and the English settlers. They also wanted some officers appointed as justices to hear grievances. The governor informed them that he would not allow them to decide where the bounds of English settlement could be. He did assure them that prices at the truckhouse would be hung in plain sight so there would be no misunderstanding. The governor offered to send a vessel upriver with goods to tide them over the winter. The Penobscots accepted the offer.

However, this uneasy alliance with the English brought new difficulties. The English wanted the Penobscots to fight their former allies and kinsmen, the Abenakis, who had fled to Canada. At this time, a new leader succeeded Loron, Wambemando (Wɑpɪ-Mànəto, "White Evil Spirit"). As his name indicates, he was a force to be reckoned with; the name suggests shamanism and great spiritual power. No doubt he gained his power through ritual and through hunting and combat exploits. We find him in the historical record in 1754 writing to Governor Shirley and telling him that the Indians in Canada will not follow his lead in making peace but that those of the St. John will follow him.[80] A year later, he again wrote to Governor Shirley: "We thought the Canadian Indians would bring us into trouble. We will join you but our wives and children must be supported."[81] Rogue Englishmen broke the peace by betraying Penobscot trust. A soldier named James Cargill led thirty-one men on a killing spree that left twelve Penobscots dead. The Penobscots felt very hurt and angry.[82] At first Governor Phipps, Governor Shirley's successor, responded to Cargill's savage act by telling the Penobscots the English were sorry and promising to bring Cargill to justice. However, in October 1755 Phipps informed them they must not come near the fort to trade or they might be mistaken for an enemy.[83] Contrarily, he advised them to bring their women and children into the fort for safety and to join the English soldiers in fighting the French and Abenakis. Governor Phipps sent Captain Bradbury to St. George to find out if the Penobscots were involved with the other Abenakis in a conspiracy against English settlements. Although Bradbury did not see or talk to any Penobscots, he advised Phipps that the Penobscots were conspiring with the Abenakis. The Massachusetts House of Representatives responded to the news by issuing a proclamation calling for bounties to be paid on Penobscot scalps—of men, women, and children.[84]

In October 1754, the English built Fort Halifax at Taconic on the Kennebec River, effectively blocking the Penobscots' route to Canada along the Sebasticook. A few scattered families lived in the Kennebec River region for many years afterward, but they never again collected themselves into a large village.[85]

David Ghere reports that the Penobscots divided into three factions at this time: those who migrated to Canada and joined French expeditions;

those who moved to the St. John Valley; and a third group who moved up the Penobscot River.[86] Small skirmishes characterized most of this war, with the exception of an attack on Fort St. George by three hundred Canadian militia, Penobscots, and Maliseets in August 1758. Although small raids against settlements continued, the Penobscots approached Massachusetts governor Thomas Pownall in hopes of reaching a peace agreement.[87]

Pownall responded in May 1759 by going to the Penobscot with 333 men and taking the former Penobscot chief Loron hostage at the St. George fort. Loron told Pownall he had no power to represent the Penobscots, as he was no longer chief. Pownall gave the Penobscots a British flag to bring home and told them that they should become English and come live in protection of the fort.[88] Governor Pownall refused to discuss peace with the Penobscots and told them they must forfeit their lives, liberties, and lands. He took the perspective that the Penobscots were now a conquered people and should subject themselves to English rule, and did not recognize them as a separate or sovereign people. Pownall proceeded up the bay by ship and sent Brigadier General Jedediah Preble overland to the head of present Belfast Bay. Preble landed at Castine and proceeded to build Fort Pownall (near present Stockton Springs). Building the fort symbolized the conquest of the Penobscots; the governor claimed all their lands by right of conquest.[89] In 1762, the new governor of Massachusetts, Francis Bernard, held a conference at Fort Pownall with five Penobscot leaders.[90]

Meanwhile, the Muscongus Patent, previously given to Samuel Waldo (who died in 1759), claimed some of the Penobscots' territory. The patent made Kenduskeag open to settlement without consent or purchase from the Penobscots. The English undoubtedly built some of their claim upon the conquest of the Penobscots by Pownall. Furthermore, the Massachusetts General Court granted twelve additional townships to settlers in March 1762.

Thus, the Penobscots began to encounter firsthand the problems the Norridgewock Abenakis had with English settlers in proximity to their villages. For the Penobscots, even in time of peace, the security of their lands and their persons continually grew more difficult to maintain as settlers moved into their territory in great numbers.

Massachusetts opened more Penobscot lands to settlement when the General Court approved twelve conditional townships between the Kennebec and Machias Rivers by 1762. Settlers in these towns often did not respect tribal ownership of land or individual Indian rights. Perhaps this was because they represented the more desperate and impoverished yeoman farmers. They were often bankrupt, had not succeeded in the more populous regions of New England prior to immigrating to the District of Maine, and therefore often represented the antisocial and maladjusted segments of society.[91]

However, even the elite leadership treated the Natives severely. For example, in 1767, Governor Bernard wrote to Captain Thomas Goldthwait at Fort Pownall, "You have two objects in view of repressing the insolence of the Indians and relieving the fears of the people—add eight men to the garrison. We hear the fort is in the hands of the Indians when they come to trade in any great number. Set the truckhouse out of the bounds of the fort. The Indians are insulting and plundering the settlers."[92] The chiefs of the tribe apologized for the acts of their young men who had stolen some pigs and sheep, and promised to make restitution for the animals.

The young Penobscot men did not harass colonists and their animals without provocation. The Down East region of Maine was a frontier for New England settlers, and most of them in this region were equipped with little more than persistence. They believed that they must tame the mysterious wilderness with plow and fence. They perceived only that there were countless trees in the forest—they did not view the trees as a limited resource—and set about felling and selling the forest. By this time, more than two hundred sawmills in forty-two towns were cutting the tall pines for British shipbuilding. As the trees came down and towns sprang up, the Penobscots' land and game resources gradually slipped away from them. As townspeople came into contact with Natives, sporadic incidents of violence and vandalism occurred between the two groups. Native leaders continued to try to find ways to resist the oppressive political decisions of Massachusetts leaders and spurious attacks by backcountry ruffians.

Penobscot leaders had previously forged political alliances with the French and Abenaki tribes in western Maine, until the English overcame both the French (1713) and the Abenakis (1724). Once their western allies could no longer assist them, Penobscot chiefs sought stronger alliances with the tribes to the east: the Passamaquoddies, Maliseets, and Micmacs. They hoped to hold on to or regain lands and continue to obtain necessary trade goods while protecting their people from attacks. Common residence, kinship, and common enemies produced both social and political bonds and conflict as factions formed. Abenaki factions devoted to French alliances tended to move to Canada; those seeking accommodation with the English and retention of aboriginal lands tended to remain in place. They could do this only if they could accomplish one important political goal: the establishment of permanent, stable trade with the English of Massachusetts.

One hundred years of nearly constant warfare created massive changes in the politics of Maine. War in Europe spilled into North America and into Penobscot territory. Although initially resisting taking sides in conflicts between the English and French, the Penobscots were left in a confused and contradictory position through their kinship ties with the French and their economic need to trade with the English. The wars ultimately removed most of the Abenakis west of the Penobscot River. The remaining Penobscots lost territory in the lower region of Penobscot River and Bay. In addition, allies were defeated and lost, and the Penobscots were forced to negotiate for peace under unfavorable conditions.

During and after such consuming warfare, the Penobscots received refugees from devastated coastal villages. Smaller communities coalesced into single villages farther inland. Much movement took place between villages. Family groups moved from one village to another because of kinship ties throughout Wabanaki territory.[93] The previous military strength that had belonged to the confederation of numerous smaller bands throughout the District of Maine significantly weakened. However, English settlers along the coast continued to fear Maine's Natives because of their perceived hostility.

The series of eighteenth-century wars in Maine altered many of the kinship networks and alliances established over a long period of Penobscot history. Penobscot allies included the Maliseets of the St. John River and the people living in villages along the other major rivers in Maine. In addition, the gradual removal and destruction of Eastern Abenaki tribes in western Maine and the uncertainty of French ability to assist their efforts to remain sovereign eventually left the Penobscots standing alone in a thickly populated field of English settlements. By the 1760s, the Penobscots were nearly surrounded by colonists and forced to trade with the English. Colonists had successfully cut them off from former allies of western Maine, who emigrated to Canada, were destroyed, or joined the Penobscot villages. They had routed the French and therefore removed the only other source of trade goods for the Penobscots. The Penobscots had become dependent on trade goods and now looked to treaty goods to supply some of their needs. Scarcity of game and other resources added to their impoverishment. Factions grew within the tribe as a result of the frustration with having to submit to their former enemy. Survival was not guaranteed, and Penobscots sought to make allies among the local English military and government officials, in hope of protection from rogue colonists who meant them harm. They no longer had any real military strength to aid in negotiations, and had to accept terms of trade and land negotiations that were thrust upon them. They would soon find themselves in a new conflict, as colonists now conceiving themselves as

Americans turned their attention away from the threats of New England's Native Americans and toward freeing themselves from the British monarchy. The newly constituted "Americans" would develop a more conciliatory attitude toward Natives who did not join with the British against their rebellion.

Chapter 5

LIBERTIES AND LANDS

Disappointment in the Promise of the New Nation

> The Great Spirit gives us freely all things. Our white brothers tell us they came to the Indians' country to enjoy liberty and life. Their Great Sagamore (the English king) is coming to bind them in chains, to kill them. We must fight him. We will stand on the same ground with them. For should he bind them in bonds, next he will treat us as bears. Indians' liberties and lands, his proud spirit will tear away from them. Help his ill-treated sons; they will return good for good, and the law of love runs through the hearts of their children and ours when we are dead. Look down the stream of time. Look up to the Great Spirit. *Sursum Corda*. Be kind, be valiant, be free—then are Indians Sons of Glory!
>
> —CHIEF JOSEPH ORONO

The rhetoric of liberty during the period prior to the American Revolution was not lost on the Penobscots—but did they share in the fruits of that liberty? As Eric Foner writes, "the Native American idea of freedom which centered on preserving their cultural and political autonomy and retaining control of ancestral lands"[1] was incompatible with that of land-hungry settlers and entrepreneurs. Jefferson and others of his generation hoped that if Native Americans abandoned their traditional ways, became Christian, and adopted a settled agricultural lifestyle, they could be assimilated into the general American population. However, the experience of the Cherokee—who adopted a constitution, lived by farming, and were republican citizens—suggests a different fate. They did not assimilate; they were excluded.[2] The meeting places of Native people and land-hungry settlers became a battleground for two opposing views of the meaning of liberty. One view was based on colonialism and the idea that only white men had full rights of citizenship, while the other view grew out of indigenous beliefs in the importance of continuity of communities and the rights of people to live according to their own traditions.

While the Native populations continued to diminish, the American population grew at an astounding rate. As a result, the major population's ideas about freedom, including the right to expand and acquire free land, meant that Indian removal became a necessary goal in the Americans' mission of spreading their own freedom. Liberty as a natural right became the rallying cry for American revolutionaries, and liberty trees, poles, and Sons and Daughters of Liberty sprang up throughout the thirteen colonies. Massachusetts was the site of much of the activism; the northern portion of that state was known as the District of Maine.

Williamson reports that Maine's zeal for liberty incorporated several violent protests, including a mob taking stamped clearances from the customhouse and burning them, and a force of thirty men armed with clubs, axes, and other weapons rescuing two persons convicted of rioting. Meanwhile, patriots carefully watched Tories and subjected them to insults and harsh treatment.[3] The Penobscots were well aware of the events taking place in their own state and elsewhere in the colonies. Under the leadership of Chief Joseph Orono, in May 1775 a contingent of Penobscot leaders traveled to Massachusetts to see whether the new government would act favorably toward them.

The Provincial Congress of Massachusetts at Watertown promised the Maine Indians protection from the British. "Captain Goldthwait has given Ft. Pownall into the hands of our enemies. We will supply you as fast as we can and hope none of your men will join with our enemies. The Indians at Stockbridge have enlisted as soldiers. We have sent Captain John Lane to you to raise a company of your men. Mr. John Preble will supply you."[4] Chief Joseph Orono, with three of his colleagues, returned to Watertown, Massachusetts, two days after the battle of Bunker Hill and tendered their services to the Provincial Congress held there on June 21, 1775. Orono, addressing the congress, said, "In behalf of the whole Penobscot tribe I hereby declare to you, if the grievances, under which our people labor, were removed, they would aid with their whole force to defend the country." The grievances concerned trespasses by the whites upon their timberlands and being cheated in trade. The congress responded by promising him that "as soon as they could take breath from this present fight" they would attend to the grievances. Concerned with keeping the Maine Natives peaceable, in June the congress passed a resolve forbidding all trespassing or making waste upon any lands or possessions of the Penobscots, beginning at the head of tide and extending six miles on both sides of the Penobscot River. This essentially reversed Pownall's hated declaration of conquest over Penobscot lands. Massachusetts authorities assigned to Captain Lane the added duties of Indian agent and established a commissary under his direction.[5] They hoped their

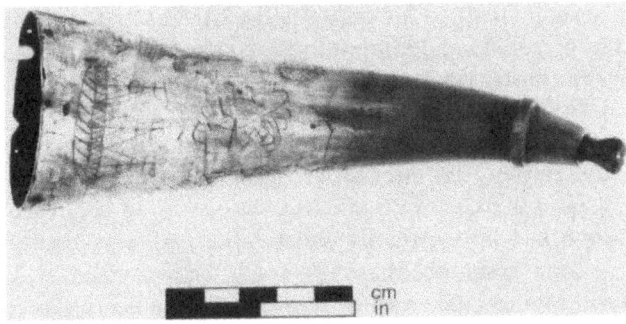

FIG. 5. Chief Joseph Orono's gunpowder flask. *From the collection of the Abbe Museum, Bar Harbor, Maine. Photo by Stephen Bicknell.*

actions would solve several problems. The Penobscots would receive needed food and hunting supplies, the agent would see that local settlers did not molest their lands and their persons, and in return the Penobscots would not attack the settlements in the region.

Penobscots wanted freedom, too. Perhaps the rhetoric of liberty influenced the Penobscots to consider making alliances with Americans against the perceived oppression of Great Britain, in hopes that the Revolution would stop the flood of immigrants coming onto their lands. Certainly the promises made by Massachusetts at Watertown gave them hope and expectation that they, too, could share in the fruits of universal liberty espoused by the revolutionaries.

The quadrille of the American Revolution in Maine included the following dancers: the Penobscots, the Maliseet-Passamaquoddies, the British (and allied American Tories), and the revolutionary Americans. Within each of the groups certain key individuals performed critical movements. Joseph Orono clearly stands out as the leader of the Penobscots. Orono was light-skinned and blue-eyed, tall and thin. While there is some controversy about his heritage, historians Williamson and Eckstorm both believed him to be of partial French descent, basing their belief largely on the word of Penobscots.[6] The rumor that Orono had been captured from a white family in York seems false, because he would have been too old to be the child who was stolen. It seems more reasonable that Orono was the son of the elder Castine's daughter. Orono himself told Williamson that his father was French and his mother Penobscot. He spoke French and Penobscot but not English, which we know because he required an interpreter whenever he negotiated with English speakers.

Orono's appearance helped him to be more easily accepted by Americans. The reason he decided to bring his people into the war probably rested on several factors. One was a desire for liberty for his people, interpreted as personal freedom that included the ability to make decisions free from the constrictions of other governments. He also hoped to gain protection from Massachusetts against settlers taking Indian land and resources. In addition, his people needed to be able to trade with the people of Massachusetts for necessities. Massachusetts promised to meet their needs in exchange for an alliance. Also, the old Penobscot alliance with the French, who eventually assisted the American cause, gave the Penobscots some assurance that they would be treated fairly. One other factor of some importance was the poor relationship between Penobscots and certain British individuals in the service of their king, especially Captains Thomas Goldthwait and Henry Mowatt.

Goldthwait commanded the military at Fort Pownall; Mowatt had been with Governor Pownall when he first declared that the Penobscots had lost all their lands by right of conquest. Goldthwait generally appeared to be afraid of the Natives. Writing to the governor of Massachusetts in 1764, he worried about the Indians attacking the fort, declaring, "The Indians had grown very surly."[7] Reporting on a conference later that year, he wrote, "The insolence of the Indians I believe proceeds from there being a large body of them together and their knowledge of the weakness of the Garrison." Goldthwait never tried to curry favor with the Penobscots, and a few years later Enoch Freeman, a local citizen, sent a letter to the governor's council reporting that the "Penobscots are highly exasperated with Goldthwait for allowing the fort to be dismantled and stopping trade."[8] Freeman was referring to the first outbreak of hostilities of the Revolutionary War in Maine. After a brief skirmish in southern Maine, the British captain Mowatt sailed the *Canceau* into Penobscot Bay and removed all the heavy guns and ammunition from Fort Pownall to his ship, thus rendering the fort unprotected and ineffective as a trading post. Locals denounced the loyalist commander, Captain Goldthwait, and rebel colonel James Cargill burned the fort in July 1775 to keep it from the British. The Penobscots thus lost their fur market and their source of provisions.[9]

The combination of the loss of the trading post, the lack of local agricultural produce, and the laws against trading with Nova Scotia left the Penobscots and their American neighbors in severe stress from lack of food. Children of both groups were dying from hunger. Local communities of whites were also quite vulnerable to the British and to privateers, since there was no protection from the Continental army and little if any local militia. The Penobscots were on friendly terms with the French settlers in the region, many of whom were related through marriage, but they were not close to the English-speaking settlers. However, Massachusetts authorities began to realize that the friendship, assistance, or at the very least neutrality of the Natives of Maine was essential to the survival of the Maine settlers.[10] They utilized local military men such as Andrew Gilman, Jonathan Lowder, Jedediah Preble (brother of John Preble), and Captain Lane. These men had joined the American cause and were familiar with the Penobscots because the men had been at Fort Pownall and met the Natives when they came to the fort to trade. Gilman and the others served as interpreters and negotiators in the effort to secure a Penobscot alliance.

Captain Lane raised a company for the army and in it enlisted five Penobscot men: Soucier, Eneas, Sebattis, Metagone, and Sewanockett. Although originally Pigwackets of western Maine, like many other displaced Abenakis they later joined the Penobscot community and are listed on the postwar census as Penobscots. These men also served as guides and aides to Colonel Benedict Arnold during the expedition up the Kennebec River to Quebec.[11]

When General Washington first planned and organized Arnold's trip through Maine in hopes of routing the British in Quebec, one local settler informed Arnold that Natanis, a Pigwacket living near present-day Flagstaff, informed for the British. This one act of mistrust greatly influenced the outcome of Arnold's military excursion. Natanis received word of Arnold's intent to kill him, probably through his relatives Eneas and Sebattis. Arnold had sent them, together with Frederick Jackins from Norridgewock, on an errand to Quebec. Thus forewarned, Natanis was able to disappear into the woods and avoid harm. He later informed Arnold's men that he had watched them as they moved through the woods. He had even driven game their way when they were hungry, probably as a means of assisting his kinsmen Sebattis and Eneas.[12]

Jackins and the two Penobscot men traveled by bark canoe. Arnold suspected duplicity from the Natives he sent as couriers to General Schuyler in Sartigan, Quebec.[13] He mentions several times in his letters and journal his concern that the Abenakis had not returned as quickly as he expected, and his suspicion that they might have betrayed him. They did return, however, informing Arnold that the Canadians had pledged their friendship and would assist Arnold's men in their attack on Quebec.[14] Arnold's suspicions worked against him in several ways. He hired local settlers as guides, rather than the more knowledgeable Natives. He relied upon an inaccurate map[15] and lost his way, spending valuable time and energy in the process. If he had relied upon his Penobscot guides to hunt on the journey, he would have experienced less hunger and hardship.

Before reaching the cabin belonging to Natanis, the expedition passed by the burned-over remains of Norridgewock. There they saw remnants of the gardens and the church where English soldiers had killed the Jesuit Sebastian Rasles and many of the Abenakis just ten years earlier. It was a grim reminder of the treatment Natives could expect to receive at the hands of Englishmen. There were as yet no incursions of settlers above Norridgewock, but other Abenakis were hunting on Chaudiere Pond.[16] Other Penobscots joined Natanis, Sebattis, Eneas, and Sewanockett in assisting Arnold's men in their march to Quebec and battle with the British.

One member of Arnold's expedition, John Joseph Henry, related in his journal that after leaving the location of the cabin of Natanis they came upon a birch-bark map set on a stake firmly driven down into the edge of the water. "This map we attributed to Natanis or to his brother Sebattis, who, as we afterwards knew, lived about seven miles up this westerly stream."[17] The crew of one of the expedition's boats found some deserted cabins of the Abenakis upstream and plundered their stores of venison, corn, and kettles. The map proved helpful, and they soon arrived at the first pond at the head of the Dead River.

Meanwhile, Arnold brought some 950 men with equipment across the twelve-mile carry using sleds and oxen. Natanis, in the company of his brothers, made himself known to Arnold's party at Sartigan, Quebec. "Natanis shook everyone's hand as if they had been long acquainted and informed the men that he had been watching them from a distance, knowing he was in danger. He, his brother Sebattis, and seventeen other Indians, the nephews and friends of Natanis, marched with us to Quebec."[18] He and the other Abenakis joined the battle for the city of Quebec. Arnold's expedition resulted in the death of 100 men and the capture of 400 others.

The failure of the expedition must have disheartened the Penobscots as much as it did the revolutionaries of Massachusetts. The Penobscots were struggling with how to comply with New England in its war with old England, realizing that they must come to terms with whichever party was victorious. For the most part, they acted in accord with their immediate needs. One need, safety of their persons, required being on friendly terms with the local settlers, a task quite difficult in the best of times. A second and very pressing need, to feed their families and obtain supplies for hunting, they could fill only through trade. While New England made demands upon them to fight against old England, only a few of the young men were willing to leave their families and go to war. The Penobscots could raise about fifty fighting men, but their families needed those men for fall and winter hunting so that they would have furs to trade for food and other goods.

The Penobscots' problem of trade needs some clarification. Calloway writes that Native Americans "had been drawn into a larger Atlantic economy that shaped their tastes, their lives, and ultimately their landscape. For many Indian peoples, the most pressing question posed by the outbreak of the Revolution was not who should govern in America but who would supply the trade goods on which they had come to depend."[19] For the Penobscots, trade was certainly one of the major concerns. The truckhouse at Fort Pownall had moved outside the fort in 1768 but was then demolished in 1775. The Penobscots were not happy trading with the fort, wanting a trading post located closer to their settlement. So they traveled to Boston to request an authorization from the governor for a new truckhouse.[20] Moving the truckhouse closer to the Penobscots might have solved much of their problem of obtaining supplies; however, British blockades of Penobscot Bay prevented Massachusetts from supplying goods to Bangor.

At this juncture Passamaquoddy and Maliseet leadership decided to join the dance by making an alliance with the Penobscots. In September 1775, Maliseet leaders Pierre Toma and Ambroise Bear of the St. John River requested that Jonathan Lowder write to the Massachusetts Council expressing friendship and a desire to cooperate with the Penobscots in opposing the British. They requested a priest, guns, ammunition, and food, which they promised to pay for with furs.[21] Toma and Ambroise appeared in Watertown with Lieutenant Andrew Gilman and Jedediah Preble. The government gave them blankets and ribbons and made an agreement with them whereby the Penobscot truckmaster would supply them with ammunition and provisions for winter in return for their furs.[22]

In November the Penobscots complained about John Preble. They wanted him replaced, and they asked for Jonathan Lowder. They also requested a priest and complained that traders mistreated them, often plying them with rum and then cheating them "in good style."[23] They expressed their dissatisfaction with truckmaster Preble and reiterated their complaint that settlers were living on their lands and poaching game. The Massachusetts Council at this time gave the Penobscots permission to go to Canada to find a priest and replaced Preble with the more popular Lowder.

Lowder was born in Boston in 1733, served as a soldier in the French and Indian Wars, and later as a gunner at Fort Pownall. As the American Revolutionary War progressed, he also served as a lieutenant colonel under Colonel Josiah Brewer. He resided in Bangor and held one hundred acres of land. His dealings with the Penobscots were honest and straightforward; they came to trust him over Preble, whom they disliked.[24] Lowder often accompanied tribal leaders and acted as interpreter at important conferences. These military men—Lowder, Brewer, and a few others who got to know the Penobscots—were the few friends the Natives found among the local settlers.

   The Penobscots were understandably cautious about throwing their lot in with the Americans but hopeful that Massachusetts would honor its promises to them. In September 1776, some of the representatives of the Penobscot tribe expressed a desire for neutrality. They stated that they could not spare any of their young men, because they were worried about defending themselves against British ships. They were hoping to avoid conflict and wait until Britain and America settled their differences. They were very concerned about whether they would be protected from the British, who, their eastern allies had informed them, had a great force at the St. John River. Finally, they did agree to act as messengers and informers. In return for their services to the war they requested that Massachusetts authorities remove the settlers living on Native lands above head of tide.[25] In spite of concerns about keeping the young men home, ten Penobscots joined a regiment with thirty-six other men under the command of Lieutenant Andrew Gilman. These ten young warriors acted independently of the rest of their village. They traveled to New York with Gilman in October 1776 while the remainder of the Penobscots declared neutrality.[26] Within the tribe there remained differences of opinion about the war. The majority eventually came to support the Americans, while others just remained at home and took a neutral position.

   In order to keep the eastern tribes from joining the British side, Massachusetts appointed John Allan "Superintendent of the Eastern Indians" in January 1777. His jurisdiction included the Maliseets, Passamaquoddies, and Micmacs, but not the Penobscots. The Penobscots remained, because of their geographical position in the center of the settled area of Maine, under the separate jurisdiction of the Court of Massachusetts. The Penobscots became involved at times with the Maliseets and Passamaquoddies and with privateers; they were accustomed to the threat of British vessels whenever they encamped with Allan. Some seized a British schooner loaded with lumber at the St. John River, stealing the supplies and then releasing the vessel.[27]

   It appears the Penobscots also wanted to join with the Maliseets. In August, some Penobscots went to Machias and met with Allan.[28] In the midst of the conference, British ships arrived at Machias. A Captain Smith, some settlers, and Indians repelled the ships' attack. Orders came in a few days later to forgo further expeditions against the British.[29] In September 1777, the chiefs of the Penobscots and the St. John Maliseets held a conference and resolved "to stand together with our brethren of Massachusetts and oppose the people of Old England that are endeavoring to take our lands and liberties from us. . . . We have no place to go but to Penobscot for support and we desire you would provide ammunition, provisions and goods for us there, and we . . . will give you our fur and skins."[30]

In spite of their pledge, Americans like John Allan did not trust the Indians. On September 22, 1777, Allan wrote, "The Penobscot Indians are constantly here making heavy complaints of impositions and extortions and Insist upon being connected with the other tribes. . . . I find there is a French merchant (Mons. Lunier) settled at the Head of Penobscot with a British Commission to Treat with the Indians, he uses every Art and means to turn them—they have had many Supplys from him and I fear they have given much Intelligence from time to time." Allan wrote further that the Penobscot Indians had entered into an agreement of trade with the Maliseet, Madawaska, Meductic, and Passamaquoddy tribes effective as of June 12 at the St. John River.[31]

With their Native allies, the Americans set up command at both Machias and Penobscot River locations. At the Penobscot, Colonel Josiah Brewer was the commander of the small garrison stationed at present-day Bangor. He received provisions to sustain thirty men and two officers from Massachusetts for three months. Lieutenant Colonel Jonathan Lowder, Lieutenant Andrew Gilman, and Ensign Jeremiah Coburn fell under Brewer's command. Ten of the thirty-six men who were stationed at Fort Pownall under the command of Andrew Gilman were Penobscots. A total of forty-one Penobscot men served at one time or another under Gilman's command. Massachusetts provided these men with two hundred pounds of gunpowder, two hundred pounds of lead, and £400 to procure supplies. The following April 1778, the House of Representatives sent Lowder more goods to trade with the Penobscots, and ordered the Penobscots' furs and skins to be turned over to the War Department for military use.[32]

Meanwhile at Machias, the headquarters of the Eastern Department of the war, John Allan employed six Maliseets as soldiers. He had a well-supplied truckhouse with five hundred bushels of corn, thirty barrels of flour, and fifteen firkins (quarter barrels) of lard. Nevertheless, he complained of the difficulty of providing for the Indians and their families who camped nearby. Allan's impoverished company was successful, however. When four armed British vessels were sent against Machias, Major Stillman's party on one side of Machias, and Joseph Neptune, chief of the Passamaquoddy tribe, with forty to fifty Indian fighters and other white volunteers on the other, successfully repelled the British.[33]

At Penobscot, both Indians and whites suffered from lack of food and other supplies. A letter from Josiah Brewer dated April 12, 1778, stated that the condition of the Penobscot tribe was very bad. Although John Preble and another trader, Major Robert Treat, had brought them some corn, it was not enough for the Indians. They were living under great hardship. There were no potatoes, for example. Meanwhile, Colonel Josiah Brewer led the local militia, and Andrew Gilman served as his lieutenant. Under Gilman's command, the militia built a truckhouse near the falls about a mile from Preble's place. Preble accused Brewer and Gilman of profiting from the Indian trade by illegally using the Indians' goods as payment for services rendered to them by white men. He also complained that the traders held lavish parties fueled with the Indians' trade rum. In spite of Preble's accusations, the Penobscots continued to trade with Lowder and Brewer. Although dismissed by the Provincial Congress on January 22, 1778, as a result of Preble's complaints to the Committee of Safety, Gilman was eventually reinstated.[34]

Meanwhile, Colonel Allan had another conference with the Penobscots, during which Chief Orono complained about two major problems they were having—finding subsistence and mistreatment by local settlers. He told Allan that the provisions at Preble's truckhouse could supply only two or three hunters, not the whole community. "We was in hopes when we acknowledged ourselves Americans, owned them as brothers, that the white people on this river would take some notice of us and not admitted any person whatever to take advantage of our disposition." He went on to tell Allan that settlers had stolen twenty-five-hundred moose hides and other furs from them during the winter, leaving them with nothing to trade. He said the men and women were given drink, their goods taken, and then "they kick us out of doors." He also related that there were many Tories living in the area who told them of the goodness of the king and many settlers moving onto their lands while at the same time treating the Natives despicably. "This treatment we did not expect from Americans, especially after lands were given us by the General Court."[35]

The Provincial Congress approved supplies for Lowder's truckhouse in 1778; Brewer applied to be truckmaster in 1779.[36] As if the Penobscots' problems with hunger were not enough, Joseph Orono and his lieutenant, Colonel John Neptune, brought news of an imminent invasion of British and Indian forces from Quebec to John Preble at the Bangor truckhouse on April 30, 1779. The threatened invasion from the north never occurred, but soon a new threat developed to the south.[37]

In 1779, the British took notice of the settlers on the Penobscot River and eastward, where they wanted to establish a military post. British General McLean and nine hundred men went to present-day Castine, landing on June 12 without opposition. Captain Mowatt was left in charge of three sloops. The British hoped that a force placed on the Maine coast would provide a resting place for the king's navy near Halifax, Nova Scotia. The force would provide protection to British subjects of Nova Scotia and other territories in the eastern part of the country. In addition, the British would establish a new province for the loyalist refugees from New England. This province was to be called "New Ireland" and would be governed by Thomas Hutchinson. (These plans were never realized.) The peninsula in the Penobscot Bay called Bagaduce, near present-day Castine, was chosen for the fortification. When the British landed, they began building Fort George.[38] This was the cause of the spectacularly unsuccessful Penobscot expedition.

The Penobscot expedition began when Americans responded to the British landing on Bagaduce Peninsula by sending nineteen armed vessels with 344 guns and twenty-four transports under the command of Richard Saltonstall of New Haven, Connecticut. Solomon Lovell commanded the land forces. The Americans appeared on July 25 and began fighting on July 28. Unfortunately for the Americans, an additional British fleet of seven ships arrived on August 13 and forced the Americans to retreat. The British overtook some ships and they surrendered, while other Americans escaped and burned their own ships.[39] The Penobscot Indians guided the rest of the retreating land forces overland from Kenduskeag to Kennebec and thereby saved many lives, although some of the men perished along the way from weakness and hunger.

A roster of the Penobscot men who served in the battle included one man who died on July 25, another on August 5, and a third who was taken prisoner. The men under the command of Lieutenant Gilman are listed in a payroll record provided to the General Court on September 17, 1779.[40] What is remarkable about this list is that it contains the names of most of the heads of families for the Penobscot village at Old Town, indicating that whatever vacillation there may have been initially was swept away once the Penobscots decided to defend their own territory in Penobscot Bay from the British. The Penobscots decided to aid the Americans because they believed that doing so would further their economic and political interests. No doubt the rhetoric of revolution fired up animosity toward King George, but more important, they had forged an alliance with people who had promised to protect their rights and their lands. Their hopes were based on the promises made to Orono by the Provincial Congress at Watertown in May 1775.[41]

Due to the British occupation of Castine and control of Penobscot Bay, Indians and settlers alike suffered from lack of food and other supplies.[42] The winter of 1780 was exceedingly cold, and Chief Orono once again traveled to Boston. Jonathan Lowder abandoned his Penobscot truckhouse since he could not get supplies through the British blockade; he established a new truckhouse at Fort Halifax (on the Kennebec River) in the winter of 1780–1781. About thirty Penobscots led by Orono and some of the white settlers moved to the Kennebec for protection and to obtain food. Massachusetts appointed Josiah Brewer truckmaster at the Kennebec truckhouse and authorized him to purchase supplies for the Indians.[43] He traveled with some Penobscot chiefs to Newport, Rhode Island, to meet with the French consul and request a priest who could minister to Maine's Indians. The party waited in Newport until they could take the French priest back to Maine with them. Brewer wrote the Massachusetts Council for provisions to support himself, interpreter John Marsh, and six Penobscot men for ten days.[44] At the same time, Chief Orono sent a petition requesting payment for the widows of four men killed by the British during hostilities. He reported that the tribe had been driven from their settlements by the enemy and requested provisions for supplies to be sent to Colonel Brewer at Fort Halifax for the support of the widows.[45] The Senate responded to the requests by stating, "we are of opinion that a large number of the Penobscot tribe consider themselves as in actual service of the United States—and that it would conduce to the Public Good, in attaching the tribe to our service to make some provision for the Families of these persons." They recommended sending provisions to Fort Halifax for the support of trade with the Penobscots living there.[46]

The new French priest, Juniper Berthiaume, began his duties at Penobscot in November 1780. Eight months later, he traveled to Boston with three Penobscots and their English interpreter requesting provisions and back pay for himself.[47] Truckmaster Josiah Brewer joined him, also petitioning for pay and rations. Brewer brought the furs and skins he had collected at Fort Halifax and turned them in to the commissary general. Andrew Gilman also petitioned the General Court and reported himself destitute and in need of back pay, clothes, and a small tent so he could travel with the Indians as an interpreter.[48]

Both the House and Senate considered Orono's petitions for provisions. Orono reported that his people were very needy, having recourse only to Fort Halifax for trade goods. Orono continued to serve the American cause by carrying letters to Machias, the St. John River, and Nova Scotia.[49]

Meanwhile, the Penobscots' new priest, Berthiaume, reported to the Massachusetts House that Brewer had been cheating the Penobscots at Fort Halifax. He wrote that the Penobscots had instead gone to trade with the British at Castine and some had gone to Canada.[50] Brewer seems to have been unaware of the problem. He writes, in a letter to his friend

Richard Devens, "Grate part of the Indians Removed back to there [sic] old hunting ground last fall and have not got in with their Spring hunt."[51] Penobscots had to return to old hunting territories for furs and skins to trade at Fort Halifax; the priest accompanied them. Clearly, the Penobscots desperately needed to find fair trading partners, and they were willing to travel great distances to do so.

There were no more military actions at Penobscot after November 1782, but keeping the Penobscots friendly continued to be a goal of the Massachusetts government. However, there was continual hostility between the French Catholic priest and the local, Protestant, English leaders. When Juniper Berthiaume went to Boston to collect his back pay, the House and Senate dismissed him.[52] This congressional action brought quick protest from the Penobscots. They reported that they heard that their priest had been dismissed upon a false report of Colonel Brewer and interpreter Gilman. They requested that he be returned to them, and asked for cannons and gunpowder to protect their village. They had been obliged to obtain a French interpreter to send to Boston and asked that this priest be paid. Massachusetts leaders seemed to be in conflict about whom to believe and whom to support. The House passed a resolve discharging Brewer and Gilman as truckmasters at Fort Halifax and reinstating Father Berthiaume in the office of instructor.[53] He did not stay in his post long, however, because in June of the following year the House passed a resolve to pay him and discharge him from any further service to the state.[54] Massachusetts ignored his protest, sent in June 1784. The lawmakers did not like to support a French Catholic, they preferred to back their own citizens, and so the legislature reimbursed Brewer for back pay and granted him land that he had improved near Fort Halifax.[55] Ultimately, the local Protestant citizens prevailed and the Penobscots, no longer a military threat, lost their priest. This significantly reduced their ability to stand firm against the local population.

On July 11, 1783, the post at Machias was discontinued and Colonel Allan discharged, as the war effort no longer needed his services. On September 3, the Treaty of Paris set the new boundary between American and British citizens at the St. Croix River. As a result, in January 1784, about six hundred loyalists evacuated the fort at Castine, after burning the barracks and storage buildings, and moved to Canada.[56] For the Penobscots, the war caused not only loss of life but loss of independence, because Massachusetts authorities would not, in the end, honor all the promises made to the Penobscots before the war. The Penobscots gained some pay and pensions for their military men and widows, and a guarantee of trading partners and trade goods from Massachusetts. Yet by creating goodwill and good relations with the new American government, they had hoped for much more. They wanted Massachusetts to keep its promise of protection of their lands, their persons, and the sovereign rights to their lands as long as they were a nation.[57] They would be disappointed.

Orono's great speech declaring his Penobscot warriors "Sons of Liberty" had bravely proposed a new political agenda. An alliance with the new American government, he hoped, would preserve Native liberties and lands. Sadly, the poverty of the new American government and internal factions within the government of Massachusetts ensured that the District of Maine would continue to be a frontier area characterized by lawlessness and acts of violence—with continued mistreatment of Native people for a long time.

Chapter 6

DANCING IN PLACE
Retaining a Land Base

> Ko na wa ya ti ge
> Ko na wa ya ti ge
> Ko cha ba la chich a
> Ni ta ge si za
>
> One of our amusements in the old days was the game of barter. Two companies would gather in separate wigwams and each dress one of their men in comic dress as *nolmihigon* or clown. The first *nolmihigon* and his company would go to the second wigwam with some article to be offered for exchange. Then the *nolmihigon* would dance and sing so comically and praise the article with so much wit that often he would receive in exchange for it something of far greater value. . . . If the *nolmihigon* were clever he might obtain a good canoe for his old spoon. . . . So we joked and played on long winter evenings in the olden days.[1]
>
> —BEDAGI

The barter dance song and game ritualized exchange, a central economic activity in Penobscot subsistence. But when Massachusetts turned its attention to gaining additional territory from the Penobscots by proposing new treaties, it was no game. New times required new strategies and new choreography in the dance of resistance. New times were characterized by the proximity of many new Americans who pressured Penobscots to assimilate. The United States sought to achieve assimilation through a process called "civilization,"[2] which can be described in this case as pressuring Native peoples to become Protestant Christians, settle in one place, take up farming, abandon the Native tongue and learn English, and send their children to English-speaking schools. All these components of assimilation were considered "improvements," and both secular and church officials led the effort. Penobscots were not unwilling to *change*; they had already adapted some European technology and

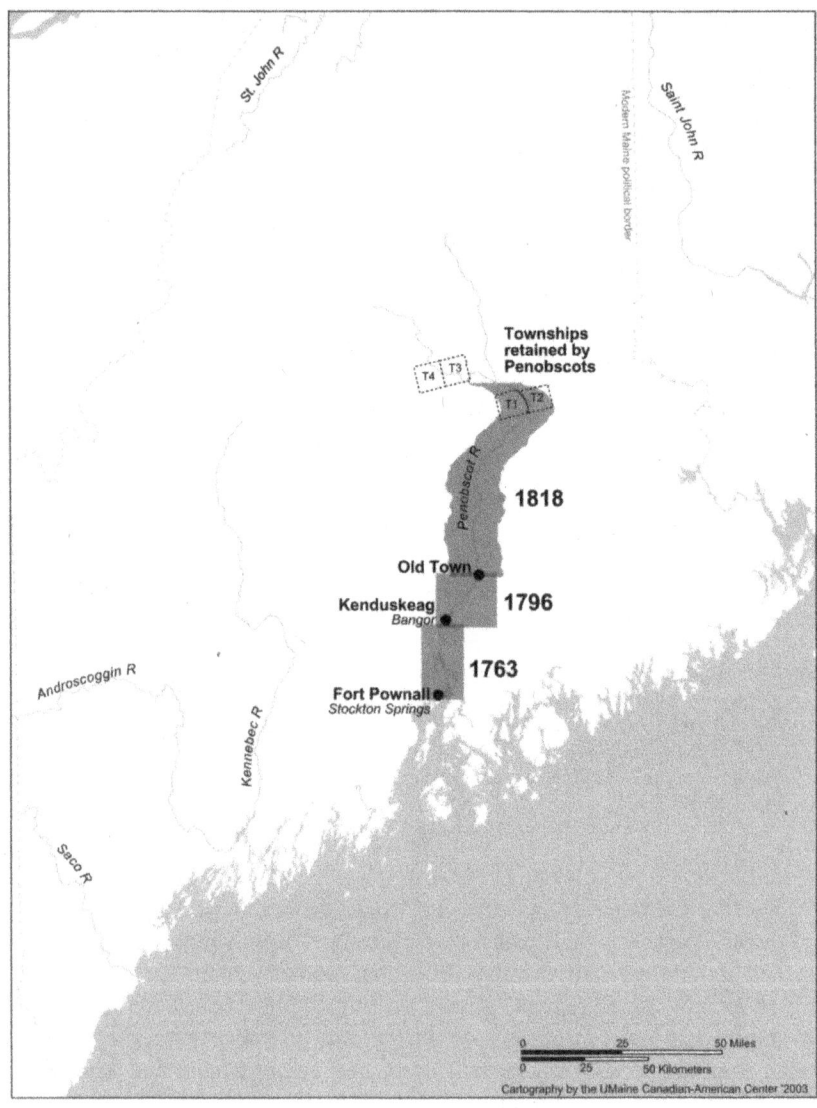

MAP 3. Lands taken by the English, Massachusetts and Maine 1763–1818. *Cartography by Michael Hermann, Canadian American Center, University of Maine.*

materials into their culture. However, they did not want to *assimilate*. They cherished their culture and traditions and fiercely resisted efforts to take their lands.

Maine Indian policy mirrored federal policies. While the architects of federal Indian policy, George Washington and his secretary of war, Henry Knox, placed a greater emphasis on the morality of Indian policy than some other political leaders, that morality must be understood in the context of beliefs of the times. Knox believed that the Indians possessed the right of the soil, and that it could not be taken from them "unless by their free consent, or by the right of conquest in case of a just war."[3] He further believed that the tribes of Indians ought to be considered foreign nations and not the subjects of any particular state. However, Knox also suggested that young white men marry Indian women and that females from large cities who had "strayed from virtuous paths" and who had "seen the error of their ways" might be found to marry the "sons of the wilderness" and consequently be rewarded with "good pensions." He saw this intermarriage as a solution for "civilizing" Indians.[4] The primary interest of the nation was eventually to absorb the Indians both politically and culturally into the American "melting pot"—or destroy them in the process.[5] The genesis of American Indian policy resides in the political and moral philosophy of the nation's founders, combined with their practical decisions based on problems facing America's new government.

Economic crisis quickly hit the newly formed nation. Left with considerable war debt and little in the way of industry or commerce, the new states sought to raise money by levying high taxes. The taxes hurt yeoman farmers the most. In Massachusetts, yeoman farmers took part in Shays's Rebellion in 1787. In the District of Maine, the backcountry farmers called themselves Liberty Men, demanding freedom from economic dependence as tenants or wageworkers. Ironically, while they dressed in Indian clothing and war paint, they ignored Indian claims, believing that all unsettled land should be distributed largely among white males so that they could raise crops and earn an independent income.[6]

Meanwhile, the large landowners, or Great Proprietors, were the capitalists who wanted to hire labor for mills and other industries, and therefore attempted to price the farmers off the land and into their service. One of three large patents in the District of Maine, the Waldo Patent, included about one million acres between the Medomac and the Penobscot Rivers. Waldo brought many Scots-Irish into the region to cut lumber and farm the lands before the American Revolution. For the most part, these coastal settlers had been cutting timber, but the British blockade during the war prevented them from selling it. So they moved inland where they could hunt game and raise crops. This brought them directly into Penobscot territory. Settlers were largely underrepresented in the General Court, so powerful men such as Henry Knox, James Bowdoin, and Josiah Little assumed control of the three great land companies in Maine. They pressed their claims to rents in courts where they enjoyed every advantage. Settlers who had built homes and barns, put up fences, and cleared fields stood to lose everything to the large landowner. As a result, the settlers rebelled and attacked the Proprietors' men and even attacked and set fire to their homes. The disputes continued until after 1820, but both groups had in common the need for land.[7]

When Henry Knox returned to Maine after the war, he was asked to assist Massachusetts leaders in obtaining additional lands from the Penobscots to satisfy land-hungry settlers. Knox himself held a vast tract of land: his wife had inherited a large piece of the Waldo Patent (about thirty square miles). Knox sold his lands to Waldo's Scots-Irish settlers after 1790. But so many settlers were moving into the central region of Maine's Penobscot Bay area that more lands were needed. Massachusetts leaders asked Knox to negotiate with the Penobscots in 1784. The settlers wanted the Penobscots to move farther upriver, thus releasing more territory for farmers and lumbermen. The General Court of Massachusetts authorized Knox, Benjamin Lincoln, and George Partridge to conduct negotiations on its behalf. In June, the three men traveled by horseback to the Penobscot settlement. Knox congratulated the Penobscot veterans on their conduct in the Revolutionary War and told them they had more land than they needed. Chief Orono responded courageously, "The Almighty placed us on the land and it is ours."[8]

Two years later, the governor of Massachusetts reported that as a result of negotiations, the Indians had agreed to relinquish all their claims and interest to all the lands west of the Penobscot River from the head of tide to the Piscataquis (about forty-three miles) and all claims on the east side of the river from the head of tide to the Mattawamkeag River (about eighty-five miles), reserving to themselves only the island on which Old Town stands and those islands in the river that had improvements, from Sunkhaze to Passadumkeag Island inclusively. He reported that they held their islands in fee (meaning they could use them but not sell them) and also islands in the bay, known as White and Black Islands near Naskeag Point. The governor reported that all the lands on the west should remain as hunting ground for the Indians (to the headwaters of the Penobscot above the Piscataquis) and east above Mattawamkeag. None of these lands should be laid out or settled by the state. In return, the state would pay the Penobscots 350 blankets, two hundred pounds of powder, shot, and flints. He claimed that the Indians would sign the treaty upon receipt of the trade goods.[9]

The governor's declaration proved unrealistic. According to a report of the committee on Penobscot Indians authorized on July 6, 1786, to conduct negotiations with the tribe, the Penobscots did not agree to sign the treaty. The committee met on July 28 with sixty-five members of the tribe and their chiefs, including Orono, Esquire Orson, Colonel John Neptune, and Neptonbonet, all Revolutionary War veterans, and reported, "early in the conference we discovered an aversion in the Indians to surrender all their claims to their lands."[10] In another letter written to the governor, the committee reported that the tribe claimed their lands by right of resolve of the Provincial Congress of June 1775. The state, however, claimed the land by right of conquest by Governor Pownall in 1760. Not surprisingly, the committee reported:

They [the Penobscots] appeared much hurt and disappointed . . . as they supposed before they had the whole width of land as far as the waters of this river extend east and west. This led them to complain that as they could not read and write they were imposed on and that writings were of no value to them.[11]

One can only imagine the frustration and disappointment of Chief Orono and the other Penobscot leaders as they realized that the Americans would not keep the promise made by the Provincial Congress at Watertown in 1775. Their own dream to share in the liberty touted by the new nation was dashed. Further, they now faced the possibility of having to relinquish even more lands to settlement, as well as the increasing difficulty of hunting and amassing a quantity of furs and skins that would pay for their necessities at the trading post.

At first, the Penobscots resisted what they viewed as duplicity on the part of Massachusetts negotiators. When the legislature sent agents to the Penobscots to obtain a deed, the tribe refused to ratify the treaty. Massachusetts authorities rationalized that the tribe had only limited jurisdiction over the lands, a right to occupy and to hunt but no right to transfer title or to sell timber from their lands. It is clear that the Penobscots believed otherwise. For example, the tribe negotiated with John Marsh in 1796 to quit their claim to Marsh Island. A deed conveying title to this land was signed by the major chiefs of the tribe, Joseph Orono, John Orson, Neptonbonet, Warrumgassett, and Soc Tomah, in exchange for thirty bushels of corn on October 15, 1793.[12]

Resisting pressure from settlers, the Penobscots refused to sign the 1788 treaty, but the negotiators did not let the issue rest. A large community of settlers grew in the area between the Indian settlement at Old Town and Colonel Jonathan Eddy's dwelling at Nichol's Rock (present-day Eddington Bend). This community pressured the state's leaders to acquire property from the Penobscots and have it surveyed into parcels for farming and timber harvesting. As a result, the General Court at Boston appointed William Shepherd, Nathan Dane, and Daniel Davis as commissioners to negotiate a treaty with the Penobscots for this territory. The result was a treaty on August 8, 1796, between the Commonwealth of Massachusetts and the Penobscot Indians. This agreement resulted in Penobscots quitting their claims to all the lands below Old Town Island but reserving all the islands. In return, Massachusetts was to provide the tribe with trade goods "as long as they remained a nation."[13]

Chief Joseph Orono, Esquire Orson, and five other tribal leaders signed the agreement. The reason they made this agreement had to do with their impoverished situation. Settlers were moving into their territory, hunting and trapping and clearing land. The long occupation of Penobscot Bay by the British and consequent warfare had left the Penobscots in a position of economic hardship. Furs were becoming more difficult to obtain and game was thinning, requiring longer travels to obtain subsistence. Not all members of the tribe were happy about these land negotiations. Eckstorm reports that Orono consequently had trouble with the tribe due to his part in the loss of this territory and lived apart from them in the little village one-half mile above the truckhouse. He died in 1801 and was succeeded by John Attean, son of Esquire Orson.[14]

By the time Attean became governor of the Penobscot tribe, their numbers were reduced to about seven hundred.[15] They were greatly outnumbered by the whole population of Maine, about twenty-four thousand, with about two hundred settlers residing several miles below the Penobscot village.[16] The small number of warriors and continuous poverty and illness weakened the Penobscots' negotiating position with the settlers. As a result, the state carved up their remaining lands except for the islands in the Penobscot River. Unlike other eastern tribes who lost all claims to land, the Penobscots remained in place. Now, surrounded by new Americans, Penobscots faced additional pressure from Massachusetts to change their way of life and become "civilized."

To New England leaders, "civilization" entailed a process of land ownership in which individuals owned and improved the land by building permanent buildings, raising fences, and growing crops. Men conducted such improvements while industrious, Christian women cooked, spun, and wove within their separate domestic sphere. New England's theological and philosophical ideals, reinforced by biblical passages,[17] provided a rationale for a civil law that declared that those who did not work the land had no right to withhold it from those who would. New England Christians believed their activities of "civilizing" the New World fulfilled God's will.[18]

Civilization included several essential components: Protestant Christian practices; industrious farming; settled, permanent homes; individualism; and patriarchal land ownership. If Native peoples did not follow all the activities prescribed, they were lost, not saved, and could be cleared from the land or killed. The mission of New England became the nation's mission, and the rhetoric of civilization would continue unchanged from the early national period on into the nineteenth century. Examples of such rhetoric are found throughout the nineteenth century, within the writings of such renowned historians as William H. Prescott (1796–1859), Lewis Henry Morgan (1818–1881), and Francis Parkman (1823–1893).

Prescott wrote about the history of the conquest of Mexico, stepping outside the established boundaries of thought about civilization by praising the cultural accomplishments of the Aztecs and other Central American peoples.[19] Most Americans believed, as Morgan did, that no indigenous peoples of the Western Hemisphere had evolved their own civilization, attributing mound building and other American wonders to lost civilizations.[20] Similarly, much of Parkman's writings presented in dramatic narrative a view of American history as a contest of one advanced society triumphing over a more primitive society. Parkman's New England loyalty and Anglo-Saxon heritage appeared in his praise of the triumph of England over France, democracy over feudalism, and Protestant faith over Catholic "tyranny." His writings portrayed Natives in all the negative stereotypical roles. Native people were "tenants of the wilderness," basically childlike, unable to work, and destined for extinction.[21] Many of these ideas come from the cultural evolution concepts of the Enlightenment, which held that hunting societies were more primitive than agricultural societies.

Nineteenth-century colonial and racist views promoted the biologically innate inferiority of "primitive" people. As an inferior race, Indians were doomed to extinction if unable to respond to the demands of a "civilized" life. Christian reformers and government agents sought to "civilize" Indian nations for their own good. Ethnologist and Indian agent Henry Schoolcraft wrote, in 1846, "it has been given to us [*whites*] to carry out a series of improvements and of moral and intellectual progress."[22] No historians made serious attempts to understand or explain the condition of Native Americans as a product of three hundred years of colonial history. Locked in ethnocentric and racial cocoons, Americans fashioned an Indian policy based on civil, religious, and racial ideals that excluded any interest in understanding the rich variety of Native cultures in the world around them. One of the proponents of those ideals and the person most responsible for the early-nineteenth-century American Indian policy was Thomas L. McKenney.

McKenney served first as superintendent of Indian trade and then as the head of the Office of Indian Affairs (1816–1830). His primary interest while superintendent of Indian trade was reform of the Indians. He conceived the government's Indian policy as first an obligation to civilize and Christianize the Indians. "It is enough to know that Indians are Men . . . that they have souls . . . and that we have the power not only to enhance their happiness in this world, but in the next also; and by our councils, and guidance, save souls that otherwise must perish!"[23] McKenney and his fellow humanitarians, many of them clergymen, missionaries, and other government officials, believed that the salvation of the tribes could best be achieved through agriculture. Farming would provide the Indians with an appreciation for private property, an incentive to work hard, and stability to organize in permanent, self-governed communities. Most reformers believed that Indians must be settled in one place so that they could regularly attend church and school and thus benefit from the teachings of the gospel.

Protestant virtues and landownership were essential to the agrarian ideals proposed in the new republic. Most Americans at this time controlled their own means of production through farming and cottage industry. The moral vision of republicans such as Thomas Jefferson described farmers as "the chosen people of God." The independent, virtuous farmer and republican liberty were essential attributes of the new nation.[24] As a result, leaders of the Massachusetts and, later, Maine governments believed they had a duty to instill in Native Americans the same core values of agrarianism, republicanism, and Protestant Christianity that they themselves held.

The settlers who resided in the District of Maine represented dissident Protestant groups and therefore were more tolerant of religious differences (within Protestantism) than Massachusetts leaders, but their tolerance did not extend to Catholics, whom they considered heretics. As heretics, Catholics were a threat to both religion and society. Generally, Protestants believed that it was desirable to work hard to amass wealth and that God rewarded righteous men and punished sinners. They believed in two worlds, the Christian, civilized, godly world and the world of nature, the wilderness, and uncivilized heathens.[25] They were especially fearful of anyone who took on the trappings of Indian culture (such as French and English frontiersmen and fur traders), seeing this as a threat to Protestant order and good living.

French-speaking priests threatened that Protestant order but continued to reside among the Penobscots and Passamaquoddies for some time. Penobscots followed Catholic religious practices and resisted all attempts to dissuade them from their chosen beliefs. Priests, many of them from

France, assisted the Penobscots with their resistance and also aided them politically by reading and interpreting negotiated treaties before the American Revolution and by writing letters for them after the Revolution. But priests also took part in the "civilization" movement.

Although discharged from service at the end of the American Revolutionary War in 1783, the French priest Juniper Berthiaume continued to serve the Penobscots on his own for several years. During these years, he continued to advocate for the Penobscots in matters concerning their rights to both their religious beliefs and their territory. When the Massachusetts Protestants tried to dissuade the Penobscots from their "Popery," Berthiaume intervened.[26]

Reverend Daniel Little, who traveled to Maine with the intent of teaching Penobscot children English and Protestant practices and beliefs, told the story of Berthiaume's intervention. Little's journal described his impressions upon traveling to Kenduskeag for a conference with the Indians in 1786. He arrived there with interpreters Joseph Treat and John Marsh. There were twenty-one canoes, with sixty-five Indians led by Orono, Orson Neptune, and Neptonbonet.[27] Little met Juniper Berthiaume there and described him as someone who spoke "broken English." The priest talked with the Indians, who refused to allow their children to attend Little's school. They also refused to ratify treaties concerning their lands. For reasons unknown, Berthiaume apparently left Maine in 1788.

The state of Massachusetts was not willing to support a Catholic missionary in Maine, but the Penobscots resisted accepting a Protestant missionary, so after Berthiaume left, the Penobscots followed an old tradition and petitioned Quebec for a priest. Their request was, of course, unsuccessful: they were no longer under the jurisdiction of the church in Quebec but under the Prefect-Apostolic of the United States.[28] The Penobscots then sent a letter to Bishop Hubert in the United States. The text of the letter reveals the reasons the Penobscots wanted a priest:

Our heart is sad. Is it not a reason for grief to see men of this age who have not yet received their First Communion? All our young folk have been baptized only by our own hands: as for our dead, we dig their graves and bury them ourselves. Nor have we any one to teach us.

We seek a priest. God knows that is the reason why we decided to undertake this long and painful journey. It will touch the heart of our father [the bishop] and he will find means of getting us one.

We know that our father [the bishop] said that he would never be able to give us one who could make his permanent residence in our village: we therefore restrict ourselves to the request that he provide us a mission of about two months from time to time.[29]

Bishop Hubert informed the Penobscots that Bishop Carroll of the United States was now their spiritual leader, and so they returned home with that news. They then sent a letter requesting a Catholic priest to the leaders of the Catholic Church in New England. In response to the Indians' request, Louis de Rousselet, a French priest who was a resident of Boston, traveled to the Penobscots for a visit, during which he ministered to their spiritual needs. The priest also brought two Penobscot boys back to Boston with him to provide them with an education. He returned to the Penobscot in March 1791 and remained there until December.[30]

Bishop Carroll tried to obtain federal aid for a resident Catholic priest for the Indians of Maine and sent a memo to President George Washington in March 1792. Washington replied that the Indians were inhabitants of Massachusetts and "any application therefore relative to these Indians for the purpose mentioned . . . would seem most proper to be made to the government of Massachusetts."[31]

The Catholic Church paid for the services of Francois Ciquart, the next priest to be appointed to the Maine missions, so that he might go to the Passamaquoddy reservation. From there, he resided and administered to the Penobscots by visiting them at least occasionally. It was not long, however, before Ciquart abandoned his post and went to New Brunswick. Once again the Penobscots found themselves without a priest.[32] The bishop was concerned about this and took steps to remedy the situation.

Francis Matignon, bishop of New England's Catholic community in 1796, invited John Cheverus to be missionary to the Indians of Maine. The bishop warned Cheverus that the post was "far advanced into the country" and that he would have "to wear the cassock habitually, because its inhabitants were used to seeing their clergymen in a long dress." He also said that part of the priest's duties would be to assist the Indians in accepting the government of Massachusetts.[33] This is significant, illustrating the change in relationship between church and state. Previously, French Catholic priests had been in a more confrontational role with colonial and state governments. Now, the church leadership resided in New England instead of Quebec. New England's Catholic leaders realized the jurisdiction of the state of Massachusetts over the future of the Penobscots and sought to assist in improving the relationship of the state government with the tribe.

During the negotiations for the treaty of 1796, Massachusetts promised the Penobscots a resident priest. In June 1797, several men from both Penobscot and Passamaquoddy tribes visited Boston to make an official request for their priest from state officials. The bishop sent John Cheverus to Maine with the following letter of introduction:

My dear Brothers,
I doubt not that you will welcome the worthy Missionary, who, influenced solely by his zeal and his love for you, leaves here today to visit you, and also to

furnish you the aid and comfort of religion, as well as to advise with you on the means of obtaining a permanent resident Missionary to act as your Father, Protector, and Guide in the way of salvation.

We had first hoped that the government of this state would contribute toward the expenses of this journey; but it has not done so. If your delegates had made a request for this and had consulted with us for this purpose, perhaps they might have obtained it. The residence of a permanent missionary among you will depend on the efforts, which you yourselves will make, together with the aid, which it is not yet impossible to obtain from the General Court next January. . . . While he is among you, we will be united in prayers that God will bless his ministry among you, may you all produce fruits of blessing and salvation, strengthen you in faith and charity, and fill you with all kinds of grace, both spiritual and temporal.[34]

The importance of the "temporal" grace brought to the Penobscots needs emphasis. Priests such as Cheverus and his successor, James Romagne, may have "saved" the Maine Indians, but not just in terms of their souls. It may have been the priests who did the most to save their lives. No one else was willing to live among them and minister to their faith, health, and social welfare. Although priests were scarce in New England, the bishop considered the Indian missions a priority for priestly service. The Penobscots had been continuing to practice their faith, holding Sunday prayer services and teaching their children without benefit of a resident priest. However, diseases, including alcoholism, cholera, and smallpox epidemics, and corruption from outside influences took their toll on the community.[35]

In June 1798, Cheverus went to Old Town. He related his experience there in a letter to Bishop Matignon dated June 7, 1798. Cheverus reported that only 220 Penobscots survived.[36] Smallpox had killed 300 in one winter. This is an astonishing figure; if true, more than half of the community was killed. Such epidemics brought the Penobscot people very close to extinction. Nevertheless, the Penobscots supported their priest, feeding him well. Cheverus reported eating salmon, partridges, pigeons, turtles, and moose. He also enjoyed the benefits of campfire smoke "when it drives away at once thousands of flying insects feasting upon my poor face."[37] To ensure his continuing presence, a delegation of Penobscots went to Boston to seek financial support for the priest. They were rewarded when the General Court prepared a resolve ordering two hundred dollars per year to pay "a teacher of religion and morality, among the Indians of the tribe of Penobscot and Passamaquoddy."[38]

During his career both as priest and later as bishop, Cheverus visited the Penobscots every year and had a church built for them. However, the bishop wanted to use Cheverus elsewhere and hoped to find an English-speaking priest for the Indians so that they could learn English from him. James Rene Romagne, born in Nayenne, France, and a longtime friend of

Cheverus, replaced him as missionary to the Indians of Maine. Romagne had spent six years in England as a refugee of the French Revolution. As a speaker of both French and English, he was in a unique position to assist Maine Indians during a time when they began to move from speaking Abenaki and French to speaking Abenaki and English. He arrived at Passamaquoddy Village in August 1799. From that time on, he remained in service to the Indians of both tribes for nineteen years. Of his visit to the Penobscot, he wrote to his bishop:

> My interpreter there is a respectable man hundred and twelve years old. He many times lamented at the behavior of his brethren. . . .
> Since I am a priest of yours, I have baptized 45 children, buried an old woman, and a child; 2 marriages; 2 women, the one Presbyterian, the other of the Church of England, have made profession of Catholic faith. Another comes to instructions. Two others seem well inclined, would to God they will embrace truth.[39]

Romagne resided in a house on ninety acres of cleared land near Pleasant Point that was granted to him by the Massachusetts legislature on March 4, 1801. The state purchased this land from John Frost and appropriated it "to the use and improvement of the said Tribe of Indians till the further order of the legislature." In addition to this residence, Romagne collected a stipend of two hundred dollars annually from the state of Massachusetts, as his predecessor Cheverus had done.[40]

True to his times, Romagne promoted a settled agricultural lifestyle, encouraging the men to plant corn and the women to spin and weave. He also preached abstinence from alcohol, at least partly due to the influence of some of the older Abenaki men, many of whom, he reported, "had never touched a single drop, and could not even be tempted to."[41]

Romagne studied the Native language, using existing manuscripts of prayers left by earlier priests. He finished editing *The Indian Prayer Book* that was printed in 1834 by order of Bishop Fenwick.[42]

Romagne also looked after the health of the people he served. In 1804, he inoculated both Penobscots and Passamaquoddies against smallpox.[43] This act may in large measure have saved the tribe from further devastation from the disease. In the meantime, the Massachusetts government pursued its goals of encouraging agriculture by appointing a commission including Romagne and agent William Jenks "to induce the Indians of the Penobscot to settle on and cultivate their lands." Jenks reported that the Indians were well disposed toward this idea after they attended a meeting at Indian Island with the priest in September.[44]

A year later, the War of 1812 broke out between the United States and Great Britain. None of the Maine Indians directly engaged in the war, although the British occupied Eastport, Castine, Belfast, and Bangor. Romagne reported to Bishop Cheverus that "he was treated very politely by the British commander and officers at Passamaquoddy." During their occupation of Castine, the British did not disturb Romagne or the Penobscots, and the bishop continued his annual trips to Maine during the British occupation. However, the British blockaded Maine ports until April 25, 1814, and some Bangor militia under the command of General Blake of Brewer unsuccessfully resisted the British occupation of Hampden, resulting in the death of three Americans. Settlers living between the Penobscot and the Kennebec Rivers shared supplies with the residents of Bangor during the siege of Penobscot Bay.[45]

In 1815, Bishop Plessis of Quebec planned a visit to New Brunswick and Maine. He stopped at Pleasant Point to confirm Passamaquoddies and Penobscots. Romagne impressed him with his command of both English and Abenaki and with his education and demeanor. Romagne informed Plessis that many Penobscots had traveled to Pleasant Point, both for confirmation and to celebrate a national Indian festival. This was probably an inaugural feast, since the tribe had just conducted an election for deputy governor. Romagne set off for France in the fall of 1818.[46]

Bishop Cheverus replaced Romagne with an Irish priest named Dennis Ryan. Ryan was sent to Maine in April 1818. The following June, economic necessity compelled the Penobscots to sign an agreement with Massachusetts that was essentially a quitclaim to all the land remaining to them in the District of Maine, except four townships and the islands in the Penobscot River. Massachusetts promised supplies, an agricultural adviser, and church repairs. On January 22, 1819, Massachusetts ordered an annual stipend of $350 for the Natives' religious teachers.[47] Ryan meanwhile served his church primarily at Newcastle.

Although Massachusetts tolerated the Catholic priests, especially now that control of those priests was with the bishop of New England, they exhibited very little tolerance for other Penobscot cultural traditions. While Penobscots practiced Catholicism, they also continued observing customs from their own aboriginal beliefs. Generally, it was not acceptable in Penobscot society for individuals to use power or wealth for themselves. All power (spiritual, magical, political, material) was to be used for the good of the whole community. When it was not, it was considered black sorcery. While Penobscots enjoyed European technology, they did not want to change into white men. They found contact with whites spiritually and morally degrading, especially fearing abuse of alcohol by their young people. They had an intimate relationship with the landscape, dividing their world into family territories for hunting, fishing, and gathering of other resources.[48] But that use did not extend to amassing wealth; their Gluskabe legends taught them the importance of leaving animals, fish, and other resources to regenerate, so that future generations would not go hungry.[49] Their social order had served them well throughout the fur-trading period because Maine's vast natural resources were not threatened by the hunting and trapping of such a relatively small population. But the Americans, who viewed Maine's vast landscape as an unlimited source of land and lumber, did not share the Native perspective.

Massachusetts first authorized Moses Greenleaf to survey the lands purchased from the Penobscots, and especially to draw out an eight-thousand-acre parcel for Thomas Johnson and others.[50] A number of persons had settled within this parcel; the legislature granted anyone who had been on the land for at least a year a parcel of one hundred acres. Amos Patten was commissioned to survey the settlers' lots within the tract purchased from the Penobscot Indians on June 14, 1814. Major Joseph Treat was assistant surveyor for this project. He would later be appointed by Maine's first governor, William King, to survey the entire length of the Penobscot River.[51]

Pressure on the Penobscots to release title to their lands intensified as a result of the new settlements. Meanwhile, treaty goods did not carry the Penobscots through the winter to the hunting season, and delegates were sent to Boston for aid. The British blockade of Penobscot Bay during the War of 1812 had kept goods from arriving, and sales of furs and skins were meager. The General Court passed a resolve in 1816 ordering that three hundred bushels of corn be sent to Old Town to offset hunger. The legislature provided the money because they were told that the hunting season was late and the people were "uncommonly unfortunate in hunting," rendering them close to starvation.[52] The corn was not enough. Game became scarcer, and the Penobscots began to turn to selling timber from their lands in order to acquire money with which to buy food.

In 1818, the commissioners of the land office reported to the General Court that the Penobscots were "illegally" selling and disposing of timber from their lands, which the state believed they had no right to do. The state believed that the Penobscots were devaluing the lands, and by excluding all settlement thereon they "present[ed] a material obstacle to the sale and settlement." In addition, they argued that the Penobscots were poor and destitute, frequently petitioned the General Court for relief, and had petitioned the legislature to release their claims to ten townships in exchange for money for food.[53] Therefore, the governor was authorized to appoint three persons to negotiate with the Penobscot tribe at Bangor the last Wednesday of June 1818.

The state used this opportunity to press for control of even the remaining Penobscot possessions—the islands in the river. The General Court

FIG. 6. View of Penobscot Indian village. Sawdust trail across the frozen Penobscot River. *Courtesy Maine Folklife Center, University of Maine, photograph no. 8285.*

further ordered that the Indians release all their lands and islands for a sum not to exceed $500 and annual articles to provide means for their "improvement." The agents were to be paid $600 to perform the negotiations (more than the whole tribe would receive for their land).[54] The treaty that was negotiated allowed for $400 and goods to be delivered immediately, with other supplies delivered annually thereafter. General John Blake, who lived in Orrington, was appointed agent and was paid for his services and disbursements to the Penobscots.[55] The legislature instructed the governor to see that the treaty was performed in good faith, but the amount of goods provided to the Penobscots was not to exceed $2,000 in one year without further appropriation by the legislature.[56]

Blake reported to the governor that he received corn and other articles allowed as annual payment to the Penobscots and distributed them "in small quantities at a time among the Indians in order to prevent them selling and bartering them away for spirituous liquors and other useless articles." He had also found that several non-Indian families had settled on the state's and Indians' land "for the purpose of plundering the same," and he reported warning them off and sending their names to the solicitor general. Blake reported that the Penobscots were very much injured by the sale of one of their islands called Shad Island (it had been sold to Joseph Treat), which was well situated for the shad fishery, upon which

Penobscots depended for their subsistence. The Penobscots requested that the government purchase the island for them. The agent also leased the meadows and took securities from the leases and forwarded them to the government.[57]

Blake's annual reports provide a glimpse into the condition of the Penobscots and their concerns—but also into the efforts the state began to make to forcibly assimilate them. In a letter from William Jenks to General Blake dated September 12, 1811, at Bangor, Jenks writes, "As one of the commissioners appointed by his Excellency the Governor to induce the Indians of the Penobscot to settle on and cultivate their lands, I have just visited them in company with Mr. Romagne, my colleague in this office." Jenks recommended that ten to fifteen acres be planted that spring under the supervision of Romagne. He further stated that the education of the children was "an object near my heart." However, he did not believe that it would be possible to begin teaching the children until the community as a whole was "comfortably provided for."[58] Jenks reported that he and Romagne were going to get the tribe started on a plan of cultivating their land and planting corn the following spring. He requested four bushels of seed corn from Indian agent John Blake.

The letter indicates that a clear mandate had been given to Jenks and Romagne by the governor to pressure Penobscots to settle down and plant corn. But the Penobscots had not requested such assistance. As a matter of fact, the Penobscots sent a letter through their agent claiming that the legislature had appropriated five hundred dollars for the purpose of introducing agriculture among the Indians but complaining that they had never received any articles from the appropriation. At this time, most of the men were still hunting and trapping and bringing the furs and skins to Blake to exchange for the goods they needed for their families. Penobscot hunters struggled to find game, however, as another letter attests. In this letter, agent Blake wrote on behalf of the Penobscots to the Senate and House of Representatives on January 31, 1815:

The Chiefs of the Penobscot Indians beg leave to represent to your honors through the instrumentality of their agent that they are very much injured in consequence of the white people's hunting on their land by reason they have become very poor; they depending on hunting for their principle support, which is of but little.... They desire that your honors would take the matter under your wise consideration and pass an act that the white people may be liable to some adequate fine for every animal they take on the state's or Indians' land in order to prevent those injuries to such Indians.[59]

In addition to distributing the tribe's treaty goods to its members, the agent was instructed to "protect" the resources on the Indian (read "public") lands. In 1817, agent Blake reported that a sawmill had been built on a branch of the Mattawamkeag River on the Penobscots' lands and that much of the timber in the vicinity had been cut. The dam of the mill also prevented fish from swimming up into the ponds and lakes for spawning. The Penobscots asked their agent to request that the government remove the sawmill and dam. The agent also reported that the Penobscots were unhappy with the measure of their land, that they questioned the state's survey. The distance in dispute was some two miles of land downriver from Old Town.

Dispute over lands was just one of several issues that arose between the Penobscots, Massachusetts, and Maine in the first part of the nineteenth century. These issues included the tribe's efforts to retain control of the resources on its lands; an enforced change in subsistence from hunting to agriculture; negotiation with Massachusetts and, later, Maine through the Indian agent; and pressure on the Indians to assimilate. The Penobscots resisted by retaining or regaining control of their islands and resources; continuing to hunt and trade in furs and skins; seeking independent means of subsistence through basket making, guiding, and lumbering; retaining small villages on islands upriver; resisting agent controls; retaining a Catholic priest; marrying their own kind; and continuing to speak Penobscot.[60]

Such resistance exacts a price. That price for the Penobscots included intratribal strife. In some cases, factions of the tribe split over the issues and moved away more or less permanently. However, as a survival mechanism, elements of cultural resistance allowed the tribe to retain some traditional practices, adapt some elements of American culture, and invent or adopt from other Indian tribes a few new items of culture, such as manufacturing fancy baskets as a means of subsistence. But of all the forms of resistance, the continuing possession of and residence on islands in the Penobscot River seems to have been the most important mode of cultural survival:

We had a natural moat that surrounded us, which was the river. And we had strict orders [as children] that we couldn't cross that unless it was known why we were going. And we didn't need urging not to cross it.[61]

Retention of the island land base provided a measure of isolation and protection from the dominant culture, which valued the lands and, as a result, frequently challenged the methods of cultural persistence practiced by the Penobscots.

Several times, the state sent negotiators to obtain title to Penobscot lands, including the islands in the river. Pressure was strong from the growing population of local settlers, who wanted to obtain title to lands owned by the tribe or who wanted to harvest timber and grasses or to fish with weirs in Penobscot fishing places. The legislature intended that Penobscot acts of ownership should be restricted to hunting, fishing, and cultivation; in contrast, the tribe presumed the rights to sell timber and convey lands to speculators when they wished.[62] For their part, the Penobscots suffered from poverty due to a great reduction in animal resources; they became willing to sell some of their lands in hopes of obtaining education, more assistance for their subsistence endeavors, and support for their spiritual leadership. In spite of a small population and enormous pressure from local settlers, the Penobscots did retain title to some of their lands, especially the islands in the river. Representatives of the larger community and the state's leaders expected the Indians to become extinct: they therefore sought to claim title to Penobscot lands, allowing Natives to live, hunt, and fish upon them like tenants. The Penobscots successfully circumvented this movement by refusing to sign a treaty that removed their sovereignty over their shrinking domain. Like the clever *nolmihigon* who hoped to obtain a good canoe for his old spoon, the Penobscots determined not to lose in negotiations with Massachusetts.

Chapter 7

BIBLE, PRIMER, HOE, AND PLOW
Resistance through Religion, Education, and Subsistence

> Yaw ni gowe yaw ni go weh yaw no go weh[1]
> —GREEN CORN SONG

From the first mother's flesh sprung the green corn and from her sacred bones the tobacco. The corn filled the people with strength, but the tobacco "gave freshness to the mind and . . . heart."[2] Penobscots honor the memory of the first mother each time they use tobacco to make a spiritual offering, and in the ceremonies of the green corn dance. During the seventeenth and early eighteenth centuries, Abenakis grew green corn in large gardens near villages along the Kennebec; as we have seen, these villages were the birthplace of many members of the Penobscot community—so agriculture was not unknown to the Penobscots. Though most of their subsistence consisted of hunted and gathered foods, corn and tobacco played important roles both in the nourishment of bodies and in the spiritual beliefs and practices of the community. However, before the historic period, aboriginal agriculture along the Penobscot River consisted of small gardens that only supplemented the major subsistence practice of hunting.

Colonial Americans believed that agriculture, Protestant Christianity, and citizenship were linked together in the virtuous citizen known as the "yeoman farmer." Additionally, they believed that such a life should be promoted among Native Americans for their improvement. When the United States and Maine governments promoted a settled agricultural lifestyle for Penobscots, they ignored centuries of Penobscot experience in adapting to Maine's climate and natural resources. The Penobscots already knew how to make a good living off the land through hunting and gathering activities, such as mammal and bird hunting in the fall and winter, fishing and gathering shellfish and plants in the spring and summer. But Europeans did not value Native knowledge.

Operating under the principles of the Enlightenment and of Christian philanthropy, in 1818 the U.S. House Committee on Indian Affairs recommended, "Put into the hands of [Indian] children the primer and the hoe, and they will naturally, in time, take hold of the plough; and, as their minds become enlightened and expand, the Bible will be their book, and they will grow up in habits of morality and industry . . . and become useful members of society."[3] The following year, Congress appropriated ten thousand dollars annually for "civilization of the tribes adjoining the frontier settlements." An additional thirty-five thousand dollars supported schools under treaty provisions by 1834. The "Civilization Act" intended to teach Indians to live like white settlers.[4] Protestant (and some Catholic) missionaries administered the fund and established mission schools. Within five years there were thirty-two such schools in operation with 916 children. These boarding schools substituted English for Native languages and taught agriculture and the gospel.[5]

These and other national Indian policies influenced life in Maine. Penobscots resisted "civilizing" efforts in a number of important ways. First, they repeatedly requested financial support for their Catholic priest and for education of their children, in the face of pressure to accept Protestant missionaries. While a number of families utilized a state-sponsored farmer to grow crops on their lands on several islands in the river, most Penobscot heads of household continued to hunt and trade in furs for the major portion of their subsistence throughout most of the nineteenth century. Not until the last quarter of the nineteenth century did those Penobscots who lived in more interior sites move to Indian Island, and that was largely a response to better educational and job opportunities than to state pressure to settle in one place and become farmers.

The Penobscots had a long-established tradition of sending leading men of the tribe as representatives to the General Court of Massachusetts in Boston, and they continued the practice when Maine became a separate state. They sent two or more representatives to meet with the governor and his council. The representatives brought with them letters, petitions, and complaints from the tribe. Before most Penobscots learned to write, the agent or priest was instructed to write on their behalf. Sometimes this caused problems because it appears that the agents and priests often wrote letters for two different factions in the tribe.

The legislature reimbursed Penobscot representatives for travel costs, but with money from tribal funds that came from the sale of timber on their lands.[6] The Indian representatives were recognized and seated with ceremony. Sometimes they addressed the body, but they did not have a vote in the legislature, even in matters affecting their own people.[7]

Maine's first and most important order of business was to acquire additional lands from the Penobscots. The Maine legislature's first resolve appointed a commissioner to negotiate a treaty with them.[8] Lothrop Lewis negotiated the same treaty that the Penobscots had made with Massachusetts in August 1820, and Maine ratified the treaty the following February.[9] Massachusetts paid Maine thirty thousand dollars to assist the new duties of Maine to the Penobscots, which included a biannual payment of goods as set forth in the 1818 treaty. Maine set up a trust fund with the funds paid by Massachusetts and used these funds to pay for the tribe's needs. In particular, the legislature used funds to pay for tribal representatives' travel to the legislature and to support a priest. Later the government authorized the dispersal of small amounts to the agent to support a school and to pay a doctor. Tribal members also received biannual payments of treaty goods. In spite of the fact that all money that was paid into the tribe came from their own funds held in trust by the state, local people viewed these payments as "welfare" and looked upon the Indians as dependents or wards of the state.

In 1821, the legislature passed an act allowing the governor to appoint from one to three persons to act as agents for the Penobscots. Agents' duties included the procurement and delivery of treaty goods, and the approval of all contracts and bargains regarding timber and grass growing on the Indians' lands. Agents were not allowed to grant leases beyond one year or to sell more than five hundred dollars' worth of timber in a single year. Agents had to be bonded, and they were endowed with the power to collect debts due to the Indians. They also had to keep a true record of their proceedings—receipts and expenditures of both money and property—and make a report of such to the governor and council on an annual basis.[10]

In 1826, the legislature broadened the agents' powers by passing an act giving them leave "to lease any of the Islands belonging to the said tribe, for any term of years not exceeding twelve, and to sell and dispose of the burnt and decaying timber upon the two Indian townships, on the west branch of the Penobscot River."[11] Although agents were required to obtain consent from the tribe's governor or lieutenant governor, the money from such transactions was placed "in the treasury of the State . . . subject to the order of the Governor and Council, whenever in their opinion, the situation of the said tribe requires its appropriation for their benefit."

The act required tribal leaders to petition the governor and his council through their agent to obtain appropriations from the legislature in order to fulfill any needs they might have either as a governing body or as a community. The act was conceived as a control measure, further removing the Penobscots from sovereignty over their own property. Although the Penobscots had money in trust from the sale of their lands, they were considered and treated as paupers. The state's leaders did not consider them capable of managing their own funds, resources, or property. In addition, as I have demonstrated in the last chapter, they hoped to force the Penobscots to comply with the state's efforts to assimilate them into the general population, primarily by means of education and agriculture. In their actions, state leaders were following policies set forth by the federal government.

President Monroe signed into law a federal "act making provision for the civilization of the Indian tribes adjoining the frontier settlements" on March 3, 1819. The president had the discretion to employ "capable persons of good moral character, to instruct them in the mode of agriculture ... [and] teach their children reading, writing, and arithmetic." The president and secretary of war spent the money through the "benevolent societies" already establishing schools for Indian children.[12] The government distributed this money almost exclusively to Congregationalist and Baptist missionary societies.[13]

Congregational ministers and laymen responded to this federal act by sending missionaries to Maine from Massachusetts and New Hampshire. They began forming various missionary societies in Maine. David Thurston and other Congregationalists associated with the Bangor Theological Seminary formed the Maine Congregational Charitable Society on January 23, 1821.[14] Protestant missionary zeal would soon turn toward Maine's Native people, who had no resident priest at the time.

When the Penobscots' resident priest Romagne left for France in 1818, no priest immediately took his place. It was not long before the Penobscot Indians gained the attention of the Maine Missionary Society. An article titled "Indians in Maine" in the *Christian Mirror* reported:

The influence of their catholic [sic] priests has been universally admitted to be one of the greatest obstacles in the way of their improvement. Since, however their former priest returned to France, this influence has been rapidly diminishing. Well informed people living in the vicinity of the Penobscot Tribe, do not hesitate to assert that a very considerable change has taken place in their feelings within two years past.

The author noted the decaying of their grave crosses, the lack of church attendance, and broken windows in the church and the priest's house as signals of this change of feelings. "Why then should not some systematic and vigorous exertions be made to raise the remnants of these once numerous tribes to the rank of Christians and men?" the *Mirror* article asked. The author then called for schools and mission families to go to the tribe.[15]

Much of the nation's missionary zeal of the time grew out of the "Society for the Propagation of the Gospel" in Boston. One member of the society, the Congregational minister Elijah Parish, gave a sermon examining the question of how best to preach the goodness of God to the Indians, "who suffer from diseases, pestilence, conquering and famine," as well as, apparently, Catholicism. He concluded that the Indians would take hold of the doctrine of Resurrection with enthusiasm.[16] Similarly, Benjamin B. Wisner delivered a sermon on the subject of proselytizing the Indians in which he examined the question "Shall we make it our primary object to civilize or to Christianize them?" Wisner argued that the gospel does not call for civilizing but only for the preaching of the gospel. Wisner entreated that his followers "employ such missionaries . . . as have learned by experience . . . and will . . . endeavor [to bring to the Indians] . . . simple testimony of the Lord Jesus as the propitiation of our sins. If we persevere in this course we will contribute to both salvation and the civilization of men."[17]

In the spirit of reform that was the spirit of the times, the Congregationalists of Bangor formed "the Society for the benefit of the Penobscot Indians." Accordingly, in March 1823 the society conducted a school at Old Town, taught by Josiah Brewer, a graduate of Yale (1821). After completing his education, he served as preceptor of the Bangor Young Ladies' Academy in 1822, teaching about thirty children.[18] Local historian John Edwards Godfrey made a visit to the Indian school and years later gave the following account:

I once visited his school and wondered how he [the teacher] could accomplish anything. The children had never been subject to control, and he could get their attention only by persuasion for a few minutes at a time. Almost any trifling occurrence would draw them from their places. However, some learned to read and write. One of his Indian pupils, at least, still lives, Joseph Polis, who is a householder and a famous manufacturer and dealer of Indian wares upon the Island.[19]

The same Bangor men who were in charge of the Indian school found themselves in financial straits at that time. Congregationalists appointed Jacob McGaw, Daniel Pike, and Thomas Hill in December 1825 to superintend the erection of the Bangor Theological Seminary. The trustees had entered into an agreement with Maine's mapmaker, Moses Greenleaf, to sell maps as a way to raise money for the seminary in 1821, but it was not enough.[20] They hit upon a scheme to combine their need for a building with the need of the Penobscots for "improvement." They approached the legislature for support. On January 20, 1826, the governor approved an act titled "an Act to incorporate a Society for the benefit of the Penobscot Indians":

Resolved, That the Agents for the Penobscot Indians be, and they hereby are authorized, empowered and instructed, to lease for and during the term of ten years, to the Society, for the benefit of the Penobscot Indians, said society first obtaining the consent of said Indians, such tract of land, as may be considered necessary or convenient, for carrying into effect the benevolent designs of said society, for improving the condition of said Indians: Provided however, That such tract, shall not contain more than one hundred acres, and that such land shall be used by said society, for the sole purpose of prosecuting their plans of improvement among said Indians.[21]

It is unclear from historical documents whether this group ever consulted the Penobscots, who apparently rejected the idea of leasing their land to the Congregationalists and contacted their own bishop. Catholic priests Byren and Barber had been making annual visits from 1822 to 1826. Byren put a stop to the seminary-sponsored school in July 1825.[22] At this point also, Bishop Fenwick stepped in and tried to obtain funds from the state to build a school and repair the churches. The legislature appropriated funds to build a storehouse and school.[23] So Virgil Barber conducted a school at Indian Island for about six months of the year. Apparently, the Penobscots, with the aid of their priests, prevented the Protestants from obtaining the land they sought. No further action regarding land sales between the Penobscots and the "Society for the benefit of the Penobscot Indians" appears in the legislative records.

The Bible and the Primer

In Maine, the Congregational Church was the official state church and therefore held much political power. Legislators found it difficult to appropriate funds for the Penobscots to receive an education from Catholics. Therefore, the state supported education for the Penobscots only irregularly. The priests taught at Old Town from 1838 to 1840 for six months of each year. There were about twenty-five students in attendance, some more than twenty years old. Strong anti-Catholic sentiments in the state from time to time led legislators to withdraw their support for the church and school at Old Town. Funds appropriated by the legislature between 1840 and 1850 supported only agricultural pursuits.[24]

Finally, in 1850, the legislature passed a resolve appropriating $125 for the purpose of educating the youth of the Penobscot tribe of Indians. The agent provided $25 for books. The Indian agent, rather than the priest, directed this effort.[25] Although boys and girls had previously attended school together, the agent organized separate schools for each sex. A male teacher taught about twenty-five boys for six weeks in 1850, while fifteen to twenty girls attended school for nine weeks in 1851. Although the Penobscots wished to continue the school, in 1852 the leg-

FIG. 7. Indian Island Church and Convent. *Courtesy Brian Robinson, University of Maine.*

islature withdrew financial support for the school, and classes were terminated. The state's agents played a role in the loss of support for education. In 1852, Indian agent Arvida Hayford reported his belief that the Indians must be encouraged and stimulated to the pursuit of agriculture in advance of any successful attempt at educating and "civilizing" them. Resolves for the several years following indicate educational appropriations of $200 in 1853, $300 in 1854, nothing in 1855 and 1856, and $350 in 1857. At this time, it seems that Penobscots desired an education but were thwarted by the state's insistence on controlling their affairs with an emphasis on teaching agriculture. The nearby Old Town school committee oversaw the school, rather than members of the Indian Island community. The committee administered the money that the legislature appropriated in 1857 and reported to the secretary of state that they kept schools at both Old Town and Mattanawcook Island: The teachers found it difficult to teach students who spoke no English, and were not accustomed to sitting for long periods of time at desks. Their priest encouraged them to attend school, however. The schools took place for 17 weeks under a male teacher and 20 weeks by a female teacher. There were 45 scholars, 3 reading in the Progressive fifth reader, 2 in the fourth, 6 in the third, 10 in the second, 12 in the first and 12 in the primer. Seven had advanced in Greenfief's Common School Arithmetic to and beyond Reduction; 21 were studying fundamental rules; 4 were studying geography from books. All of the students received oral instruction from outline maps. The students ranged in age from six to thirty-five.

A number of the scholars resided on other islands but came to Old Town for the express purpose of attending school. Evening schools were held for the benefit of older Indians who were unable to attend during the day. The usual number in attendance in the evening was from twenty-five to thirty. The Old Town school term took place during the summer. At least on one occasion an outbreak of smallpox interrupted the school. The Penobscots feared a more severe outbreak among themselves than among their neighbors, and thus they all fled away from the Island.[26]

The committee reports the difficulty teachers had in teaching students who spoke no English, yet the curriculum included reading, arithmetic, and geography, all taught in English. No efforts were made to provide bilingual teachers, so clearly students must have found it difficult to learn from teachers who spoke no Penobscot. Still, Penobscots wanted an education. It is clear from such reports that Penobscot adults attended school to learn to read and write in English and wanted their children to attend school. In addition, the 1857 report indicates that people deliberately moved to Indian Island from some of the other, smaller villages like Olamon and Mattanawcook expressly to attend school. Finally, the mention of an outbreak of smallpox and the necessity that Penobscots felt to flee the epidemic reflects the inadequacy of health care, since smallpox vaccines were available at this time.

The number of inhabitants in the Penobscots' northernmost village, Mattanawcook Island, grew to such an extent as to warrant the establishment of a second school. This could be done only at those times when most of the people were home and the teacher could travel without too much difficulty. Apparently, some adults had traveled to Old Town in previous years in order to attend school. Some of the older scholars had previously learned reading and math at Old Town. The agent considered establishing a school at the middle village on Olamon Island, but the legislature did not appropriate enough funds to support a third school at this time.

The school committee reported that the Penobscot students achieved the same level of success in their studies as children in other schools. They also reported good attendance, even among older students who had never attended before. They attributed this success in large part to the advice of the Penobscots' missionary priest, Eugene Vetromile, who encouraged them to attend school and learn to read and write.[27] The committee reported:

In order to form a just estimate of the difficulties under which these schools labor, and the advancement made, it is necessary to keep in mind that the school is composed of those, who, outside the schoolhouse, talk in their own, a different language from that there taught—that most of the smaller scholars at the commencement of their attending school do not understand one word of English—that they are of a roving disposition, and their frequent hunts, fishings and tours in basket-selling, cause great interruption in their attendance at school. Yet, notwithstanding all these difficulties, some have learned to read with ease and fluency; about one to every six in the tribe can read. A few take weekly newspapers. The first principles of geography and arithmetic they learn readily. A few have studied English grammar.[28]

The report indicates a rapid acquisition of literacy by midcentury. Penobscot chiefs and councillors read newspapers and kept informed about important news about, for example, Indian wars in the West, and local news about the lumber industry and legislative acts that might effect their lives. Educational efforts broadened as the legislature appropriated funds for schools at Old Town and Lincoln in 1858–1859. The legislature also passed the following resolution relating to the Olamon community near the town of Greenbush:

Resolved, that there shall be paid to the superintending school committee of the town of Greenbush the sum of two dollars for each and every Indian child that shall attend the schools in said town for a term not less than two months in each year, and that said superintending school committee shall return the number of such scholars so attending for said term of two months to the secretary of state; and the governor is hereby authorized to draw his warrant for such amount on satisfactory evidence being adduced to governor and council.[29]

Prior to the Civil War, the education of Penobscot children received more attention and larger appropriations from the state than would be the case later. In 1860, Maine's legislature authorized the governor and council to pay the following sums for the education of Penobscots: "Two hundred and fifty dollars to be expended by the superintending school committee of the town of Old Town, and one hundred dollars to be expended by the superintending school committee of Lincoln for the purpose of maintaining among the Penobscot Indians, a school or schools for their education." The legislature required the committee to report "All items of expenditure and such other facts as they may deem for the interest of education among the Indians, or in such manner as the governor and council may direct." In addition, the legislature appointed a committee to study Indian affairs. James Purinton, Indian agent, reported that a female instructor taught at the school at Old Town from May 14 to October 12; the school was interrupted for two weeks by a case of varioloid (smallpox).

Fifty-four Penobscots attended the school, but not all attended at all times. As for the school's success, the agent reported, "On the whole I have no hesitation in saying that the money has been judiciously expended, and the result of the school fully answers all reasonable expectations, and justifies legislative appropriations; let the system adopted be continued, and it will be a powerful means of improving the language, elevating the character and improving the condition of this people."[30]

In 1861, agent Purinton reported in more detail on the progress of the schools. "From the best information I can obtain by observation and inquiry, there are now in the tribe more than one hundred who can read understandingly—for instance they obtain and read the newspapers which contain the current news of the day, in which they take a deep interest. About forty can write legibly, and some of them write and compose good letters, and can draw in respectable form, common business agreements."[31] Literacy in English strengthened Penobscots' ability to negotiate with the state. As a result, they became politically more independent from the priest and the Indian agent. They also moved into better positions in the marketplace and advocated for better education for their children. But in spite of their success, the state continued its paternalistic policies.

The superintending school committees of Old Town and Lincoln, who reported to the secretary of state, directed the schools. In 1861, the teacher conducted the Indian Island school for seventeen weeks during the summer and fall; there were eighteen scholars in Lincoln who studied from May to September 14.[32]

The state reluctantly provided meager funds for Indian education by passing an act of the legislature in March 1862 authorizing the agent of the Penobscot tribe to "lease the public farm on Orson Island and to appropriate the accruing rents to the use of the schools of said tribe."[33] The appropriations for Old Town and Mattanawcook remained very low from 1862 to 1864.

In 1864, agent George F. Dillingham called to the attention of the legislature the need for a new school building. "The building used for a school house on Old Town Island was built by the State many years ago for a storehouse, and has become so decayed as to be unsafe. The expense of suitably repairing this building would be about the same as of building a new one, better adapted for this purpose."[34] Again, in 1865, the agent reported the old storehouse unsuitable for a school. "In the Spring I was called upon to provide some suitable place in which to keep the school on Old Town Island." He reported that the building was unsafe and that parents objected to sending their children there. He had the building inspected by competent persons who concluded that there was great risk in using it. The only public building the agent could find was the public hall; the Indians did not like having the hall used for this purpose, but under the necessity of the case, finally consented. The hall had been built expressly for public meetings and meetings of the governor and council and thus was not suitable for a school. The agent implored, "A small appropriation would build them a house large enough for a school, and is very much needed. The desire to improve the advantages of school education appears to be increasing and more general among the Indians."[35]

With the war over, the state returned to its regular business. Finally, in 1865 the legislature appropriated four hundred dollars from the tribe's funds to build a school. The agent's report of 1866 described the new school. Located in a central and convenient place between the two villages on Indian Island, it was completed in time for summer school. The legislature appropriated enough money to pay for the building and furnishings of the schoolhouse. The agent reported, "Most of the adult members of the tribe manifest a commendable zeal and interest in the welfare of their schools."[36] The schools continued at the same level of support until the 1870s, when an economic depression hit Maine. However, after 1878 the legislature assigned jurisdiction of the school to the Catholic Sisters of Mercy, at the request of the bishop, and provided a more regular appropriation for the school's support. With these improvements, many Penobscots moved downriver to send their children to the school.

The legislature appropriated $450 for education in 1878. The Sisters of Mercy introduced singing and gymnastics to the children's curriculum. According to the agent, "The religious hymns as sung by the scholars, present already a very creditable performance. The total and average number of scholars under her [the sister's] careful and judicious exertions has been increased, and in the opinion at least of the older members of the tribe, more progress has been made by the school during the short time it has been under her charge, than for any previous year since its establishment."[37]

The nuns held adult education courses in the evenings for about twenty-five young men engaged in daytime occupations. They held another class for young women both married and single, to learn "sewing and other domestic duties." This level of attendance attests to the value the people of Indian Island placed upon gaining an education.

The following year, Indian Island received the same allotment for education, while the smaller schools at Olamon and Mattanawcook received a smaller sum. The legislature also provided thirty dollars for the purchase of a stove and repairs to the schoolhouse at Mattanawcook Island. At this time, the Indian agent and the resident priest at Old Town shared responsibilities for expenditures of money. The school committee at Old Town was no longer involved. Sister M. F. Borgia directed the school at Indian Island for thirty-five weeks. The agent reported, "The Sisters of Mercy have won the confidence and love of parents and children, and the result is, more desire to attend than the house will hold." The results of Penobscot efforts to obtain an education bore fruit when, for the first time, the agent's report included a written account by a member of the

Penobscot tribe, Joseph Nicolar, the agricultural superintendent, concerning agricultural activities of the community.[38] Speaking, reading, and writing skills in English provided Penobscots with some advancement in their ability to control their own affairs.

Legislators increased appropriations to the schools in 1880. In addition, the agent supervised the building of a new schoolhouse for the Old Town students. Although the legislature did not appropriate sufficient funds for a large enough schoolhouse, the agent sold the old school and added the funds from the sale to the appropriation.[39]

Indian agent Charles Bailey reported in 1881 that classes were taught at all three of the established schools. The Sisters of Mercy had charge of the Old Town school, "and the success of these untiring workers must be of great encouragement to them in their labor, so forbidding in many of its aspects."[40] Again, in the following year, the agent reported that the moral and educational effects of the teachers' work became more apparent each year, especially among the younger members of the tribe. "The prospect that this institution is permanently located in the tribe affords a hopeful and encouraging view of their future."[41] In addition to their secular teaching duties, the sisters also gave religious instruction and daily chapel services. Pastor F. X. Trudel of Old Town provided spiritual services to the tribe, as no priest resided on the island at that time.

Without clear reason, the legislature reduced appropriations for education in 1884, so that only a few weeks of school took place at Olamon Island in the springtime. In two years, so few scholars attended school at Olamon that parents sent their children by canoe to public school across the river at Greenbush. By 1888, a new Indian agent, John H. Stowe, had taken office and reported that three of the Sisters of Mercy had a permanent home on Indian Island. One of these, Sister Christina, took charge of the school. Stowe reported that both students and teacher seemed to enjoy their time together and that older members of the tribe frequently admonished younger members to stay in school and study:

> Indeed, so well are they succeeding in their schoolwork here that, as I learn, every year some of the older and brighter scholars outstrip the limited course of study and leave the school, for the sole reason that the teacher's time does not suffice to take up new and higher branches.

Stowe suggested that the school sorely needed an assistant teacher and requested that the legislature consider a larger appropriation for this purpose.[42]

The following year the agent reported that since nearly nine-tenths of the Penobscots had their homes on Indian Island, the school there was the largest and "most prosperous." Fifty-seven children were of school age (six to eighteen) and, of those, forty-five were registered. The principal, Sister Christina, reported improved attendance and punctuality, with an average daily attendance of forty. Teachers obtained new maps, charts, and blackboards that greatly facilitated their work. Fewer than ten students enrolled in the Mattanawcook school, so the school committee of Lincoln decided to open public schools for the first time to the Indian students located there. An appropriation for Indian education paid their tuition.[43]

In 1890, Sister Christina reported that parents' interest in the school was constantly increasing. As a result, punctuality and regularity in attendance improved. She reported rapid progress and intelligence in her students. One of the boys entered the Hampton Institute in Virginia in September. She reported that the boys had an aptitude for bookkeeping and added it to the curriculum. I find it odd that she did not mention teaching the girls bookkeeping even though most women engaged in basket and craft sales throughout the summer months, supplying a major portion of family income.

Of course, it was in her interest to promote the school by pointing to her progress; however, she hinted that the school's success might be limited: "The most serious obstacle to success" she declared, was "the difficulty of retaining scholars who have arrived at the age of fifteen or sixteen." The boys preferred to work for wages or go hunting rather than attend school. The girls were needed at home to help with child care and basket making. The survival of the family often depended on the work of these older children. Sister Christina suggested a winter school for the older class to combat the problem.[44]

Teachers presided over two terms at the Olamon school. Of the students at Mattanawcook who attended Lincoln schools, the supervisor of Lincoln reported, "They go to school every day that school keeps, don't miss a day and are doing very well indeed."[45]

The inadequacy of the school buildings continued to create problems. The following year the legislature appropriated two hundred dollars to repair the Old Town school. Agent John Stowe reported that once again the schoolhouse was too small, too cold, and poorly ventilated, and was thus inadequate to meet the needs of the children. In addition, the community needed to move the school to elevated ground to combat flooding. Stowe suggested a site along the common, next to the convent. He proposed a playground and modest park in addition to a school building there. He also requested one thousand dollars to build the school and suggested using funds already appropriated for repairs, proceeds from the sale of the old schoolhouse, and other means, in addition to an appropriation from the legislature to conclude this project.[46]

After fifteen years of teaching at Indian Island, the Sisters of Mercy lent their voices to the agent's request for an improved facility. The new agent in 1892 repeated the previous agent's request for funds for a new school building, reporting that the older students dropped out partly because of the crowded, inconvenient, and sometimes cold quarters. The agent requested that appropriations be made in 1893 to fix the problem. Meanwhile, in the past two years most of the families from Mattanawcook had moved to Old Town Island. The agent therefore suggested a reduction in funds to Mattanawcook, matched with an increase to Old Town.[47] The legislature delayed granting his request for one year, but in 1894 they provided funds, and the agent supervised the building of a new school, twenty-eight feet by forty-one feet, with separate entrances for boys and girls. New single seats and slate blackboards were installed. A combination of wood and coal heated the school. Showing their support for education, members of the Indian community raised four hundred dollars to match the state's appropriation from their trust funds for the school building. The Penobscots sold baskets initially to raise the money to repair the church but instead used the funds for the school.[48] The legislature fell short of even minimal fulfillment of the state's treaty obligations, stingily using the Penobscots' own money rather than state funds for the children's education.

Meanwhile, teachers conducted school at Olamon for two terms of seven weeks each for a number of years. This was clearly not an adequate term to allow for reasonable progress of the young scholars who attended. Therefore, the agent requested an increase in appropriation to allow the teacher to conduct school for a single term of twenty-four weeks a year. At the same time, Mattanawcook no longer required funds, since there were no more students of school age. The last student to attend school there was Francis Stanislaus, who now, at the age of twenty, was attending a business college in Poughkeepsie, New York. The agent granted the entire appropriation for Mattanawcook to Stanislaus to defray his college costs, although this amounted to only one-third of the sum needed. His parents raised the rest of his tuition.[49]

The sisters in charge reported good attendance, averaging forty-eight of a possible fifty-two students. The pupils ranged in age from five to sixteen. Older boys preferred "to rove through the woods with their guns," while older girls had to stay at home to help their parents with basket making, as sales from their craft provided a substantial portion of the family's income. Teachers reported excellent conduct and effort on the part of students. The library purchased a few new textbooks and some reference books. Also, at the prompting of the local American Legion, teachers purchased an American flag for the classroom.[50]

At least one outsider visited and commented upon the success of the schools at the end of the century. Anthropologist Montague Chamberlain visited the Indian Island school in 1898 and wrote a report of his impressions of the progress of that institution. He found that the school suffered significantly from a lack of "proper and sufficient books." He reported that the children were bright and responsive and their conduct was above reproach. He noted that the many students who went on to the public high school in Old Town ranked among the best students there. The sisters taught the children to play the piano, and some of the larger homes sported pianos. One little girl entertained Chamberlain with a song that she sang "in a sweet sympathetic voice and with tasteful expression,"[51] while accompanying herself on the piano. Chamberlain made a significant personal donation of books to the school.

As the century came to a close, the legislature once again appropriated funds to build a school on Olamon Island, because the community there had grown. At Olamon, twelve students attended the school, taught by Mrs. M. V. Harris for seven weeks in the summer and eight weeks in the fall. The new schoolhouse measured sixteen feet by twenty-five feet with a porch, woodshed, and outhouse.[52]

Meanwhile, at the urging of Montague Chamberlain, some parents sent their older students to the federal government's Indian School at Carlisle, Pennsylvania. Four boys and three girls secured admission with the aid of Chamberlain, who had become very interested in Indian affairs. The government supplied round-trip transportation, board, tuition, and clothes. Students hoped to learn trades, but the school also attempted to assimilate them into American culture by removing them from their own tribal culture. The difficult transition caused some pupils to become very homesick soon after arriving there.

Of the seven Penobscot children who attended the school at Carlisle, three persevered. At this time, the agent also reported that one boy was in his sophomore year at Dartmouth College and another was taking a year at preparatory school. In 1902, the three Penobscot students at Carlisle had completed three years of their course. Three more Penobscot boys traveled to Carlisle to join them. Hamilton (the Indian agent does not tell us his first name), the young man attending Dartmouth, completed two years there and then went to Boston to study medicine. The agent reported that while modern Penobscot healers still practiced their ancient art using natural herbs and roots, Hamilton represented the first Penobscot to study the European style of medicine.[53]

In 1906, only three scholars remained at Olamon; they soon joined the scholars at the Indian Island school. The two teachers at Old Town conducted school for thirty-three weeks, for a salary of less than $7 per week.

The agent requested that a larger appropriation be made to pay them $550 for the term. He noted that special students who attended school in Old Town paid $100 each to do so. He therefore felt that it was reasonable to increase the salaries of the teachers at the Indian Island school.[54]

Apparently, some of the parents' interest in sending children to school waned at this time, because the agent reported that some parents were not cooperating in sending their children to school or made excuses for them when they did not attend. There were fifty-eight registered, with an average attendance of forty. The tribe appointed a member of their community, John Ranco, to serve as truant officer. He apparently performed his job well; attendance improved in 1909, when the total number of students was sixty, with an average attendance of forty-five.[55]

For the most part, Penobscots embraced the idea of sending their children to school. They recognized the importance of reading and speaking English as a means of providing leadership to their people in negotiating with the Maine government; in gaining access to newspaper reports about issues that concerned their community; and in providing other means for subsistence besides hunting. A number of Penobscot men and women could read by the mid–nineteenth century, and many of them subscribed to newspapers in order to be informed of issues pertaining to themselves and to other Native American people. Literate Penobscots wrote letters to the legislature, and some began writing in their own language. Speaking English gave them the advantage of being able to speak for themselves; no longer did they need to rely on agents or priests to speak on their behalf. While state leaders believed that learning to speak English would aid Penobscots' ability to join mainstream American culture, they were only partly correct. Penobscots continued to be marginalized after they began to speak English, because they did not have the political and economic power they needed to be recognized and taken seriously by the state. The state continued to control their funds, keeping them in a position of economic dependence. While the tribe sent representatives to the legislature, they were unable to vote. Therefore many of their needs went unmet. Gaining an education eventually would provide them with additional tools to gain power over their own lives, but it would take time. Meanwhile, the state continued to promote agrarian ideals that failed to meet the expected goals.

The Hoe and Plow

The state's efforts to promote European-style agriculture met with mixed results. Maine, following the prevailing republican ideals of instituting an agricultural democracy, encouraged the Penobscots to settle in one location and to practice agriculture and relinquish hunting and fur trading. Indian agents played a pivotal role in controlling tribal funds and directing those funds into agricultural efforts. Indian agents set about ordering goods for the Penobscots. In an attempt to encourage agriculture, they ordered seed and directed the plowing of land for gardens. They also purchased firewood for families, sold the Penobscot hunters' furs to local merchants, and traveled to Pea Cove (just above Orson Island) and Sunkhaze to appraise the worth of logs taken from Indian lands. For example, Samuel Call reported going to Pea Cove in May 1826. He made the following notations in his annual report to the governor and council:

> May 5 pd. G. Reed 1.25 expense.
> May 13 — 3 days at Pea Cove, Old Town and Sunkhaze
> May 17 — 2 days at Pea Cove (White's Logs),
> May 20 — 1 day at Pea Cove (Webster's Logs),
> May 27 — 2 days at Bangor selling furs.[56]

He also collected payment from those who were cutting timber on Penobscot lands. For example,

> Cash received of William Neil for Board Logs $200
> Pillsbury and White 460
> JI&C Crown 149.97
> Webster and Rogers 350
> Jones and Rogers 200
> Herman and Fisher 47[57]

Monies collected by the agent for logs and shore leases went into the state's general fund; then, Penobscots had to seek appropriations from the legislature to obtain funds from the state for their needs. These appropriations were meted out grudgingly by a legislature that insisted upon putting those funds into agricultural efforts. Meanwhile, agriculture necessarily held a marginal existence in Maine because of the weather. Short, cold summers meant unreliable harvests for corn, wheat, and other grains. Natives and non-Natives alike could not place their trust in agriculture for all their subsistence, so most settlers supplemented agriculture with lumbering, while most Natives relied upon hunting and the fur trade. Nevertheless, the concept of the yeoman farmer strongly shaped Indian policy among eastern reformers. These concepts were doomed to failure because the dominant culture was unable or unwilling to consider the wisdom of the lifestyle of the Native people and insisted upon patronizing them by controlling their assets through a system of agents.

While Americans began clearing the land of its Native people in the East, they also speculated on western lands. Such speculation led to financial panics, and many eastern farmers, discouraged by high prices and low returns, moved west.

Maine followed a similar pattern. There, frost throughout twelve months of the year in 1816 discouraged farmers; many quit or went west. Those who remained specialized in dairy, apples, and vegetables rather than growing grains. While the scarcity of money resulting from the recent war with Great Britain prevented capitalists from investing in new industry, lumbering continued in Maine, with about one-third of the trees cleared from the state's forests during the early part of the nineteenth century.[58] Penobscots, too, took part in the deforestation, working in the lumbering industry while their families tended gardens.

By 1820, several Penobscot families grew crops on their lands. The agent hired a farmer who plowed and planted for the Penobscots. To what extent men worked the land is unknown. Since most men engaged in hunting, guiding, and lumbering, I suspect that women and children tended most of the gardens. They could easily do this until they started traveling to tourist areas to sell baskets after the Civil War. Until then, however, the agent reported the successful harvest of substantial crops. For example, in 1820, the Mattanawcook community raised sixty bushels of corn, two hundred bushels of potatoes, and other crops.[59]

Although there were pressures from outside the community to settle and raise crops, at least some members of the tribe may have wished to learn modern agricultural methods. In 1835, the leaders of the tribe wrote to the legislature requesting that the agent spend the money paid to the tribe to hire someone to teach agriculture and to assist them in buying stock and seed. However, this may have been in response to pressure from the agent, as the letter sounds as if he conceived and wrote it:

To the Senate and House of Representatives in Legislature assembled:
Your petitioners Indians of the Penobscot Tribe humbly pray that the agent of said Tribe be instructed to expend all money hereafter to be paid said Tribe in the manner following—to employ a sufficient number of men acquainted with farming to instruct said Indians in farming and cultivating their land—to purchase stock to be divided equally between said Indians, without power to said Indians to dispose thereof without consent of said agent. Said stock to be divided between the families equally in proportion to the number in each family—to direct the land owned by said Tribe and not now actually occupied by any Indian, equally between the families of said Tribe and give such quantity to each as said agent may think proper, reserving a sufficient quantity for the families which may hereafter arrive—said division to be made in such manner as not to disturb the possession of any Indian, as aforesaid, and to grant to said Indian such title as to enable him to hold the same, when this his farm, without power to sell or forfeit the same—unless by consent of said agent.[60]

The legislature ordered the agent to divide the land, as the letter requested. He did so, assigning a plot for cultivation to each family. The legislature ordered that any Indian who later surrendered his possession of this plot would be compensated for improvements he had made upon the land.[61] Legally, the land had to go back to the tribe; no lands could be sold outside the reservation. Again, in 1836, the tribe petitioned the legislature, asking that the agent be allowed to use their funds to teach them agriculture.[62] The state responded by further promoted farming through the institution of a system of paying bounties for the crops the Natives raised.

In spite of all of the seemingly well-intentioned efforts of the agent hired to teach the Penobscots farming, the Penobscots found devotion to agriculture difficult. Beginning in 1838, the state encouraged the Penobscots (and Passamaquoddies) in their agricultural efforts by paying them bounties on wheat, potatoes, and other vegetables. The agent paid the bounty to the individual upon being presented proof of the amount raised. The paying of this bounty continued well into the twentieth century. Presumably the state then would sell or otherwise distribute the produce.[63]

The Penobscots grew mostly potatoes, although they received separate payments for hay cut from their lands. The annual number of bushels of potatoes grown varied to a considerable extent, as reflected in the agents' narratives. Agents often reported, for example, that agricultural efforts did or did not yield the expected crops in any particular year.

While the state's leaders expected agricultural practices to improve the situation of the tribes, agriculture actually had little effect on their lives. The resources of the Penobscot tribe in 1838 consisted of the Indian fund of $58,356.49 held in trust for them in the state treasury. The tribe received an annual payment of the interest from this fund. Even by midcentury, that interest consisted of a mere $1,500, a little over $3 per person. For comparison, a birch canoe was worth about $10 in 1820.[64] The legislature paid bounties on agricultural products and made special appropriations for particular tribal needs, still out of the tribe's own funds. The Penobscots also received some money from the sale of grass and shore privileges on their islands up and down the river.

The legislature allowed $300 to pay the superintendent of farming an annual salary. During the period between 1835 and 1862, a farmer kept the land under cultivation with the help of some of the Penobscots. In 1866, the legislature abolished the office of superintendent of farming, and the agent received an additional $150 above his regular salary to assist the Penobscots with agriculture.[65] This arrangement continued until 1869.

According to the agent, at that time the total Penobscot population included about 150 able-bodied men and their families. About 100 held cultivated land. In former years, the agent had reported that large numbers of the tribe scattered in the spring before planting, returning in the fall to draw their dividends. If this were the case, it would seem that they took very little part in the actual cultivation of the land. The agent continued to encourage everyone to stay at Old Town, but he had little success in the first half of the nineteenth century. Part of the state's strategy to persuade Penobscots to stay at home was the establishment of a public farm.[66]

In his report for 1823, agent Samuel Call wrote: "the Indians are aware that they can no longer depend on hunting for subsistence and are desirous to engage in agricultural employment. They make large demands for ploughing . . . some of them extend their ideas to the keeping of cattle."[67] The agent attended to the plowing, cultivating, soil improvements, and seed. During the years 1823 and 1824, Call reported plowing four acres on Tree [Birch] Island, and on Freeses Island for Sockalexis, Colonel Peol, John Orono, and Orono's mother. He plowed Joe Pineas's Island for Joe Pineas Francis, Peol Tomer, and Francesway. He also plowed two and one-half acres for Etienne and Sock Susep, and Costigan Island for Joe Sepsis Swasson, Lewis Swasson, and Captain Francis. This seems to indicate that a substantial number of individuals living on islands above Indian Island were also engaged in agriculture.[68]

In 1835 the state had a survey made of a suitable tract of land for a farm ostensibly to keep the old, infirm, and orphan Indians. Clearly, the legislators did not understand that such a farm was unnecessary; the Penobscots always took care of their elderly and infirm within the extended family. The state farm was never used for its intended purpose. The state chose a site on Orson Island and employed a superintendent of farming, who cleared the land of trees and tilled the soil. The superintendent supervised the building of a barn and house. Mark Trafton of Bangor laid out the farm and served as the state's agent to the Penobscots in 1832. Agent Joseph Kelsey of Guilford finished building the house in 1836.[69]

In that same year, the Penobscots, led by Peol Nichola, petitioned Maine's Senate and House. They stated that although they wished to pursue agriculture, they were too destitute to do so. They prayed for an appropriation to build a suitable house and outbuildings for each family. They also requested farming utensils, one cow and other stock, suitable clothes, and support during planting season. They also reported that some members wanted to follow some mechanical employment and requested assistance such as tools and instruction for this purpose.[70] The state never relinquished its control by providing those things to individuals, but rather supplied the agent and hired farmer with the implements and supplies.

When James Purinton undertook his duties as Indian agent in 1860, he found the public farm in a dilapidated state, with buildings needing repair. There was one yoke of oxen, some farming tools, and twenty-four bushels of potatoes of poor quality that he sold to buy better seed. He also found ten tons of hay and six bushels of buckwheat. Purinton supervised the tilling and sowing of eight acres to oats and grass. He employed a superintendent to work on the farm and also to act as teacher to the Penobscots on their several lots in the spring. Under his supervision, the Penobscots raised a crop of twelve tons of hay, 100 bushels of potatoes, 8 bushels of carrots, and 175 bushels of oats. The crops were worth in total about three hundred dollars.[71] Agricultural pursuits grew for a time insofar as the Penobscots cultivated a total of about a thousand acres by the following year.[72]

In the 1860s and 1870s, about a hundred Penobscot families farmed the land in the summer. At other seasons of the year, the men were more or less employed in hunting, in the logging camps, and in driving lumber in the spring. In this, they followed the same pattern as other Maine farmers. Agriculture was marginal in central Maine, and income supplements from hunting and lumber work were sorely needed. Of the rest of the Penobscot population, a portion engaged in making canoes, baskets, moccasins, and snowshoes. Women often took the leading role in basket making and other crafts. As the manufacture of these items became more lucrative, Penobscots turned their energies and attention toward the tourist trade and away from agriculture.

The larger economy changed rapidly in midcentury. Maine's population increased by one hundred thousand during the 1850s but lost two thousand by the 1870s. Farming and lumber continued to dominate Maine's economy, but generally business slowed and capital investment declined. Logging reduced Maine's forests to about 65 percent of the land by 1860. With the pines nearly gone, Bangor shipped mostly spruce. Bangor became a major lumber capital and the labor recruiter for woods workers, but the labor shortage due to the Civil War stopped the drives for a time. Steamboats traveled the Penobscot River from Old Town to Lincoln until 1867. As early as 1864, a railroad line was built from Bangor to St. John, New Brunswick.[73] New industries developed, including paper and tourism, and lumber gradually became less important. Penobscots took part in the economic changes, using traditional skills to their advantage in the lumber trade.

The Penobscots' agent reported that most of the men were engaged in driving logs in the spring and early summer, and would later visit the summer resorts to sell their crafts. Consequently, they had no time or energy left for farming. This problem was common to all Maine farmers even earlier, as the secretary of agriculture reported. In his 1856 report to the legislature, Secretary Goodall complained that farmers sometimes neglected their crops when they worked on the spring river drives. He argued that farmers should consider that returns from lumbering might be deceptively speedy, leading to wasted manure that could have nourished the soil, lost time, and exhaustion of men and cattle. He admitted that lumbering provided a market for agricultural produce and wage work for farmers. However, he believed that a farm yielded a surer and more reliable income than lumber.[74] As a whole, Penobscots and many other Maine people were never convinced that farming was the best or only livelihood they should pursue, and many moved west in hopes of finding better land for agriculture. The so-called civilization efforts that promoted agriculture failed in Maine because, in spite of solid efforts by Penobscots in growing crops, the Maine government did not supply consistent support. Penobscot men and women found ways to circumvent state control and followed their own course in raising money for community needs and family subsistence, employing their own traditional skills.

The failure of agriculture, the foundation of reform for Maine's Indians, was due to several factors. One was Maine's cultural insensitivity to the Penobscot mode of life. Another was the state's lukewarm support for the efforts made by some individuals to give agriculture a try. In addition, the Penobscots experienced some unique problems engaging in agriculture because of their geographical location. Natives complained that cattle owned by mainland farmers waded through the river and grazed on Penobscot crops; they were so discouraged that they had no desire to make any further effort at agriculture. Even when they appealed to the owners of the trespassing cattle, they received nothing but abuse in many instances—in consequence of which some abandoned their lands and many moved to other places.[75]

Another hindrance to successful farming was the lack of manure. Few Penobscots kept cattle. In 1879, the agent and the first Penobscot superintendent of farming, Joseph Nicolar, reported that the whole tribe kept only six oxen, six cows, five horses, and a few hogs. None of the tribe kept chickens or other fowl. After the lands were farmed for several decades, the soil was infertile, diminishing both the quality and the quantities of crops.[76]

One unexpected but related source of income improved the lives of Penobscots after the Civil War: the boom in lumber. In 1868, the agent advised the Penobscots to lease the public farm to a farmer and the shorelines of the islands to the lumber association that drove long logs down the Penobscot River. The agent advertised the leases in the *Bangor Whig and Courier* in 1868. These leases brought in $5,000 in revenue, more than the interest on their trust fund, which at this time provided $4,200 annually. The lessees paid the lease money into the state treasury. The agent requested that the legislature distribute this cash equally to each Native family in February and March, when other resources were scarce. The legislature granted this request.[77]

The funds from the shore leases supported the tribal schools, salaries for the tribal leaders, and per capita payments to individual members of the tribe. In 1874, the schools and salaries used $5,756; the per capita payments were $4,631, or somewhat less than $100 per person. This was a substantial increase of capital for the Penobscots, who found it very helpful as a resource for building their craft businesses and improving their homes. The agent reported that this payment had been very beneficial to the tribe, since businesses were depressed and there was small demand for labor in the lumbering operations. Also, crops were below average because the lack of manure had impoverished the soil. The sales of baskets and toy canoes met with more success. The shore rentals became so important that by 1876 the agent reported:

The dividend from shore rents coming to them in midwinter enables them to procure credit and means of subsistence all winter and is their principle means of subsistence not only at Old Town and vicinity but also along the whole river— Olamon, Mattanawcook and other permanent settlements. They save their productions of baskets and other wares that they make all winter to sell at seaside and other resorts where they make larger prices than if they had to sell in winter.[78]

However, this source of income soon diminished drastically. Depression in the lumber business in the 1870s caused the lessees to ask the agent to release them from paying shore rentals, so that by 1877 only a little more than $1,000 was paid to the tribe, not enough to pay for the schools and administrative salaries. This severe national economic depression forced wages down, and the agent reported that, as a result, more men turned to tilling the soil for subsistence. At Old Town alone, eighty-two members of the tribe received seed and assistance with plowing, as did eighteen farmers at Olamon and sixteen at Mattanawcook. More farms arose on the east side of Indian Island. Low prices for baskets, low wages, and decreased demand for labor continued. In 1879, the agent reported that basket making and farming were the principal means of livelihood for the Penobscots. Those young men who had been getting forty to a hundred days of labor river driving and whose services had been in great demand were offered few days of work and lower wages in the depressed economy.[79]

Penobscot crops, like those of every other farmer, were also subject to the whims of nature. In 1880, severe drought and a Colorado beetle infestation reduced yields.[80] Throughout the 1880s, the agent reported fair success at farming, but by the end of the decade nearly three-quarters of the entire tribe departed in July for the rapidly growing summer resorts to sell their manufactured goods. Potatoes and other root crops did fairly well in spite of the neglect. However, the summer trade also suffered from periodic economic depressions, and in some years individuals returned with a large surplus of baskets and little money to show for their work.[81]

Other forms of subsistence proved more lucrative at times. River driving for the lumber companies returned to paying good wages until 1894, when once again depression hit the industry. Fortunately, hunting and fishing as a middle-class sport had begun to grow in Maine by this time, and men found ample opportunity to earn wages as guides.[82] Farming was hardly mentioned in the agents' reports after 1883. Agricultural bounty payments dropped: by 1889, only two hundred dollars in bounties were being paid annually, and to only a few dedicated individuals who enjoyed growing crops. Family plots continued to be tended by those who were at home in the summer, but most families were engaged in the far more lucrative tourist business at the summer resorts. By the turn of the century, the agent reported that many Penobscots were employed in woolen and pulp mills, canoe factories, and construction.[83]

Appropriations for fertilizer and seed came from the interest on the Penobscots' trust fund, as did the bounty payments. The Indian agent handled all the Penobscots' money, so he was the person who paid for agricultural supplies. The crops that were grown consisted of potatoes, carrots, and turnips, and yellow-eye beans that were dried for baked beans. A few people kept pigs, and some kept chickens.

Federal and state Indian policies reflected nineteenth-century thinking that agriculture was the cornerstone of civilization. However, the Penobscots' efforts at farming continued to be frustrated by a lack of state support, too little fertilizer, seasonal flooding, and destruction of their crops by cattle belonging to people on the mainland. More important, Penobscots continued to enjoy hunting for furs, developing their basket-, canoe-, and paddle-making crafts, using boating skills in the lumber and tourist industries, and guiding sportsmen in the woods. A few individuals found some success at farming, but most Penobscots preferred to use other skills to carve a niche in the larger economy.

Penobscot families eventually settled primarily in one location. They were not settled in one community during the first part of the nineteenth century; they continued to resist state control and efforts to force them to accept state-mandated changes. By the end of the nineteenth century, agriculture remained a part-time pursuit, and hunting remained the subsistence activity of choice for Penobscots. They resisted assimilation by continuing to speak their native tongue to their children, even when their children attended school and began to learn to read, write, and speak in English. They also retained their right to worship as Catholics in spite of pressure to adopt Protestant beliefs. If we measure the efforts by the state to assimilate Penobscots by their success at integrating them into the larger culture of Maine, then those efforts utterly failed. However, Penobscots did make significant changes in their lives throughout the nineteenth century. They indicated some willingness to accommodate the state's leaders by giving agriculture a try, although with minimal success. By marketing baskets and other items to tourists at various tourist spots, they resisted the state's efforts to keep them in one place year-round. Some of the men worked for wages in the woods and lumber mills. Penobscots were quite anxious to learn English, though not to abandon their own tongue. Speaking English and reading newspapers especially gave them an advantage they hadn't had in the past, whether it was negotiating with the state for funds for tribal needs, protesting the breaking of treaties, simply obtaining a job, or negotiating a fair price for a canoe or a basket. But the Penobscots remained a separate people living in a separate place. They did not permanently integrate or disappear into the melting pot.

Chapter 8

SPIRIT OF A NATION
Retaining Political Sovereignty

> Dancing was not only regarded as a thanksgiving ceremonial . . . but . . . a divine art. It was cherished . . . for keeping alive the spirit of the nation.[1]
>
> —LEWIS HENRY MORGAN

Lewis Henry Morgan's statement, which refers to the Iroquois, applies equally well to the Penobscots. No outsiders ever really understood the strength of connection that Penobscots felt to their homeland and their desire to govern their own affairs. Generally, state officials believed that Penobscots had already abandoned their aboriginal ways after the American Revolution and represented impoverished, uneducated people who could be molded into membership in the mainstream culture. They could not have been more wrong. Through political means, Penobscots continually resisted assimilation. They protested by sending tribal representatives to the legislature and developed factions that confounded state efforts to manipulate their affairs. By retaining a belief in their own sovereignty, they refused to accept the role of state "ward." In Ward Churchill's summary of the scholarship about the issue of Native sovereignty, he states, "While the sovereign rights of any nation can be violated . . . it is never extinguished by such actions." He also points out that even in the case where nations surrender (for example, Germany and Japan after World War II), their loss of sovereignty is considered temporary, to be restored at some future time.[2] In addition, numerous treaties between the Penobscots and the United States (sometimes with the state of Massachusetts or Maine) define the relationship between the Penobscot Nation and the colonialists.[3] Penobscot leaders kept the spirit of their nation alive by aggressively petitioning the legislature for assistance in fulfilling their treaty rights. Their interest in doing so brought them into conflict with the interests of the state.

Shortly after Maine became a state in 1820, the governor sought to control the Penobscots by appointing an agent to care for and manage all the tribal property, allegedly for the sole benefit of the tribe. As the Penobscots' "legal guardian," the legislature passed a resolution on June 20, 1820, authorizing Maine's governor and his council to appoint an agent to provide treaty goods owed to the Penobscots from the treasury of the state as fixed by the governor and council.[4] The state moved very quickly to take firm charge of the Indians' property under the guise of improving their situation. They guarded Penobscot property, resources, and funds, while allocating meager amounts of money and goods to their care. Initially, the governor appointed agents to collect Indian furs and incrementally dispense their treaty goods and money. The governor did not believe the Penobscots capable of handling their own funds.

Agents visited the tribe every six months and reported the tribe's condition. The state paid the agents out of the funds belonging to the tribe (from the sale of some of their lands). The state provided authority to the agent to lease Indian lands and to sell tribal resources. Without any recognition of tribal sovereignty, the agent also could overrule decisions made by the tribal governor and council.

Agents had a great deal of control over Penobscot financial resources. During the first part of the nineteenth century, the Penobscots had few other means of subsistence besides hunting. The agent returned to state coffers any money collected from the sale of hay or timber from Indian lands or used the money to fill the needs of the tribe for a teacher or priest when authorized by legislative appropriation. Occasionally, in addition to providing basic services such as treaty goods and a physician's care, the agent would purchase a little something extra. For example, Samuel Call reported purchasing red-top and vulture plumes for the Penobscots in 1827, and he paid for the Indians "to go and see an elephant."[5]

The Penobscots, though overwhelmed economically and outnumbered, did not accept such control of their lives without protest. They governed themselves with a hereditary chief or governor, a lieutenant governor, and a group of councillors made up of the leading men of the tribe. These tribal leaders sent letters to the governor of Maine requesting an agent who would represent the Penobscots' interests and not the interests of local lumber barons or merchants. In 1828, several councilors of the tribe wrote to Governor Lincoln asking that their agent, Samuel Call, be removed from office and someone else be appointed to replace him. They reported that Call had assembled a council of Penobscots to advise and direct him in the distribution of supplies but refused to listen to their advice; that he neglected to obtain and distribute their supplies; that his residence in Bangor was too far away to be convenient and often caused them to have to wait several days for needed supplies; and that he neglected their lands, allowed trespasses, and took no interest in their improvement in agriculture and education. They also complained that he had neglected to build their new church, pretended that there were no funds, and refused to give an account of the funds. They requested an agent who resided in Old Town.[6] However, this letter was followed by another, signed by the Penobscot governor and councillors, which contradicted the first and asked that agent Call be retained.

Neither Penobscot governor John Attean nor lieutenant governor John Neptune signed the first letter, indicating that another faction supported Call's removal. Some clarification of the events surrounding this protest can be found in a letter to Samuel Call from a local settler named Waldo Pierce. Pierce attested that the letter against Call "was made at the instigation of Peol Molly and one white man—Peol Molly supposing you was [sic] the means of his removal from the office of counselor. . . ." Pierce also wrote that the whole tribe, with the exception of Peol Molly, "expressed satisfaction of [Call's] management of their business."[7] The legislature continued to support Call and authorized him to cause a storehouse, schoolroom, and church to be paid for out of the proceeds of the sales of timber and leases of lands.[8]

The following June, the Indian Court, consisting of the tribal governor, councillors, captains, and most of the hunting men, met and passed several resolutions that were signed, witnessed, and then sent to Maine's governor and council.[9] These resolutions do not reveal submission to state patronage but rather reveal that the tribe recognized the necessity of having an agent for protection from local settlers who took their resources or perpetrated violence upon their persons:

> Resolved, That it is necessary to have an agent to take care of the property of the Tribe particularly the Timber and Grass, and to aid us in the protection of our persons; also for the purpose of building a Church and Store agreeable to a Law or Resolution of the last Legislature of the State of Maine—and whereas we have waited a long time for the appointment of one by the Governor of the State of Maine, during which time our property has been plundered and several of us violently beaten and abused therefore
>
> Resolved, That Samuel Call our former Agent be applied to and requested to act as our Agent and that the Governor of the State of Maine be petitioned to appoint the said Call Indian Agent.[10]

The opinions expressed by these contradictory letters represent longstanding disagreements that eventually culminated in the development of a two-party system for electing tribal leaders. In their struggle to find a way to defend themselves against state leadership, some members of the tribe accepted guidance and direction from outsiders, while others did not. In his thesis on seventeenth-century Abenaki-English relations, David Ghere named two of the factions in the tribe during that earlier time, "conciliatory and confrontational in their relationship to Massachusetts."[11] However, late-eighteenth- and nineteenth-century documents indicate that the factions could not be divided neatly into two sides and that the factions were no longer confrontational but resistant. Neither faction was entirely conciliatory—they never compromised with the state over rights to govern their own people and land ownership. Members of one faction and then another were inspired by their own beliefs but were often influenced by the priests, ministers, Indian agents, and local merchants who advised them. Historically, the factions were mutable—not always strictly falling into clearly defined family groups.[12] People changed sides on different issues.

The issue of the honesty and integrity of the Indian agent masked the true concerns of the factions involved. The basic argument centered upon the degree of sovereignty that the tribe held over its own lands and destiny. One side strongly encouraged education in trades, speaking English, and participating in American culture while remaining firmly loyal to Catholicism. Another resisted major changes, seeking public education and religious freedom but otherwise holding on to traditional ways. The two factions played an important role. Compromising between the two sides led the tribe to adapt to a changing world. Nineteenth-century Penobscot society incorporated some elements of American technology, politics, religious reformation, education, and language while retaining other Native elements, surviving as a unique Native American culture.

The Penobscots sought control over who would be their agent. When Maine appointed Colonel Joshua Chamberlain[13] as agent without consulting the Penobscot leadership, tribal leaders quickly responded in protest. Just a few months after Chamberlain's appointment, the tribe sent a letter to the governor and council, expressing dissatisfaction with his appointment without the knowledge or approval of the Penobscots. In addition, the tribe argued that Chamberlain was a perfect stranger to most of the tribe and had no acquaintance with their habits, manners, and customs. Furthermore, he resided thirteen miles away (in Brewer) from the Indians' village, and his visits were therefore expensive. The tribe expressed a desire to keep such expenses at a minimum, because they reduced tribal funds needed for their subsistence. They complained further that the agent did not keep satisfactory accounts and charged bills more than once; his conduct indicated a lack of judgment in the Penobscots' interests. In addition, his advanced age precluded his changing. They requested that Chamberlain be removed and be replaced with

Thomas Bartlett of Old Town. Penobscot governor Attean, Francis Lorun, and twenty-three leading men signed the letter.[14]

However, in just a month's time, another letter was sent, stating that "there has been art and deception used to make our minds disaffected against Colonel Chamberlain . . . and by their means they have wrongly obtained our names to a petition requesting his removal." This statement suggests that someone had persuaded the tribal leaders to protest Chamberlain's appointment. The letter also stated that the Penobscots were well satisfied with Chamberlain. Tribal governor John Attean and twelve leading men signed the letter; Peal Molly did not.[15] Who fomented the act of protest cannot be determined by any of the documents in the council reports. I suspect it may have been someone such as Thomas Bartlett, whose interests were at risk by the appointment. Or it may have been due to shifting factionalism within the tribe. The state dismissed Chamberlain in spite of the supporting letter and appointed Samuel Hussey as agent.

Then, in March 1830, Virgil Barber, the resident priest, composed a letter to the state governor and council requesting that Samuel Hussey be discharged from the duties of Indian agent because he lived far away. Undoubtedly, the state government officials wanted to exercise greater control over their agents by having them live close to the seat of government, but in doing so they necessarily neglected the needs and desires of the Penobscots. Barber listed justifications for removing Hussey from his post: he was advanced in age and infirm; his residence in Portland was too far away to know the needs of the tribe; the farmer he employed to help the tribe had been of little or no value, since his residence was at a great distance from them; the store Hussey had built for the tribe was constructed poorly with inferior materials; the articles he furnished to the tribe, especially powder, shot, chocolate, and blankets were of poor quality; the corn distribution for the past year was short fifty bushels; the distribution of goods was incorrect and unequal; and the sale of $1,700 in timber had produced a loss of 50 percent to the tribe because the contractors were not supervised. Furthermore, Hussey allowed the contractors the privilege of lumbering during the winter without consulting the tribal authority. Two thousand dollars' worth of timber was removed, over and above the five-hundred-dollar limit stipulated by law, and the agent's expenses were unjustly charged to the tribe, even including personal travel.[16] Both the appointment of Chamberlain and the actions of Hussey regarding tribal lumber were conducted without consulting Penobscot leaders. Tribal protests concerning these issues centered more on the paternalism of the state than on the specific character of the agents. Penobscot political resistance to these assaults took the form of written protests concerning the tribe's ability to control their own affairs.

The state council responded on March 6, 1830, after receiving replies and explanations from Mr. Hussey "in vindication of his doings as Agent of the said tribe." They did "not find any disqualification in the said Hussey for this duty." The council stated that they had solved the problem of having an agent at a remote location by placing a farmer to reside with the tribe. They also believed that the farmer had not been with the tribe long enough to prove himself and therefore should continue with them in conformity with the treaty. They stated that "the equitable settlement and satisfactory acceptance of the same by the parties concerned" canceled the complaint about the materials and workmanship of the buildings. The inferior articles supplied to the Indians were not the fault of Hussey but were incurred "by unseen casualty." The shortage of corn could not be accounted for, but the Indians usually received a surplus and that, the state thought, brought things into balance. The distribution of goods, they believed, was under the jurisdiction of tribal leaders. The losses from timber sales were of no fault of the agent but could be redressed through legal arbitration. Hussy's journey to Old Town that the Indians paid for was part of his duties as agent to the tribe. Finally, the state declared, "While the wishes of the Indians are generally to be consulted when practicable, yet the very fact that they are under the guardianship of the State, & the care of a public agent, presupposes them to be bound by & to the doings of the agent in some other things nevertheless."[17] In other words, the state overruled the tribe's objections.

Although the state discounted Penobscot concerns and justified its own position, the Penobscots took matters into their own hands and began selling their timber themselves. This caused great alarm among state officials. Ebenezer Pope wrote a letter "to esteemed friend Samuel F. Hussey" stating that "Peol Tomer and Sabattis are selling timber on Oald Laman [Olamon Island] 100,000 feet of hemlock and hardwood." Pope expressed his belief that "if the Indians have leave to cut in this manner they will soon destroy all of their timber on their island." But Tomer and Sabattis had a right to cut the timber—they had been granted permission to cut seventy to eighty dollars' worth of timber by the priest and the governor of the tribe.[18] The struggle over who owned and controlled tribal lands and resources continued unabated. State and timber interests prevailed over the protests of the tribal leadership.

The state Committee on Indian Affairs met to discuss and make recommendations regarding the Indians' petitions. In 1829, they ordered that Joshua Chamberlain pay back to the state the fifty dollars that Samuel Hussey had given him for the Indians and responded to Samuel Call regarding his charges for services. Hussey reported to the state council that local merchant Major Treat was selling the Indian privileges. The legislature ordered Hussey to turn over the Penobscots' funds to a new agent, Mark Trafton of Bangor. Although Trafton lived closer to the tribe than Hussey did, he was still not a man from Milford or Old Town, as the tribe had requested. They asked for "no owner of sawmills, no logging man, no trader... please take a smart, sharp-eyed man."[19] Apparently, the Penobscots felt that Mark Trafton fit the bill in all other regards, as there was no further protest.

The state continued its pressure on the tribe to release title to tribal lands. The state appointed John Deane of Ellsworth to negotiate with the Penobscots for the release of two townships at the mouth of the Mattawamkeag River[20] needed for the lumber industry.

While the first logging on the West Branch of the Penobscot River took place in 1828, most logging initially occurred farther south. In just a few years Maine was furnishing three-fourths of the pine lumber exported from the United States. The Penobscot River was the center of this trade. By 1836, Orono was the site of more than two hundred mills for wooden boards. The mills sawed more than 1.5 million feet of lumber daily.[21] Each landowner was responsible for cutting his own timber in the woods and marked his logs with a distinctive mark before the logs were sent downriver. All the logs flowed down the river together to the booms, which were sorting areas set off by logs chained together. There, river drivers sorted the logs, loaded them onto ships, or floated them to local mills.[22]

As a result of the large log drives, logs covered the shorelines of the islands in the river, making it impossible for Penobscots to launch a canoe. Since tribal members traveled exclusively by canoe and could not get their canoes off the islands and into the water, they protested to the Maine governor. Also, as logging continued and trees were removed in southern areas, the loggers gradually moved upriver into the West Branch of the Penobscot River. The Penobscots requested that they be allowed to keep their islands in the West Branch and reported that the rafts for log driving that were tied to their islands in the region of Old Town "plagued them very much indeed." They wished to collect rents from those using their shorelines for such purposes, and complained that the Great Boom[23] above Sunkhaze caused flooding of several islands. Finally, they asked that the state government bring to justice those who did them harm.[24]

However, business interests prevailed at Maine's legislature; the tribe had to continue to aggressively petition the governor and council with their concerns. In 1831, they protested the loss of Shad Island, an important fishing station, and the islands near Naskeag Point in Sedgwick, which had been reserved for their use under a Massachusetts treaty. Non-Indians now inhabited the islands and refused to allow the Indians

FIG. 8. Indian Landing and Indian Island in the log drive era. *Courtesy Maine Folklife Center, University of Maine, photograph no. 8704.*

to land their canoes. The Penobscots protested the removal of the timber and grass from their lands and asked for just one agent to keep careful accounts of timber and grass sales.

Between 1830 and 1835, lands transferred to the state from Penobscot holdings included Shad, Nicatow, Smith's, and Pine Islands, and four townships.[25] Although the state considered the Penobscots their wards, the government provided very little money to the tribe and every request for assistance had to be discussed, with funds appropriated by legislative act. Penobscots protested by letters, sending them via their representatives to the governor and council in Portland.[26]

During the 1830s, as the Cherokees suffered removal from their ancestral lands in Georgia, the Penobscots in Maine experienced a less drastic form of upheaval. But the Penobscots were in some ways at a greater disadvantage. They had neither the population nor the political allies of the Cherokees. They had fewer leaders who spoke and wrote fluent English in 1830, necessitating that they negotiate through interpreters. This dependence on others enhanced tribal dissent due to some factions' mistrust of other factional spokesmen chosen for various negotiations. The internal divisions of the tribe often were also at odds in their trust of either the agent or the priest. These factions confused state negotiators but allowed the tribe to rescind agreements made by one faction and not agreed to by the other.

Negotiations with the state culminated in an especially significant event in the 1830s that led to even more severe factionalism. The state surveyed the Penobscots' islands and assigned individual plots of land to individual families. First, a portion of land was reserved for the Catholic church on the point of Indian Island facing Old Town. Both the allotment of lands and the permanent location of a Catholic church site seem to have been supported by a group of Penobscots who were dissatisfied with hereditary tribal leadership.

These disaffected Penobscots, calling themselves the New Party, appointed their own governor, lieutenant governor, and representatives to the state legislature in 1835. Leaders of the New Party included the Sockalexis and Sockbeson families, Peal Molly, Lolar, Luey, Susups, and others. They were mostly Catholic Penobscots, some of whom had lived in Quebec for a time but had returned because they were closely related to other families at Indian Island. This group mostly represented immigrant refugee families from now extinct Abenaki villages of western Maine. They had no traditional territory or place on the Penobscot reservation and, although welcomed into the tribe, did not always agree with the entrenched leadership. In contrast, the Old Party, led by Attean and John Neptune, did not recognize the new leaders and objected to their petitions and representatives.[27]

In June of the same year, New Party members wrote a letter to Bishop Fenwick telling him that they had elected a new governor, Peal Nekalo Francis, and a lieutenant governor, Paul Joseph Orson. They told the bishop that "we conclude, that it will be, Proper and be good and it will be more Secure and it is more safe of our Souls, and, our religious duties, that we [are] going to leave our Church and lotts [sic] onto your hands, One on Orson Island the other one on Old Town Island." They further stated that Mr. Conway (the priest) knew how large the lot was. The letter was signed by fifty-three men but not by the Old Party leaders, Governor Attean or Lieutenant Governor John Neptune. By this means, the small piece of land on Indian Island near Old Town upon which the church still stands became property of the church.[28]

The following year, representatives of the New Party wrote to the Senate and House requesting that their lands be divided and assigned to them by the state in severalty, "so as to enable them to hold them and the same descend to their several heirs in the same manner as Citizens of the State of Maine." They did not request that sales of their lands be restricted or that permission to do so should be determined by the Indian agent.[29] This request makes sense in light of the fact that most New Party members had no traditional territory on the Penobscot.

These requests provided the state with a rationale for greater intrusion into the tribe's affairs. On March 2, 1838, the legislature authorized the payment of fifty thousand dollars into the tribal fund in exchange for the four townships of land north of the mouth of the Piscataquis River.[30] This parcel was the last large tract of land that was negotiated away from the Penobscots into the hands of the state. State authorities still wanted the islands in the river, and to some extent believed they already owned them. On January 30, 1839, the House of Representatives ordered that the Joint Standing Committee on Indian Affairs authorize and direct the Indian agent to allot to the several male Indians tribal lands for cultivation in proportion to their families. "Whenever any Indian surrenders his possession he shall receive compensation for such permanent improvements on the land."[31] Apparently both the Old and New Parties were in accord regarding this action, because in February 1839 the tribe sent a letter to the legislature signed by representatives of both parties. The letter requested that the lands previously surveyed as public lands (forty-four acres and 145 square rods on the point of Old Town Island) be surveyed into lots so that each Penobscot family might have a piece for its house and garden. The tribe further requested that any improvements made by certain Indians be appraised and reimbursed to them from the common fund.[32]

Why tribal members would support such a radical step can be understood only in light of the loss of so much of their territory. Non-Indians now controlled most of the tribe's hereditary hunting territories. Settlers moving into coastal regions and the areas along the Kennebec River, Moosehead Lake, and Penobscot Bay had displaced whole Native families. Many displaced Native families returning to Maine from Canada and represented by the New Party had no traditional location for their homes. Allotting areas of land or family plots would at least provide home sites for displaced families. Allotment, as an Indian policy in America, is best known from the 1887 act, sponsored by Senator Henry L. Dawes of Massachusetts, that divided tribal lands west of the Appalachian Mountains into family plots.[33] The act resulted in the greatest loss of lands from tribal holdings, because lands not allotted to heads of families were sold to whites, and Indian families could sell their lands to non-Indians. The Penobscot situation differed, because no family could sell its holding to anyone who was not a member of the tribe, a policy that continues to this day. The tribe's policy became law when the legislature responded to the tribe's request by passing another "Act for the better regulation of the Penobscot Indians." The legislature ordered the agent to survey and set off lots in the public area of Indian Island but further instructed him not to allow Indians to convey their lands to anyone who was not a member of the tribe.[34] This latter contingency undoubtedly saved the last of the tribe's holdings from being extinguished, unlike those lands of the western tribes that were allotted under the provision of the Dawes Act of 1887.

After this period of land negotiations and of adjustments to a series of Indian agents, factionalism among the Penobscots emerges as the major event reflected in the public documents. At least by 1836, there were two tribal governments struggling for power, each with its own governor, lieutenant governor, and councillors. The issues that divided the two groups were undoubtedly complex, but at least one issue concerned education, especially the manner in which Penobscots supported education. Another issue, related to the first, concerned religious affiliation, preference, and liberty.

During the 1840s, the two parties sent numerous letters and petitions to the legislature on various matters. Attean and his Old Party followers objected to elections, which superseded Attean's hereditary authority but also represented "white man's" ways, as opposed to traditional Penobscot habits. Both parties protested actions of the Indian agents. In 1839, the New Party wrote a letter to object to agent Henry Richardson, complaining that he had reduced the corn dividend.[35] In 1842, the Old Party wrote to ask that Richardson *not* be discharged, saying that such changes caused the tribe to be "liable to losses and mismanagement. New Agents not being acquainted with the Indians . . . cannot manage as well as one who is acquainted."[36]

The confusion over who represented the true leadership of the tribe continued to plague state officials. War Department official Hartly Crawford wrote to Maine's governor, John Fairfield, concerning the matter in 1843:

Sometime since two medals, such as are usually given to Indians as presents were handed to Joseph Polis, then on a visit to this city, for the purpose of being delivered to the first and second chiefs of the Penobscot Indians; it appears that there are two parties, each having appointed chiefs, claiming the right to these medals.[37]

Crawford asked Fairfield to receive the medals from Polis and deliver them to the persons entitled by virtue of their offices as chiefs. Nothing in the documents clarifies whether his wishes were ever carried out.

Disputes over fishing rights and shoreline leases added to the confusion. In 1843, the Old Party objected to agent Arvida Hayford's leasing fisheries without their consent and not looking after their shorelines, which were still so obstructed by logs that Natives could not land their canoes.[38] A group of New Party supporters, led by Solomon Swassin, also wrote objecting to Hayford as agent, partly because he lived in Bangor and partly because of general dissatisfaction with his activities. New Party member Peal Molly then wrote that Jo Sockbeson was their true representative, not Sol Swassin, who was sent by the influence of the priest, indicating that the New Party was also divided. In a related letter,

Old Party member John Attean wrote that John Neptune had been chosen as representative to the state and that most of the New Party had agreed to be governed by the Old Party. Only a few dissenters still held out.[39] However, another letter, signed by the New Party governor, Tomar Sockalexis, Lieutenant Governor Attean Orson, and fifty-one New Party supporters, was sent to the governor and council in support of agent Hayford. Furthermore, the New Party complained that Solomon Swassin had attempted to cut a quantity of valuable timber from the public lands of the tribe and had been prevented by the agent.[40]

In the midst of these disputes, violence erupted: the Old Party reported to the legislature that the New Party had committed acts of vandalism against Governor Attean's house.[41] In another letter, agent Thomas Bartlett described a council meeting in which Tomar Sockalexis, Attean Orson, and other members of the New Party declared Solomon Swasson, not Peal Molly, their representative. It is not clear why Peal Molly was out of favor. Perhaps it was due to his temperament. Apparently angered at being removed from that post, Molly tore up the paper on which the vote was written.[42]

Two years later, a letter was sent claiming to be from all the tribe except four or five who supported "Old John" Attean. They declared that Peol Polis opposed the priest and they did not want him to be paid. Yet another letter reported in favor of Peol Polis.[43]

Once again in 1846, Old Party governor Attean asked the legislature to remove agent Hayford. He wrote that the Old Party families were not treated fairly, because Hayford favored the New Party in every respect. He said that the Old Party members had refused their dividends in protest, and he requested that "some good man who lives in Old Town" should be appointed.[44] Another petition was sent declaring that the tribe was now united in wanting a priest and retaining Hayford. Frustrated by their inability to understand or clarify the dissent from the numerous letters they had received, the state requested that the Orono selectmen observe an election to determine whom the tribe wanted to follow. On June 7, 1848, the Orono selectmen certified that the majority of the tribe favored retaining their old laws and customs over democratic elections.[45] Ironically, an election decided against an election.

By midcentury, the issue of finding a suitable agent subsided for a time. Those Penobscots who sought democratic changes within the tribe were unsatisfied and sent a petition to admit Indians to rights of U.S. citizenship in 1851; this was found "inexpedient" by the state legislature. Although some Penobscots clearly favored the citizenship idea, others may have wished to cling to their independence; however, at this point their jurisdiction was greatly diminished in terms of territory, customs, and financial matters. The Penobscots did not petition for citizenship or suffrage after 1851—perhaps because their concerns over safety and subsistence took precedence.[46]

Members of the Old Party, many of them having fine farms and producing substantial crops upriver from Old Town, seem to have remained somewhat apart from the citizens of Old Town. Perhaps because Governor Attean and some of his supporters lived much of the time at Mattawamkeag, those who resided at Indian Island near Old Town undermined his authority at times. The agent took actions, sometimes in concert with other Indians, without first seeking approval from Attean and his councillors. Priests may have committed the same mistake from time to time. Except for Joseph Polis and a few others who were firmly Protestant, even the Old Party members who usually were autonomous from Catholic influence could be induced to follow the priest in spiritual matters. However, the Old Party strongly objected to the priest involving himself in politics except for his advocating for specific privileges for the Penobscots.[47] Then along came the Civil War.

During the Civil War, the Penobscots sent twenty-seven of their young men to fight in the Union army, nearly a quarter of the entire male population. The men who remained at home continued to hunt, fish, farm, or make canoes. The women principally were engaged in making baskets, snowshoes, and moccasins, which they mostly sold for insufficient compensation, though some could receive good prices in the fashionable resort areas. The remaining men assisted their wives in these crafts. The Indian agent reported that members of the tribe who scattered away in the spring before planting and returned late in the fall "gained but a scanty subsistence, and in many instances required aid from the different localities in which they were found."[48] With few opportunities, it may be that young Penobscot men joined the Union army to receive bounty payments and hoped for military pensions.

After the war, veterans returned home, and they (or in some cases their widows) applied for military pensions. Two Penobscot men are listed on a Civil War monument in Lincoln, Maine, alongside the citizens who also served. They are Joseph Stanislaus, son of Mary Attean and Stanislaus Nicolar, and John Tomar. Two men who signed a petition to the legislature in 1865, Thomas Danna (Dana) and Thomas Neptune, both served in Company B, First Maine Heavy Artillery. Others who served were Peter Newell, of Bangor, and Sebattis Mohawk, Frank Susup, Samuel Newell, John Swasson, Sappiel Orson, and Peter Dennis, all of Old Town. John Glossian served in a Connecticut regiment, and the son of Beloni Thibodeau served in a New Hampshire regiment. There are a number of others who served whose rank can be seen on gravestones in the Indian Island cemetery.[49] They represent nearly a quarter of the men in the tribe, a significant contribution of population to that war effort. However, returning veterans did not receive benefits of citizenship in the nation or the state, although they did received pensions from the federal government. They would continue to struggle to maintain their landholdings, their political independence, and their culture in the face of unceasing racial and ethnic discrimination and oppression.

In Maine, Passamaquoddy and Penobscot lands were reduced to reservation holdings, defined by but steadily encroached upon by the state. Natives were pressured to conform to American ideals of republican government, Protestant Christianity, English language and culture, and agricultural subsistence. Though small in numbers, the Penobscots resisted the cleansing of their culture with some success in all the areas listed above: politics, religion, language and culture, and subsistence.

Ignoring the tribal tradition of a hereditary chiefdom, the state established annual elections for the Penobscot tribe by an act of legislature in 1867 that required only one party to vote and hold elections on alternate years, beginning with the Old Party in 1867.[50] Therefore, for several years afterward, Old Party and New Party governors served alternate annual terms. Later, about fifteen of the dissatisfied members from each of the two parties united, calling themselves the "third party" or "outsiders" and claiming the same rights of election as the two established parties. At the election of 1874, two sets of candidates were voted for, and the defeated party joined the third party. In 1874, the tribe petitioned the legislature to do away with Old Party and New Party elections, and an act was drawn up providing for elections by majority vote. However, Maine's legislature indefinitely postponed the act. Factions of the tribe continued to be divided even on this issue. A letter from the Old Party requested that election laws not be changed, while the New Party wrote asking for election law changes. In addition, the New Party made it known that they were also against the institution of an Indian constable, although the state instituted the constable anyway, to help keep order on the island.[51]

Other issues that arose in the latter half of the nineteenth century included a request from the New Party that treaty goods be paid in cash. The Old Party opposed this action. Eventually the request was honored. Penobscots living in a late-nineteenth-century society with wood-framed homes, store-bought clothing, tools, and utensils no longer wished to be paid in red and blue cloth, powder and shot, molasses, and corn. In only one issue did both parties write letters in accord: in 1874 and 1875, both sent letters requesting that preexisting treaties should not be renegotiated.[52]

Historical documents suggest that Penobscot leaders repeatedly requested that they be consulted whenever the state's governor or legislators made decisions about their lives. They had a traditional hereditary chief and subchief and a council of leading men who made important decisions about their community. They recognized the necessity of having an agent of the state who could protect them against local settlers but wanted someone who was responsive to their needs and would listen to their advice. They resisted the paternal actions of the state by continually sending letters of protest to the state leadership. The degree of sovereignty that they held based upon treaty rights was (and still is) the underlying issue of the time. Within the tribe, however, factions divided over issues of education, religious freedom, and whether the tribal political leaders should hold hereditary or elected offices. At first, the state set up an independent election that determined that most of the tribe wanted to continue the hereditary chiefdom, but eventually the state required alternate elections from each faction. Political factions thus became political parties as the state forced democratic elections on the community.[53] The state continued to view the Penobscots as its "wards" and controlled their property and funds with the help of an agent who acted as "legal guardian," until these ideas were challenged in the Maine Indian Land Claims Case in the 1970s.

Chapter 9

PADDLING SONG

Traditional Skills as a Tool of Resistance

Yo hi ko hyo we heh yo hi ko hyo weh heh
Yo hi ko hyo we heh yo hi ko hyo weh heh[1]
—PADDLING SONG

The paddling song may be the only surviving example of a work song for the Penobscots. The Penobscots had more than one such song in their repertoire, since canoes were their primary means of travel.[2] This song was not for dancing. Rather, according to Linda Davenport, singers originally used it to help keep a steady beat while paddling a canoe, and perhaps to smooth their way spiritually through the waves.

An essential tool for workingmen and -women, the canoe provided transportation in all seasons but the depths of winter. Tools, work, and the traditional skills associated with work provided a means of resistance for Penobscot men and women. During the first part of the nineteenth century, their work continued to center upon hunting. Later, men applied traditional canoe-handling skills to river driving and guiding as a way to carve a niche in the local economy. Ronald Trosper suggests that work, choices about work, and tribal economic policies reflect Native traditions of respect or reverence toward the world around them; the importance of community and of relationships between people, animals, and plants; a knowledge that the spiritual power in the world can cause trouble if not treated with respect; and concern for future generations.[3] The historical record suggests that this is true of the Penobscots, as their traditional values were invoked as a tool of resistance whenever dominant cultural restrictions were imposed, including economic life.

While the state-appointed agent was plowing and planting the Penobscots' larger islands in hopes of making farmers out of them, most of the able-bodied men, on the other hand, were spending their time in the woods hunting and trapping furs. By doing so, they followed practices established two centuries before, when Europeans first brought their goods to the shores of the new land to trade for furs. Traditional hunting and gathering skills changed during the fur trade era. Penobscots adopted firearms, stopped making and using bows and arrows, and increased stress on the populations of fur-bearing species.

Hunting

Throughout most of the nineteenth century, in the face of pressure from the state to settle and adopt agriculture, Penobscot hunters continued to hunt and trap for furs and skins they could bring into trading posts. Fur trade scholarship generally follows the trade as it moves westward; little attention has been paid to eastern trade. However, the eastern trade continued because the northern woods remained unsettled until late in the nineteenth century. The Native population, greatly reduced by disease and war, did not destroy the local game populations early on, as some scholars have reported for eastern Canada.[4] A relatively small population of Penobscots and Passamaquoddies hunted for furs and skins. They also continued to trade with local men such as the Hardy family of Brewer well into the nineteenth century. This is not to say that they never experienced problems from lack of game. The historical record indicates sporadic complaints by Penobscots about the deficiency of game near forts and other settlements. But the greater part of northern Maine allocated to kin groups by Penobscots as hunting territory usually yielded enough furs to make the practice worthwhile.[5]

Hunting continued to be the most important source of subsistence for the Penobscots until sometime in the 1870s, in spite of government efforts to induce Penobscot families to reside in one year-round location and grow crops. Maine reformers and government agents led the way in the United States in promoting an agrarian lifestyle for the Indians but failed due to the marginality of Maine's agriculture. The Penobscots fared no better than other Maine farmers in growing crops. Not only were the Natives adept at hunting; non-Indian hunters sought their assistance as guides. In spite of agricultural reform, the fur trade continued to be viable; local merchants collected furs and skins from Penobscots as well as from local settlers who hunted and trapped to supplement their incomes.

The domestic fur market ensured a successful fur trade for Penobscot hunters throughout most of the nineteenth century. Congress had regulated trade with the Indians, restricting trading licenses to American citizens after 1783. Thus the fur trade grew rapidly, with centers of trade in the eastern United States. Eastern markets were especially open to receiving goods from northern New England. Bangor and Brewer traders responded to the market by sending furs collected from Indian and other hunters in central and eastern Maine to New York and to Boston.[6]

European demands for furs actually increased after the War of 1812. Numerous fur-bearing animals thrived in western New York, Pennsylvania, and northern New England. The Indians who lived in these areas continued to bring furs and skins to trading posts. The furriers who set up businesses in Philadelphia, New York, and Boston sold finished furs domestically and in Europe.[7]

One reason for the growing trade in animal skins in the United States was the lack of domestic clothing manufacture. Imports from Europe were scarce. Families sewed their own hats, shoes, and clothing, since textile manufacturing had not yet developed to any extent throughout the United States. When London fur prices dropped, traders in the United States shifted their trade to China. After 1840, Europeans began to use silk to make hats in Europe and relied less upon beaver and other furs. The industrial revolution brought textiles to the entire Western world.[8] Still, the trapping and exporting of fur skins to Europe and China continued to be an important industry until 1900. After 1900, domestic consumption of furs and skins grew more than exports.[9]

The American market in furs provided a good income for some merchants in Maine. Local merchants such as Jonathan Hardy of Brewer "fitted out" Penobscot hunters in a contract that guaranteed the merchant payment in the form of furs collected by the hunter at the end of the season. In return, the hunter received food and hunting supplies for him and his family (a gun, ammunition, and sometimes a canoe and snowshoes) for the winter months. This worked out very well for the hunter, who usually could rely upon the trader to feed his family members while he was away hunting, and he could often get additional credit when hunting brought meager returns. However, several poor hunts could lead to mounting debts for the hunters.

Indian agents reported hunting as an important occupation for Penobscots as late as 1866. George Dillingham wrote in his report to the legislature that the Penobscots "have received good wages for their labor and have found ready sale for the results of their hunting expeditions, and also for their home productions."[10] However, this is the last mention of hunting as a means of livelihood in the agents' reports for nearly fifteen years. In 1879, the agent reported a marked change in the Penobscots' livelihood. Agent Samuel W. Hoskins reported: "In years past large numbers of [Penobscot men], being supplied by our merchants, repaired to the forests, in the fall and winter, to hunt, returning in the spring with furs and skins often to the value of $500.00. It is not so now; the game has disappeared, and with it the inclination and the skill to hunt. The tanning of moose, deer and caribou skins, and their manufacture into snow-shoes and moccasins, has gone into other hands."[11] Game disappeared largely because of market and sports hunting.[12] By the end of the nineteenth century, Penobscot men and women pursued canoe manufacture, basket crafts, guiding, and lumbering as their principal means of subsistence.

For the first half of the nineteenth century, however, hunting remained the most important means of subsistence for Penobscot families. The custom of supplying Indians with goods and credit before they went hunting was common throughout the fur-trading industry after 1826. In Canada, this was called the "Keith system" and involved equipping the Indians with a fixed standard of debts. Traders gave goods to the Indians, who then brought in furs to cancel their debts. Traders paid additional goods for any excess value of the furs. Also, the merchants gave gifts such as beads, knives, gunflints, or ribbons to the hunter as a gratuity. The custom was for 20 percent of the outfit to be in gratuities. An honest trader could rely on his hunters to bring him enough furs to make these gifts worthwhile. Unfortunately, dishonest traders often cheated Indian hunters in the American West and Northwest, with the result that Congress eventually prohibited private trade, restricting all Indian trade to government truckhouses by 1790.[13]

However, the federal government never enforced restrictions on Indian trade east of the Appalachians. Maine fur merchants such as Jonathan Titcomb Hardy and his son Walter "Manly" Hardy of Brewer engaged in fur trading with both Indian and non-Indian traders. The greatest bulk of their trade with the Penobscots occurred between 1835 and 1870. The Hardys' business records reveal enough details to reconstruct significant portions of their business with the Penobscots.[14] For example, Manly Hardy reported in his 1868 journal that he "fitted out" Peol Necola and Mitchell Francis on February 15 to go to Union River hunting. Likewise on March 23, he supplied Joe Loring, Peol Necola, and Mitchell Francis to hunt muskrats at Sebasticook.[15]

Prices for furs were established in advance of the hunt, at the same time that the trader gave supplies to the hunter. An example of such an agreement between Penobscot hunter Newell Lewis and Jonathan Hardy follows.[16]

Bangor, February 2, 1844
   In consideration of J. T. Hardy and W. Woodman having agreed to supply us with supplies for a hunting excursion this month, I hereby agree to let the said Hardy and Woodman have all the furs I may get this winter at fair prices with this agreement that the following prices shall be paid for the kinds of skins mentioned—namely:

Otter	$4.00
Lucivee [wildcat]	2.50
Fisher or black cat	3.00
Sable	1.50
Muskrat	0.08
Mink	0.50

Signed,
Newell Luis

Supplies given by J. T. Hardy:

2 bls flour @ 6	$12.00
1 bl pork @ 16	16.00
6 gals molasses @ 0.30	1.80
1 keg @3s	.50
2 lbs tea 3s	1.00
1 knife, saleratus, buttons, thread	.50
5½ yds hard twine	2.28
3 lbs best tobacco	.30
1 pr drawers	.75
paid rail road	.75
Total:	$35.58

In case of a poor hunt, Indians could also pay their debts to traders with a portion of their semiannual "dividend" of treaty goods. Usually the Indian agent paid Hardy directly in exchange for a note or invoice signed by the head of the family. Therefore, the "fitting out" of hunters held little risk for the trader.

"Dividends" were payments in goods made to each family by the state of Maine as a fulfillment of treaty obligations. The annual dividend consisted of corn, flour, pork, molasses, chocolate, tobacco, red or blue cloth, and, for hunting men only, powder and shot. A small amount of cash ($1 to $5) was allotted to each family. The total value of all of the goods was small. Each person received a bushel of corn, one and one-half pounds of pork, six pounds of flour, one quart of molasses, and so on in two or more payments per year, usually in the fall and spring.[17] Therefore, when their debts were due to merchants, the Penobscots would pledge a portion of their dividend or a pawn to clear the debt, and the Indian agent would pay the pawn holders.[18]

Another way Penobscots paid their bills was by selling hay or firewood from land occupied by the family that owed the debt. For example, Newell Polis pledged eight tons of hay from his land to Hardy to pay for his hunting necessities.[19]

Hardy also employed Penobscots to craft moccasins and snowshoes that he in turn marketed to the lumber industry. For example, Peter Sockbeson received $2.50 for tanning a moose hide, $0.10 each for making a pair of moccasins, and $1.50 for each pair of snowshoes he made in November and December 1845. He cleared his debt of $19.85 by tanning two hides and making sixteen pairs of moccasins and nine pairs of snowshoes.[20]

Jonathan Hardy took his furs to Boston, where he visited several furriers in order to obtain the best price.[21] Boston and New York furriers quoted no prices for moose skins, because the moose skin trade was strictly a local business (at least in the 1840s). It is difficult to determine just how lucrative the fur trade was for traders in Maine in the nineteenth century. There do not appear to be enough records of fur pelts taken in Maine over a long enough period in the nineteenth century to reconstruct the volume of the fur trade. Penobscot hunters brought in the only beaver pelts during this period, as well as the major portion of moose hides, which became a very lucrative part of the business beginning in 1846: lumber camps needed a great many moccasins.

It appears that Hardy was in the habit of encouraging his hunters to bring back the specific kinds of furs that the big-city furriers were willing to buy. When Hardy "fitted out" Newell Lewis, the fur prices he quoted were for a limited number of species: otter, lucivee,[22] fisher, sable, muskrat, and mink. He did not specify beaver, fox, moose, deer, or bear. Hardy did not necessarily discourage the taking of other species, as witnessed by the fact that he did pay good prices for most pelts in good condition.[23] Similarly, Hardy kept receipts for furs he purchased from hunters and trappers; from these it is possible to learn the abundance or scarcity of fur species. Surprisingly, trappers received payment close to and even sometimes equal to the price that Hardy received for the furs from the Boston merchants.[24] Fur prices fluctuated annually. Locally, moose and mink prices rose, while deer prices fell. The demands of the rapidly growing lumber industry for moccasins and snowshoes inflated prices for moose skins.[25]

During this same period elsewhere in North America, beaver, mink, muskrat, and other species were being harvested for furs in very large numbers. Americans could not catch as many beaver as Canadians, but they made up for it by catching vast numbers of mink and muskrat.[26] This same pattern of the hunt is seen in the Hardy accounts. Penobscot men who brought their furs and skins to Hardy during the first half of the nineteenth century made anywhere from $0.12 to $25.00 per winter's hunt.[27]

Although the amount of money paid to Penobscots for their furs and skins seems small by today's standards, it was actually a substantial sum in terms of their total economy. For example, forty pounds of pork could be purchased for less than $5. A canoe and paddle cost $10.50. A barrel of flour cost $6.00. A whole winter's supply of basic goods (flour, pork, molasses, tea, etc.) could be purchased for about $30.00.[28] These goods supplemented the goods from the annual dividend paid to each family by the state through the Indian agent.

It is worth noting that, while hunting provided a substantial portion of the Penobscot family subsistence, men could also earn extra money hiring out as guides for sport hunters. Employing their traditional knowledge and following traditional hunting customs continued to be more enticing to Penobscot men than farming or wage work.

Though the state bemoaned the lack of permanent settlement by the Penobscots, local traders continued to encourage the hunt as long as they could sell the furs. However, Penobscots had much competition from others.

Jonathan Hardy's records show that both white and Indian trappers were bringing large numbers of furs into his trading post at Brewer. By the middle of the nineteenth century, whites captured the larger portion of skins and furs, while the amount of furs collected by Indian hunters declined.[29]

Manly Hardy enjoyed hunting and often went into the woods with Indian and white hunters alike. One such excursion, described in the journal Manly kept, was a trip to the West Branch of the Penobscot River in 1858. Manly set out for Tobique. He first took the sixteen-hour steamboat trip to Kineo, where he and his friend Leonard got in their canoes to go to the West Branch. From there they set out to Chamberlain Lake, where they joined Pial Antwine Tomah, who was camping with a man from St. Francis.[30] Manly's account illustrates the extent to which Indian hunters still inhabited the woods, and the "woods hospitality" accorded from one hunter to another.

On September 10, Joe Obaumsawin (an Abenaki from Quebec) came to their camp, ate dinner, and afterward sang. Manly recalled that the Indians sang very well in French. Manly himself was studying *Alnambay Uli Awickhigan* (Indian Good Book).[31] Three days later, when Manly and his companions arrived at the thoroughfare between Eagle and Churchill Lakes, he found Abenakis building canoes there. Pial hailed them in English, French, and Abenaki. Throughout the month of October the party trapped for beaver, otter, mink, and muskrat.

The next year, Manly set out for Caucomgomoc Lake with several of his hunting friends, in a serious expedition to bring back furs. He published his journal entries in an article, "A Fall Fur Hunt in Maine," in *Forest and Stream* magazine.[32]

In his article, Manly recounted his friendly relations with the Penobscots. One day, he spotted a mink running on some logs, and just as he was about to shoot at it, the mink jumped upon a canoe covered with snow. So as not to ruin the canoe, Manly waited until the mink moved away from the canoe and then shot at it. When he and his companion turned over the canoe, they saw that it was Indian, as evidenced by the headboard lashed to the middle bar. There was a large bag of steel traps in it. The sound of the gunshot brought the canoe owners out from the woods. Manly described the first as an old and very lame Penobscot man. Manly spoke to him in Abenaki and ascertained his name, Brassua (Abenaki for Francis). Brassua recognized Manly and asked, "Why the devil don't you stay home long side old Jonathan?"[33]

According to Manly, all the unwritten laws of the woods, both white and Indian, gave a hunter claim to the land he occupied. If one hunter found any new spots and saw the name of another hunter or the totem mark of an Indian, he respected the first rights of the occupant. Manly knew that the Penobscot hunters would use someone else's camp and their belongings well. "For I much rather trust two strange Indians than two strange white men."[34]

Beginning in 1866, Manly took a more active role as merchant, buying and selling furs. According to his daughter, Fannie Hardy Eckstorm, he continued to do so at least until 1870.[35] After that, the records are unclear about the extent of his local business. He did continue to trade with Penobscots until his death in 1910. Some of his journal entries mention his continuing business with Penobscots. For example, for January 15, 1868, he wrote, "Thermometer is below zero. Bought 4 Deer, ... lent $20 to Newell Neptune. He pawned two double guns 'till June to pay 24$. Jan. 17. Cold. Bought 2 deer of Little Joe Francis. . . . Lent Joe 23$ for himself and 30$ for Lewis Ketchum. Sappial Soccalexis brought my snowshoes yesterday and I lent him 30$ and a pair of moccasins at 2$. Feb. 14 bought 2 deer of Saul Neptune at 9 cents each. . . . Feb. 15 bought 3 deer of Lewie Ketchum. Fitted out Peol Necola and Mitchell Francis to go to Union River hunting. Mar. 23 Fitted out Joe Loring, Peol Necola and Mitchell Francis to hunt muskrats at Sebasticook. April 28 bought a lot of furs of Sappial Soccalexis."[36] These notes suggest that Penobscots continued to rely on Hardy for some measure of income from the sale of animal skins and furs.

After 1900, the fur trade supplied only a small portion of the Penobscots' subsistence needs. Men continued to hunt for game, as they continue to do today, supplying moose and venison to supplement food supplies from grocery stores and gardens. Many of the Penobscot hunters became guides for sport hunters and made a little extra money in the process, but most men worked in the woods in the lumber trade or in some other local industry.

River Driving

In spite of the decline in income from hunting for the fur trade, Penobscots continued to resist assimilation by finding other ways to employ their own traditional skills in the market place. The latter part of the century found them moving away from agriculture and the fur trade and into the market economy by offering their boat-handling skills to the river drive bosses of the lumber trade for pay, hiring out as guides for the burgeoning sport hunting industry, and developing traditional crafts for the growing tourist industry. In doing this, they were consciously or unconsciously preserving significant portions of their traditional way of life.

After the fur trade declined, skilled hunters used their knowledge of the woods to guide sport hunters and their knowledge of inland waters to ferry lumbermen in bateaux or to make canoes and paddles. By holding onto their language, telling their tales, and finding occupations that utilized traditional skills such as making and selling baskets and canoes and working on the water, Penobscot men and women continued to resist giving up their culture.

Fannie Eckstorm wrote about an Indian crew who worked for John Ross,[37] the famous drive boss for the West Branch from 1864 to 1885.[38] He employed a crew of 150 drivers from Bangor. These included 18 Penobscots from Old Town, who handled the bateaux when they went with Ross to Connecticut in 1876. The Connecticut River was difficult to drive, and the Bangor and Old Town drivers were in demand because of their great skill.[39] The fact that the Old Town Indians were hired specifically for bateaux work indicates that they had the reputation for excellence in boat handling. Fanny Eckstorm described it best: "all our head lumbermen have been bossed first or last by Indian boatmen, and have started at the foot of the ladder without favors."[40]

The Penobscot Indians' reputation as boatmen sometimes led them to take unnecessary chances. Eckstorm related an example in the story of the running of Canaan Falls by Sebattis Solomon, Mitchell Soc Francis, Sappiel Orson, and Sebattis Glossian. Canaan was a dangerous falls, one that should have been avoided, but as Eckstorm paraphrased the words of Joe Orson, "You see we had to go. There was a young man, old man, boy, girl, all sorts were looking right down at us. Old Town Indians have a great name for river driving. We had to go. We knew it was possible to die that time, but we couldn't go back on our name!"[41]

Apparently the Connecticut River drive paid better than the Penobscot River drive.[42] However, it was more than money that brought the crews from their favorite West Branch to the treacherous Connecticut. It was pride, as well.

The Indian agent reports contain other evidence of Indian river driving and its dangers. In 1861, the agent reported that there were about 150 men employed in the summer, some in agriculture, hunting, and logging in the swamp, and in the spring, river driving.[43] In 1866, he reported deaths from exposure in the woods and driving logs.[44] Unfortunately, the Indian agents reports are very brief and do not include information about who those men were or how much they earned. In 1879, the agent stated that many of the young and active men were good river drivers. They could get forty to a hundred days of labor, but lumber market failures meant their wages were low.[45] Still, Penobscot men found work in the woods more lucrative and more in keeping with their traditions than farming. The Indian agent's report of 1883 states: "The fact also that the larger portion of the active male members [of the tribe] are engaged in driving logs in the spring and early summer, and later in the season visit the summer resorts, prevents them from undertaking the cultivation of the soil to any great extent."[46] The report of 1885 notes the death of one man "who was drowned while driving on the east branch of Penobscot River last spring."[47]

In 1887, agent Charles Bailey wrote: "There was ample opportunity for labor at log-driving during the spring and early summer at good wages, and as the Indians are expert drivers their services are always in demand for that class of labor."[48] Again, in 1888, he reported: "The young men of the tribe who are among the best river-drivers of the State, especially efficient in swift waters, made for the most part, long and profitable drives."[49] The situation was the same in 1889, but in 1894 agent George Hunt reported that "the general business depression has made itself felt in the wages and profits of Indian workers, no less than in the case of the whites. Driving wages were reduced last spring from twenty to thirty percent."[50]

The depression in lumbering apparently continued for some time. The heyday of the Penobscot River drives was over. It was not until 1919 that agent Ira Pinkham again mentioned this type of labor, stating: "The men who worked on the river, in the saw mill and canoe factory have had unusual good wages."[51] The wages of the Penobscot men were as good as or better than the wages paid to other ethnic groups on the waterways, proving that the Penobscot men were truly highly esteemed for their ability in the lumbering industry.

A few payroll records for the Penobscot Logging Association do exist and help us reconstruct wages for a time.[52] Unfortunately, most of the nineteenth-century records are lost. However, the ledger for 1906 lists

Sebat Nicolar, Susap Mitchell, and Joseph Swasson as employees, apparently working seven to ten days in July and ten and a half days in August, for wages of $2.50 per day, the same wage paid to other employees. The ledger for 1908 lists a number of other Penobscot men working from four to nineteen days in September. For 1909, I. W. Bussell at Costigan listed Asa Mishal (John Mitchell), Sr., and Asa Mishel, Jr., who worked for six days a week into November. Mitchell Sr. was paid $4.00 per day, while Mitchell Jr. was paid $2.00. Other men were paid from $1.25 to $4.00 per day, although the $4.00 rate was rare.[53] This document demonstrates that the Indian men were among the highest paid of the river drivers, surely a tribute to their skills.

Unfortunately, there are not enough of these payroll records available to determine just how many men worked the drives or when they started and finished. For that kind of information we can, however, turn to some of the men who worked the drives and who have been interviewed on the subject. Cindy Lamb interviewed eight-two-year-old Nick Ranco in 1975 as part of the project that resulted in the publication of *Argyle Boom*. Ranco had started working on the river drives at the age of ten, probably in 1903. It was not unusual for boys to work the drives. Ranco described his first season: "I was rafting then. And before the Spring was over I was checking. I checked and rafted and worked on the dams up there." A checker stood on a log or a raft and checked each log for its log mark as it came downriver. If it had the appropriate mark for his beat,[54] the checker would pick it out from the others with his pick pole and push it toward shore to be rafted.[55] A detailed description of the work is already very clearly and thoroughly discussed elsewhere, so I will not go into any great detail on the matter here.[56]

Roy Dana, who is the grandson of the Joseph Daney listed above in the 1906 payroll records, talked to me about working on the river drives as a boy. He remembered some of the older men who worked as the boatmen at that time. "These older men," he says, "were in charge of the boats, they had big long poles."[57]

One of the most difficult jobs was "carding the rear." Roy remembered, "It was our job to clean the river of the logs and see that they all got through. We brought up the rear." As to when he began in the season, he said:

Sometimes I went when it was in progress, picked it up in Piscataquis, West Branch, Pleasant River, Sebec River. We always worked together on the Indian crew. We were more comfortable with each other. Frenchmen would talk about ya in their own tongue and we'd do the same to them. Young guys went into town and went to dances and fought over the girls with the townsfolk. But the crews didn't fight each other.

It was apparently not always the case that the Indian crew brought up the rear. Ernest Kennedy related that he remembered the Indian crew always being on the first line when sorting logs at the booms, the checker being a man by the name of Joe Thibodeau. "He was a little fellow, ... smart as a cricket on logs. Yeah, the Indian fellows, they'd always put them in the Indian crew. They always wanted to work together."[58]

The Indian men were renowned for their special skills in boat handling but also for their speed and agility in the sorting process. Each crew did the same jobs but had different areas of the river to work. The crew members ate and slept together in the boom houses but stayed with their own group, perhaps because of their common language and their cultural and kinship bonds. This type of work was available to them almost every year, although at times depressed lumber prices or war disrupted the availability of jobs or reduced the wages.

Naming all the men who worked the log drives would produce a very long list. Penobscot men worked the drives for one hundred years or more. Families sent fathers, sons, and grandsons to do this work from spring into fall; they earned good wages at it. They also earned a grand reputation among their peers, if not among the general public. When a man such as John Ross wanted good boatmen, he found them in the Indian community. The Indians knew the river, were highly skilled in handling bateaux, and lacked neither daring nor skill. Many lost their lives over the years, the most famous perhaps being Governor Joseph Attean, who drowned when his boat swamped in 1870.

Guiding

In addition to boat handling, Penobscot people had an intimate knowledge of the woods and waters of Maine. The Penobscots spent most of their lives navigating the rivers and streams by canoe. Often when hired as guides they were paid to make a bark canoe or two and the necessary paddles. Then they would be paid a daily wage to accompany the party on whatever excursion it undertook, or they might be given supplies for their families for the period they would be gone, plus a bit of cash.

The demand for guides grew toward the end of the nineteenth century, as more middle-class Americans acquired disposable income and leisure time, and as sport hunting became quite popular. As a result, as the century drew to a close, Penobscot men could find lucrative summer and fall employment doing work they loved. The Indian agent for the Penobscots reported in 1894 that, in spite of a depressed business environment, "the only industry that shows real improvement this year is guiding wherein

FIG. 9. Athion Lewey, Indian guide, Grand Lake, Maine. *Courtesy Maine Historic Preservation Commission, Augusta, Maine.*

more members of the tribe found employment—and without reduction in pay—than ever before."[59]

However, in 1907, the same agent reported a poor year for guiding due to unfavorable weather conditions.[60] While guiding opportunities in earlier centuries existed primarily for surveyors, explorers, military men, and occasional sportsmen who hired guides, the sport-guiding opportunity for Penobscots grew out of the tourist industry that developed in Maine after 1870. The industrialization of New England resulted in a class of well-to-do sportsmen who wished to bring home trophies to decorate their homes. Northern Maine supplied the prizes to hunters, as moose, deer, and numerous species of fish were abundant enough to guarantee success to the sportsman.

The inventions of industrialization such as mass transportation enhanced sport hunting as well.[61] The horse-drawn stage provided transportation north of Bangor. Later, the steamboat and the train brought faster and more comfortable modes of travel to the area. In fact, the Maine Central Railroad was chartered as early as 1856 and laid rails from Auburn to Bangor in 1863. By 1893, the train created access to a point forty-five miles south of Ashland, deep in the interior of central Maine.[62] Wilderness resorts were built, such as the Kineo House on the shore of Moosehead Lake. Enterprising Maine hunters built smaller sporting camps along lakes and rivers, and formed numerous sportsmen's clubs.[63] As sport hunting grew, so did opportunities for Penobscot men to find work as guides.

Often guides were among the leading men of the tribe. For example, John Neptune, lieutenant governor of the tribe, guided Joseph Treat on his surveying journey along the Penobscot River in 1820. Neptune built the canoe for their trip, while Treat supplied provisions for the travelers as well as for Neptune's family.[64] Treat paid Neptune $1.00 per day and $10.00 for the birch canoe and paddles. They traveled for fifty-five days, from September 26 to November 19, beginning their journey at Bangor and continuing to the St. John River. Neptune accepted partial payment in goods from Barker & Crosby to the sum of $34.04. Treat paid the rest of the $65.00 to Neptune in cash.[65]

Likewise, it was Louis Neptune who was hired by the state geologist, Charles Jackson, in 1837. Jackson conducted a survey of Maine in order to assess the agricultural and mineral resources (soils and rocks), as ordered by the legislature.[66] Henry David Thoreau also tried to hire Louis and another man in 1846 at Mattawamkeag, for his trip to Mt. Katahdin, but they were unable to get together at the appointed destination at Five Islands. Thoreau described Louis Neptune as "a small, wiry man, with puckered and wrinkled face, yet he seemed the chief man of the two; the same, as I remembered, who had accompanied Jackson to the mountain in '37. [They were] slightly clad in shirt and pantaloons, like laborers with us in warm weather."[67] Thoreau seems to think they were underdressed for the weather, but his guides were used to being outdoors year-round and probably hardier than he.

Thoreau immortalized the skills of another well-respected guide, Joseph Attean. Thoreau described Attean at his first meeting, which took place at Moosehead Lake in the fall of 1853:

He was a good-looking Indian, twenty-four years old, apparently of unmixed blood, short and stout, with a broad face and reddish complexion, and eyes, methinks, narrower and more turned-up at the outer corners than ours, answering to the description of his race. Besides his underclothing, he wore a red-flannel shirt, woolen pants, and a black Kossuth hat, the ordinary dress of the lumberman, and, to a considerable extent, of the Penobscot Indian.[68]

Thoreau noted that Attean whistled "Oh Susannah," demonstrating that he was familiar with American popular music of the time. It was customary for the Penobscots to learn the songs of their fellow workers. Many of the men who worked the river drives sang Yankee songs in the evening, sometimes in the Penobscot language.[69] Attean spoke Penobscot and told Thoreau the Indian names for birds and places.

In addition to supplying and paddling the canoe, Attean also made a birch-bark moose caller to aid in the hunt. When one of the sportsmen shot a cow moose, it was Attean's job to track the animal down and butcher the carcass. He removed a portion of the meat to bring along and left the rest on the bank, along with the skin, for the return trip.[70] As they traveled along, at times they had to carry their canoe and provisions across land in order to avoid rocky areas of the river. Thoreau described Attean as "twirling his canoe in his hands as if it were a feather, in places where it was difficult to get along without a burden."[71] In other areas of rapids, Attean navigated the canoe alone, while the others walked along the shore to lighten the craft that it might easily go over the rocks.

On Thoreau's third excursion to Maine in 1857,[72] he hired Joseph Polis to guide him to the Allagash and the East Branch of the Penobscot. He was lucky to get Polis, as it was late in July when Thoreau arrived in Old Town, and most of the Penobscots were gone to the seaside or to Massachusetts to sell their baskets. Thoreau described Polis as "stoutly built, perhaps a little above the middle height, with a broad face, and, as others said, perfect Indian features and complexion."[73] Polis's house was a good-looking two-story wood-framed structure, surrounded by a garden and fruit trees. Thoreau agreed to pay Polis $1.50 per day, with an additional $0.50 per day for his canoe. Polis brought along only an ax, a gun, his blanket, and his new pipe and tobacco. They loaded their canoe atop the stage and proceeded to Moosehead Lake. Polis was forty-eight years old in 1857 and by this time well known as a guide and hunter. In fact, hunters on the stage had told Thoreau that Polis was the best.[74]

Polis paddled his canoe with his three companions and some 160 pounds of baggage. At every camping stop, he took the canoe out of the water and turned it over, placing a log on top so it would not blow away. He took charge of the campfire, finding dry bark to kindle it and large logs that would keep burning overnight.[75] Polis entertained the group with a song in his native tongue, which he then translated into English. It was a simple religious hymn. He also sang another in Latin. Polis told Thoreau that he made his living from hunting. He had been hunting the West Branch of the Penobscot River toward the head of the St. John since he was a boy, and knew it well. He hunted beaver, otter, fisher, sable, and moose for their skins. To feed himself, he captured partridges, ducks, and hedgehogs, and dried moose meat. What may have seemed to Thoreau a romantic natural lifestyle was in fact fraught with hardship. Polis related that he had nearly starved to death as a boy when hunting with two grown men. They had to abandon their canoe because of ice, with winter coming rapidly upon them.[76]

Louis Ketchum, another Penobscot guide who was well known as a tribal leader and as a river driver, owned and operated hunting camps at Namacanta Lake and was a good friend of the Hardy family of Brewer. Fannie Hardy Eckstorm (the daughter of Manly) referred to him frequently in her writings as "Uncle Louis." Her father related that Louis Ketchum served as guide to the Maine Scientific Survey in 1861. Ketchum took nine naturalists to Mattawamkeag to catch insects, gather flowers, sledge rocks, and collect animal and bird specimens.[77]

Other Penobscots also built their own hunting camps to attract sport hunters. These were built to some degree within traditional hunting territories, although the extinction of some families altered the structure of this somewhat. Also, these camps were built on land that had to be leased from large landowners, since the land was no longer part of Penobscot territory. Most were on the mainland. For example, Debsconeag Joe had a camp at Joe Mary Lake west of Millinocket in Piscataquis County, in the Swasson family territory (his surname was Francis, but he married Elizabeth Swasson, allowing him to hunt in Swasson hunting territory). Other camps were built in present Argyle, along Birch Stream and Hemlock Stream. Another frequented hunting area was along Olamon Stream, northeast of Old Town.

Penobscot hunters and guides ran into trouble when Maine began passing laws regulating hunting and guiding in the state. Sporting interests lobbied the state for better control of game resources. In 1897, Maine's legislature passed hunting and fishing laws, including a statute requiring the registration and certification of guides by the commissioners of inland fisheries and game. The law imposed a penalty upon any person who engaged in the business of guiding without such registration and certificates.[78] The Penobscots petitioned the legislature to be allowed to hunt moose and deer year-round, as was their custom. The legislature turned them down.[79] By 1900, there were many hunting lodge businesses; sportsmen could hire many licensed, non-Indian guides to take them hunting and fishing. The Penobscots, led by Mitchell Attean, petitioned the legislature for exemption from the guide license law.[80] But the state stood fast in requiring Penobscots to be licensed; many went without a license and were not bothered by game wardens about it. In this case, tradition overrode written legislation for many years.

Every Penobscot man and woman knew how to paddle a canoe and find his or her way about in the woods. Knowledge of the land and streams and willingness to lead others resulted in opportunities for paid employment using skills that the Penobscot Indian both excelled at and enjoyed. I know of no Penobscot women hired to act as a guide until the 1970s, though they certainly would have been capable of it. I believe it was considered improper for women to guide men in most instances.

Also, women were employed in a more important trade: for the most part, they managed the family basket business.

Roy Dana, Sr., told me about his male ancestors, who ran hunting camps and earned a living as guides:

My father and my grandfather, and great grandfather, they were all guides. They guided up around Baxter Park, Debsconeag lakes; they were all outdoor people. They had two hunting lodges up there and they lived there practically year-round. Joseph Dana [also written Dennis] was the family name. They hunted and guided in the 1920s and 30s, guiding on Mt. Katahdin.[81]

Other opportunities for employment for Penobscots included domestic work, piecework, and working in saw and textile mills. The evidence for such employment is thin, but a few interesting sources assist in recreating a glimpse of Penobscot working life. For example, someone who signed himself "Down East" wrote a letter to a newspaper describing a trip to Indian Island in 1845. Traveling by railroad, he started in Lynn, Massachusetts, spent the night in Portland, Maine, and went on to Augusta and Bangor. He wanted to buy some potatoes, and since the potato rot had made them quite scarce, he was advised to visit the Penobscots. He found, however, that they too had lost potatoes to rot. He said that the Penobscots had given up hunting and basket making, and were learning to make shoes. "While I was there, an express came in, loaded with boxes from Lynn; and when they were opened, it looked just like Black Marsh. The boxes were marked from I.B., N.B., M.C.P., S.B., &c."[82] These were boxes of shoe pieces to be sewn together and shipped back to Lynn.

Certainly, the Penobscots had not as yet given up hunting, nor had they given up making baskets. Basket making was not yet as important to economic survival in 1845 as it would be in the later part of the century, but there were several basket families who traveled to resorts to sell their wares.[83] Also, Penobscots were skilled moccasin and snowshoe makers. No other reference to Penobscots making shoes for Lynn occurs among Indian agents' reports specifically, so it seems that it was a brief or rather unimportant undertaking. A number of Penobscots engaged in moccasin making for Manly Hardy; Penobscot men and women may have worked for other merchants as well. As noted, the moose-hide moccasin was in great demand in the lumber trade. It seems a short trip from moccasin making to shoe making.

Some of the women took advantage of opportunities to earn money in domestic work. For example, Joseph Nicolar's mother, Mary Malt (Martha) Neptune (daughter of Lieutenant Governor John Neptune), was left with six children to support when her husband died in 1837. She worked for a Mrs. Thomas in Rockland and was able to send her children to school in Rockland. Later, she turned to making baskets.[84]

Manly Hardy had a Penobscot Indian woman for a nurse when he was a child, and one of the Indian women did the washing for their family. At that time, there were a large number of Penobscots residing in Brewer, some next to the Hardy home. Hardy did not name the women who worked for the family.[85]

It was not until 1877 that an Indian agent first mentioned mill work: "Severe depression of business generally and the lumber business in particular led to decreasing demand for labor in mills, woods, and on the river."[86] His statement seems to indicate that some Penobscots sought work in mills. However, in 1879 the same agent stated, "the young and active Indians will work river-driving, yet very few, if any, ever hire for the woods to use an ax, or to assist in any other way in a lumber operation."[87] Presumably, he meant few if any would work in sawmills. The Indian agents did not mention mill work again until 1907. During the long business depression of the 1890s, many of the men found employment guiding for sportsmen, and of course the basket trade continued to bring profits. However, the agent reported that members of the tribe worked in woolen and pulp mills, canoe factories, and construction. Again, in 1911, the agent reported: "While fewer have worked on the drives than formerly, more have gone to the summer resorts and more worked in the mills and factories. They have long been known as expert guides, and quite a few find ready employment as expert canoe and paddle makers."[88] In 1919, the agent again reported "unusually good wages paid to men who worked on the river, in the saw mill and canoe factory."[89]

By the end of the nineteenth century, few Penobscots continued to hunt as a primary means of subsistence. However, they used their own tools and traditional skills associated with work as a kind of leverage of resistance against assimilation. Hunting and fur trading probably continued to be important occupations for the Penobscots throughout most of the nineteenth century, in large part because of the financial support provided to them by traders. However, as this means of livelihood became less viable, Penobscots found themselves interacting more and more in the workplace with whites as they moved into mill work. They were able to use their boat-handling skills and knowledge of the river on the river drives; they found some work guiding and constructing canoes and paddles for the sport hunters. Skilled woodworkers went into the lumber mills, and skilled moccasin and snowshoe makers did piecework for local merchants and for the Lynn, Massachusetts, shoe companies. However, even as they worked with whites in these various Maine industries, Penobscots retained separate social lives and political identities. They continued to send protests to the governor and legislature of Maine whenever they believed their treaty rights were being assaulted.

Chapter 10

BIRCHES AND BASKETS

Commodification of Culture
and Economic Resistance

> In making the necessaries of life, Gluskabe told man to take the skin off the white wood tree, and make for himself a vessel that will bear him upon the water.[1]
> —JOSEPH NICOLAR

At the beginning of the twentieth century, Old Town was a bustling if small industrious city, with textile mills, lumber mills, shoe factories, and a canoe factory. One traveled to Indian Island only by watercraft or over the "sawdust trail" on the ice in winter.[2] The community maintained a separate existence from the dominant culture. Few whites ventured onto the island except to seek baskets to purchase or a guide for some inland excursion. Penobscots paddled their canoes "over," as they say, to the mainland to work and to shop. A good portion of the men found employment in the Old Town Canoe factory, just one of several commercial entities that took part in the appropriation of Native American culture that persisted throughout much of the twentieth century.[3] Penobscots resisted the commodification of their culture by gradually becoming more secretive, protecting their culture from inquisitive persons by not talking about it to outsiders in fear of being ridiculed for their beliefs. The canoe became an important commodity to the burgeoning sports industry in the twentieth century, while Penobscots, like other northeastern Native communities, turned to the production of souvenir art as a mainstay of their economy, thus taking advantage of growing tourism in Maine.

Penobscot canoe makers played a significant role in the development and marketing of the Old Town canoe. During the nineteenth century, a number of Penobscot men built canoes to sell. But Penobscot Indians also assisted in the industrialization of canoe making. At first, they made birch-bark canoes for sports enthusiasts coming to Maine for hunting and fishing. They also made them to transport men and supplies in the lumber trade, where the larger bateau was impractical.

The birch-bark canoe would occasionally spring a leak because of a bump, and as birch trees became scarce due to lumbering, at some point some unknown person patched and reinforced the birch-bark canoe with cloth. Gradually, the wood and canvas canoe evolved, built essentially the same way as the birch-bark canoe and using the traditional Penobscot design.[4] In spite of the birch-bark canoe's wonderful utility and more than three centuries of use, sportsmen were slow to accept the boat as a gentleman's craft. However, the eventual adoption of the wood and canvas canoe by sports enthusiasts explains in large part the success of Old Town's recreational canoe industry and the role of Penobscots in that success.

In 1874, *Forest and Stream* printed a response to a reader who had inquired about birch-bark canoes. "We are reluctant to inform our anxious inquirer that the birch bark canoe is not named or known in the category of civilized craft which our modern canoe men paddle and sail. . . . It is the peculiar toy and vehicle of the aboriginal redskin and although it is light and buoyant and full of poetry and well adapted to his requirements, the palefaces are conceited enough to believe that they can manufacture something better in all respects."[5]

Native Americans, professional guides, and woodsmen widely adopted the wood and canvas canoe in Maine and Canada. However, the recreation industry continuously ignored the craft. In 1876, *Forest and Stream* magazine reported: "A person from Nova Scotia reports a previously unknown canoe style that was brought to Yarmouth by a Joseph Johnson from Bangor, Maine." This was a canvas-covered canoe. The established canoeing world called these "rag" canoes, but by 1910 wood and canvas canoes flooded the market. Meanwhile, *Forest and Stream* and the American Canoe Association wondered where they had come from.[6]

As the local demand for the canoe grew in response to the needs of the lumbering industry, Indian builders were unable to keep up with orders. Some white men also began manufacturing canoes for the lumber business. In Old Town, Guy Carleton built bateaux and bark canoes. In Lowell, Maine, two builders, Jonathan Darling and Bill McLaine, built more than seventy-five canoes per year during the 1870s. Wood and canvas gradually replaced bark largely because birch trees large enough to make a canoe had become scarce as a result of the lumbering in the region.[7]

In 1885, *The Industrial Journal*, a Bangor newspaper, reported: "About ten years ago canvas began to be used in place of bark as a covering for canoes and a great many of this description are now made in Bangor."

Several men laid claim to the canvas canoe. By 1898, Evan H. Gerrish of Bangor could boast of twenty years of experience building the canvas canoe. In 1922, G. E. Carleton of Old Town reported that his model of canvas-covered canoe was a reproduction from a birch-bark canoe belonging to the Penobscot tribe of Indians. It had been on the market for more than thirty years, the pioneer of the modern canoe. In 1901, B. N. Morris, of Veazie reported, "I wish to impress that this style of construction is not a new idea, but one which has been in practical use at least twenty-five years." In 1910, E. M. White reported, "The White Canoe, pioneer in such craft, is among the earliest descendants of the birch."[8]

But it appears that the earliest commercial builder was E. H. Gerrish of Bangor. In 1875, he manufactured fishing rods, canoe paddles, and canvas-covered canoes. By 1878 he was making eighteen canoes per year, by 1882 he had hired an employee and was making twenty-five canoes per year, and by 1884 he manufactured fifty per year and sent canoes to the New Orleans Exposition. He hired a number of Penobscot men to assist with his manufacturing business. This early construction of canvas-covered canoes used tacks in place of lashings, but decorative lashing remained well into the 1890s. Linseed oil and layers of paint first covered the canvas.[9]

Meanwhile, in Old Town, *The Enterprise* suggested in December 1894 that "a canoe factory would pay well in Old Town." There were already seven or more builders in Old Town who were manufacturing about three hundred canoes per year in the mid-1890s. Then, in 1901, an entrepreneur named George Gray hired Henry Wickett and established the "Indian Old Town Canoe Company" in a four-story shoe factory. The following year he hired a superintendent, J. R. Robertson of Auburndale, Massachusetts, and formed a corporation with himself as president. Robertson changed the name of the company to Robertson–Old Town Canoe Company, but in 1904 the owners changed the name to the Old Town Canoe Company, its name to the present day. This company enjoyed a large measure of success. By February 1909, Old Town Canoe had built two thousand canoes.[10] Their catalogue tells the story:

The test of time and the ingenuity of the white man have found nothing of comparable size superior to the Indian model of a water craft, be it for pleasure or for service on stream, river, lake or ocean bay. Until, however there was substituted cotton duck or canvas for his birch bark covering, the use of canoes was restricted to those localities where the materials could be easily obtained, and where there were Indian workmen to apply them. Fundamentally in lines and model the watercraft of the red man survives.[11]

In 1909, scores of "Old Town Canoes" were sold to miners prospecting in northern Ontario, and many went to Alaska. A number of Penobscot Indian workmen were employed in making four models: the HW (Henry Wickett); the I.F. (guide model); the Robertson; and the Charles River. By 1912 and 1914, major four- and five-story brick additions were made to the factory, and hundreds of canoes were made per month. Penobscots found employment in the Old Town Canoe Company making canoes and paddles. A *National Geographic* magazine article in 1937 featured a picture of Penobscot men working in the Old Town Canoe Company. The caption reads:

Penobscot Braves Still Make Canoes—but of Wood, Not Birch Bark. From 10 to 20 percent of the employees of the Old Town Canoe Company are Indians living on the island reservation. At work here on the white man's adaptation of their ancestors' craft, the man at the left drills holes for screws which the other inserts as he fastens strips of red cedar to the ribs. Canvas, in place of birch bark, will be stretched tightly over the hull.[12]

The Old Town Canoe Company catalogue of 1910 highlights the role of the Penobcots, who are known as "Old Town Indians." It reads:

By our Indian workmen—and a number are included in our employees—there is infused into our canoe all that is possible of the old Indian romance such as Hiawatha felt in the lines given us by Longfellow:
"I a light canoe will build me
that will float upon the water,
Like a yellow leaf in Autumn,
Like a yellow water lily."[13]

Another source suggests that the company continued to exploit the reputation of Penobscot canoe makers, keeping them employed primarily as a marketing strategy. WPA writer Robert F. Grady recorded the following oral history in 1938.

"Henry Mitchell, an American Indian canoe maker, lives on the Penobscot Reservation on Indian Island . . . on a road recently improved by a small crew of Indian WPA workers. His home is a small, one and a half story house painted red but in need of a fresh coat."[14] Mitchell was born on the reservation at Old Town in 1884, married, and had three children. Both Henry Mitchell and his wife attended the Carlisle boarding school after high school. Upon graduating from Carlisle he found employment in Derby, Maine, but moved to Old Town in 1907 and worked in the Old Town Canoe factory for many years.

Well, I ought to know something about canoe making. I worked in that shop a good many years. But last year I couldn't get in there. I went to Perley (Cunningham, the manager) but it was no use. When a man gets to be over fifty they toss him out in favor of a younger man. . . . Henry, my boy, worked during the college vacation season in the canoe shop the last year I worked there, but he couldn't get a job there last year either. . . . Last year was a "bad year" at the shop, but this year shows promise of being a good one. I got this little job as a janitor at the schoolhouse, and I don't know what we'd do without that. It's government work.

Mrs. Mitchell added,

Henry generally worked in the railing room at the canoe shop. That shop has certainly helped the Indians a lot—so many of them work there in the summertime. Almost every one who works there has a canoe, and it is quite a sight to see all those canoes coming across the river when the men are coming over to lunch or when they're returning from work in the afternoon.

Henry reported to Grady that he was sorry he didn't take up paddle making because paddle makers could work year-round. When he started making rails he got fifteen dollars per week:

After I worked on canoes for a while they put me down on flat bottom boats and then on motorboats, putting on rails, decks and combing. I got about four dollars a day on the boats.... It costs us twelve dollars a week to live, and that job [the janitor work] pays only ten. The baskets we make help a little, but not enough. There isn't much profit in making baskets and ornaments compared to the work that goes into them.

However, this seemingly bright picture of Indian employment in the canoe factory had its darker side. When layoffs were necessary, Penobscot men often were the first to be cut.

A lot of Indians lost their jobs, but of course, he [Sam, the canoe factory manager] had to keep some of us. There was a picture of an Indian on the outside of their catalogue, and the book told about how the patient Indian craftsmen constructed the successors to their birch bark canoes. Sightseers need to come in and sometimes one of the women would say, "Oh, I want to see the Indians!" Sam would look wise and lead them around to where a few of us were working and say, "To be sure. Here are a few of them right here. We would never be able to run this place without them, I assure you."

But then when layoffs came, "Sam got us thinned out pretty well. He'd come over to some of us and say, 'Well boys, I'm sorry to have to lay you off, but we have heavy taxpayers here,[15] you know, and we feel that we should keep them at work.'" Penobscots, of course, did not pay property taxes, because they lived on the reservation, and consequently were not allowed to vote in state and national elections. Maine people believed that taxpayers should be employed before others. In spite of the uncertainty of employment and the discrimination suffered in the work place, Penobscot men have continued to work in the canoe factory throughout its eighty-year history, into the present time, as laborers, craftsmen, and designers.

The story of Penobscot men making Penobscot canoes in a factory is unique among stories of Native Americans in industry. Deep in their past,

Penobscots had invented a watercraft design so suitable for Maine that it was widely adopted by whites, who reworked the craft using different kinds of materials but retained the design. These entrepreneurial whites then created a successful business by manufacturing the canoe for a worldwide market. Penobscots took part in the commercialization of this aspect of their culture out of economic need, while the company committed a kind of cultural imperialism by promoting the craft as "Indian" and keeping Indian workers on as a tourist attraction and marketing ploy. Cultural imperialism appropriated and distorted elements of Indian culture, resulting in a loss of ownership of, for example, the Old Town canoe.[16]

Penobscots experienced conflicting feelings of pride and resentment: pride in the demand for their indigenous craft and resentment toward those who exploited them to make a profit. However, the choice to work in the canoe shop as opposed to some other wage-earning business was a form of resistance. It allowed Penobscot men to use traditional skills, to travel from home in their own canoes, and to work close to their homes while earning money so they could purchase necessities for their families.

Another kind of commercialization of Penobscot culture took place in the Indian art trade that exploited Indians by promoting their culture for consumption. According to Erik Trump, Indians' arts appealed to white American concerns about labor, modernity, and lost values. They believed that lessons from the "primitive past" could cure modern ills. In addition, Indian reform organizations promoted Indian arts and crafts as a means of assisting Indians to become economically self-sufficient.[17] Traders also promoted arts and crafts through catalogues and arts-and-crafts magazines as well as in their stores. But Penobscots were also able to resist some of this exploitation by directly marketing their wares to tourists and thus keeping the profits for themselves.

In Maine, one result of the spread of the industrial revolution was the growth of tourism, due to an increase in leisure and money among those of the middle and wealthier classes. Entrepreneurs built hotels and resorts; people flocked to Maine to enjoy the country. Penobscot artisans were there to greet them with their souvenir arts: model canoes, pincushions, fancy baskets, and toy tomahawks. As Ruth Phillips reports, souvenir arts came to dominate the artistic production of the indigenous peoples of North America throughout the twentieth century.[18]

Maine provided a welcome haven to tourists as the twentieth century began. Entrepreneurs responded to tourist demand by building hotels and boardinghouses along the coast or on the shores of Maine's many lakes. Some of the resorts, such as the Poland Spring House and the Kineo House, provided "luxury in the wilderness" for Maine's summer

FIG. 10. Chief Blue Jay Warburban in front of Penobscot Indian workshop and store. *Courtesy Maine Folklife Center, University of Maine, photograph no. 8290.*

visitors. Tourism provided income for hotel managers but also for domestic workers, restaurant workers, and craftsmen. Groups such as the Shakers and the Native Americans developed crafts designed specifically for this tourist trade—a lucrative enterprise that provided more return than mere subsistence.

While men constructed large utilitarian baskets, especially potato and pack baskets, Penobscot women primarily made the fancy basket, evolving numerous designs and forms in response to market demands. Other scholars have written about the impact of commercialization on identity formation.[19] According to Ruth Phillips, Native people successfully "commoditized" their arts, reinventing constructions of Indianness that achieved wide distribution. They had to reimagine themselves in terms of the conventions of Indianness current among the consumer group.[20] Yet Indian self-determination relies on economic independence; arts, crafts, and other traditional pursuits provide that economic independence. While the goal of priests, agents, and other reform organizations was to assimilate Indians by integrating them into the marketplace, it is clear that the goal of the Penobscots was independence. They gradually gained control over their sales by going to the consumer directly.

Baskets were widely sold and promoted by Indian traders' catalogues and in arts-and-crafts publications,[21] but Penobscots preferred to sell directly to tourists. At first the priests and the agents helped with the selling, but by the twentieth century, the growth of tourism and the popularity of tourist spots such as Bar Harbor drew forth the basket makers. They would pack their families, tents, and basket-making supplies and travel to the resorts, where they would set up camp and prepare and sell baskets directly to tourists.

According to Ruth Phillips, "Souvenir arts began as a small part of the larger hunting and fur trade subsistence. As the fur trade declined, commodity productions closely tied to the expanding tourist trade grew.[22] Penobscot families began selling baskets at summer resorts like Newport, Rhode Island, as early as 1848.[23] While Penobscots engaged in making utilitarian wares such as canoes, work moccasins, utility baskets, and ax handles, the tourist market demanded artistic commodities such as decorative clothing, ceremonial war clubs, model canoes, quill boxes, pincushions, and toys. The Penobscots, like other northeastern Indians, responded.

To meet the demand, families held basket and braiding parties in which everyone would bring food and talk and laugh and tell stories while they braided the sweet grass or made additional baskets for market.[24] Penobscots successfully took part in the commodification of their arts, reinventing constructions of "Penobscot" by reimagining themselves in terms of the conventions of the stereotypical Indian current in the early twentieth century.[25] The convention resulted from a popular belief that Native Americans were disappearing and losing their culture, and that the culture needed to be preserved. But these ideas destabilized indigenous concepts of identity as the twentieth century wore on, and Penobscots became identified with their crafts as relics of a past way of life.

People purchased baskets because they expected Natives to disappear; this gave their crafts both rarity and authenticity. Baskets and other Native crafts that had been functional became purely decorative around 1900. The fancy basket evolved from the earlier utilitarian basket technology as a response to market demands. Penobscots created (and still create) many original and peculiar designs. One nineteenth-century invention, in which a strand of weft is twisted, became a hallmark of Penobscot baskets. Later the twists were doubled. In English, this was called "Porcupine work."[26] In Penobscot, each twist was called čákık̆ıs, "little wart," attesting to the wonderful sense of humor found among basket makers. Baskets became glove boxes, napkin rings, scissors cases, candy dishes, and creamers. Numerous and varied shapes required the invention and manufacture of unique blocks to form the baskets. Often the men working in the canoe factory would make the needed blocks on the company lathes.[27] Other popular items included bookmarks, place mats, button baskets, flat handkerchief baskets, purses with folding tops, thimbles, acorn-shaped baskets to hold yarn, and many others. Penobscot men and women also made bark-and-wood model canoes, quill-decorated boxes, bark picture frames, bows and arrows, Indian dolls, model wigwams, snowshoes, sweet grass whisks, model toboggans, and moccasins.

Penobscot women brought their belongings and their children to tourist locations and set up camp in the late spring and early summer, selling souvenirs until vacationers returned home in the fall. Women and children traveled to resorts throughout New England and eastern Canada. Julia Dana Newell (née Saul) had her summer camp at Rye Beach, New Hampshire. Later she moved to Poland Spring, where she and her husband built a cabin that they covered with sheets of birch bark. Mary Swasson traveled all the way to Narragansett Pier, Rhode Island, her usual summer rendezvous for the basket trade.[28] Other families went to Belgrade Lakes and Bailey Island, Bar Harbor, and Deer Island.[29] Often the men would join them on weekends if they were working during the week, or they would find employment nearby. A great deal of work was necessary to prepare enough materials for the market. Theodore Mitchell, who was born November 20, 1919, and grew up on Indian Island, remembers the significance of the basket trade and the preparation required for the move:

> The main source of income was the basketry.... A lot of the families went to what they called "Salt Water." They scattered all up and down the coast. The set up tents and made and sold baskets. They also went and gathered sweet grass to bring back, and so they did this all summer. And then at the end of the summer they came back and the men went into the woods and got the ash logs for the winter and brought that up....[30]

Resorts appropriated Native culture in order to attract tourists, advertising the Indian artisans. The Penobscots cooperated in the cultural appropriation by building birch-bark-covered cabins and donning headdresses or other culturally distinct clothing to attract summer visitors to buy their wares.[31] Making baskets allowed women and men to earn money to help support their families while retaining some measure of cultural integrity. If this required being identified as stereotypical "Indians" in order to attract sales, they were willing to make the compromise.[32] About 100 Penobscot people left Indian Island every spring to sell their wares at summer resorts. Others set up stores on Indian Island or sold to retailers in Old Town. In the U.S Census for 1910, 85 out of 107 Penobscot women listed their occupation as basket maker, and also 13 men. (Most men listed their occupation as woods or mill worker.)

Local resorts promoted the Indian basket makers by using romantic notions of the noble savage in their publicity. For example, the following article appeared in a local publication at Poland Spring resort:

The Indians—members of the Penobscot tribe of Old Town, Me.—are here for their annual visit.

Follow one of the winding paths, leading past the golf links, past the spring, into one of the sylvan lanes which Poland Spring abounds and you find—the Indians! Here, also are tables piled with baskets. . . . For these are Indian baskets, exquisitely woven—and differing little in workmanship and pattern, probably, from those in the days when America's forests swarmed with red men, and Pocahontas, John Smith and their friends wove romances that poets have immortalized.[33]

The romance of the exotic Indian was a great draw for the city-dwelling middle-class and wealthy individuals who came to rusticate at Poland Spring and other New England resorts. At the same time, Natives participated in tourism with increasing entrepreneurial energy as producers of souvenir art. The message they were receiving from the dominant culture was to assimilate but at the same time retain ethnicity in an archaic sense. Obviously, this contradictory message created painful confusion about identity. Nevertheless, participation in the commodification of culture is one resistance strategy for economic and cultural survival that has prevailed throughout most of the nineteenth and twentieth centuries.[34]

During the 1930s, economic crises and social change disrupted the basket-making industry. American businesses devastated by the Great Depression laid off many workers, and fewer had money for extra items such as fancy baskets. Those basket makers living on reservations marketed their goods to fewer and fewer tourists.

The stock market crash created only a ripple among Maine's mostly rural populace. By 1932, however, unemployment rose to 15 percent, while income from tourism dropped about 20 percent. Pulp and paper employed about twelve thousand people in the 1930s and was not set back as much as other industries. Markets tumbled for lumber, textiles, and shoes, and many mills closed. Old Town's two woolen mills closed, for example.[35] In the face of financial difficulties, Maine's mostly Yankee population remained stubbornly independent and Republican, reflecting characteristic attitudes toward federal welfare programs and a long-standing mistrust of outside control.

However, by 1933, many communities were hard-pressed to provide relief for the growing numbers of unemployed. The first relief program, the Civilian Conservation Corps, established in 1933, recruited young men who built four hundred miles of roads, completed most of Maine's section of the Appalachian Trail, constructed campgrounds, and fought forest fires. Other relief programs provided work-relief projects; the Works Progress Administration helped many of the poorest, especially women, and Maine's Indian tribes.

Some women canned foods for school lunches; others sewed garments or nursed the sick and elderly. Bangor women sewed five thousand quilts and put up fifty thousand school lunches per week.[36] Cultural programs employed artists, writers, and musicians at various tasks. In Maine, a traveling orchestra employed one hundred musicians, while fifty writers took part in preparing *Maine: A Guide "Down East."*[37]

The *Guide* includes a description of Old Town (population 7,266) as "formerly a lumbering center":

Industrial activities today include the manufacture of woolens, wood products, paper, pulp, and toilet preparations. Better known, however, are the canoes manufactured here and sent to all parts of the world. . . . The presence of Indians working with modern equipment recalls the romance that hovered over the silvery birch craft so skillfully fashioned by their forefathers; they bring to mind the lines of Hiawatha in Longfellow's beautiful poem:

> I a light canoe will build me,
> That will float upon the water,
> Like a yellow leaf in Autumn,
> Like a yellow water lily.

The *Guide* also includes a description of the village at Indian Island:

The village, which centers around the main street extending back from the wharf, has a drab appearance, only the church, school, and parochial residence being painted. The Indians live in unplastered, weather-beaten structures, though the meagerly furnished rooms are scrupulously neat. Although some of the Indians are employed at Old Town mills, they do not like to work in factories, and the men usually find employment in the woods, on the river, and as guides during the hunting and fishing season. Each spring a great many of the Penobscots leave the island for the seashore and mountain resorts, where they camp for the summer, selling baskets, handiwork, and curios to tourists. Both men and women are skilled in basket weaving and the products of their handiwork are for sale in the shops on the island and near the ferry landing in Old Town.[38]

The *Guide* writers reinforced the romance of the "disappearing noble savage" so popular in American culture at this time and the idea that Indian men found employment in activities they excelled in: making canoes, river driving, hunting, and guiding. They also reiterated the seasonal movement of families to the resorts to take part in the tourism markets.

Glimpses into the thoughts of Maine's Penobscot Indians during the Great Depression can be found in interviews with men and women who lived through that difficult time. Henry Mitchell reported to WPA writer Robert Grady that whites seemed to think that the Indians were somehow "on the dole" and received government aid without having to pay any taxes. However, Mitchell pointed out that the Penobscots reaped none of the rewards of the property tax system, either:

We pay no direct, or property tax, but on the other hand we don't share in things that taxes help to pay for—police protection, fire protection, etc. We have our own police force, fire department, and political system. There are a lot of things we don't get unless we pay for them—clothing, amusement, lighting, water, etc. Our fuel is cut on our own land. If any one wants a radio, a lamp, or a rug, he simply has to pay for it. We have felt the depression like every one else. Before the war [World War I] a lot of us used to go to the seashores every summer to sell baskets, but very few of us go now. The people aren't buying them.

People could always get a job when I was a young man, and although that is not true today, still I think working conditions have improved since I was young. We work fewer hours a day now, and employers admit we ought to get a little more than living wages.[39]

Discrimination in the workplace probably explains to a large extent the reason that few men and women wanted to join the white man's industry. Mitchell explained:

The Indians before my time didn't work much on the other side [on the mainland in Old Town]. About all there were then were sawmills, and there were plenty of whites to run those. The old Indians used to hunt, fish and serve as guides. They made birch bark canoes and baskets.

In addition, the WPA and other relief programs were helping the Penobscots a little. There was relief for hunger, and building projects brought community improvements:

They didn't get any food allowances from the government as they do now. Living conditions, of course, weren't so good. There were more shacks, no electricity, and no city water. We've had lights for two years now. Almost every house has a radio.

Discrimination against and segregation of the Indians took place not just locally but at the state level as well. Indian representatives to the legislature were paid one-third the amount of other representatives (although Maine's representatives were not paid much to begin with, because of a tradition of citizen-legislators). The officials in Augusta said that the Indians did not do as much work as the others and consequently did not deserve as much pay. Indian representatives could not work on committees, nor could they vote. Mitchell told Grady, "Just why the Indians shouldn't vote is something I can't understand. One of the Indians went over to Old Town once to see some official in the city hall about voting. I don't know just what position that official had over there, but he said to the Indian, 'We don't want you people over here. You have your own elections over on the island, and if you want to vote, go over there.'"

WPA workers brought roads, electricity, and water to Indian Island. Radios brought news of the larger world and popular culture. As long as people remained separate, on the islands, working independently as hunters, guides, and basket makers, they could maintain a certain autonomy of politics and culture. While Penobscot culture changed and adapted to changing circumstances, the community resisted external control, making changes to suit themselves whenever possible. Consistently misunderstood and maligned, Penobscots sought education and training to improve their lives, but not to integrate themselves into mainstream America on anyone else's terms.

A summer pageant was begun on Indian Island that brought summer visitors to purchase souvenirs. By the 1930s, there were seven craft shops on Indian Island. Used to living on very little, many families were able to survive in large part by selling their home productions and by swapping or bartering. According to Ted Mitchell, families who moved into the woods to collect ash and make baskets in the wintertime got by in this manner: "They swapped, and bartered. They'd go to the farms around and swap for potatoes and different kinds of produce or maybe a ham shoulder or something. Of course, they were very frugal in terms of what they ate."[40]

When World War II began, many men and women signed on to fight, while some families moved to southern New England to work in war industries and send money home. Even then, they often made baskets to supplement their wages. Madeline Shay reported that she and her husband William Shay often made baskets "to pay the electric bill."[41]

As I have mentioned in the first chapter, after World War II few young people wanted to make baskets. However, today basket making is a great source of pride and cultural identity to the Penobscots and their other Wabanaki neighbors. So we have danced a full circle.

The story of the dance of resistance proves that cultural continuity does not mean cultural sameness, and cultural change does not result in total assimilation or extinction. Clearly, the Penobscots made numerous changes in their lives as a means of resisting assimilation and extinction. Sometimes the changes meant accommodating to the larger culture or dominant politics. But they were always accommodations under protest, with a realization of an underpinning of cultural differences. In other cases, resistance meant taking a separate path to subsistence, while recognizing a need for taking part in a market economy. Men found work that gave them some sense of autonomy because it required specialized skills in canoe making, paddle carving, hunting, or knowledge of the woods and waters. Women found work that allowed them to continue creating crafts and baskets for sale, making a living by selling to whites but not having to work for wages. As a result, they could continue to retain and pass on to their children their crafts, their language, folklore, and other aspects of Penobscot culture they wished to preserve. This is how the Penobscots resisted the overarching popular belief that they would soon be extinct.

EPILOGUE

The Role of Tradition
in the Story of a People

> Through folklore, we learn much that is otherwise concealed about the human condition.[1]
> —RICHARD M. DORSON

The dance of resistance takes place at the core of the Penobscot cultural system, which consists of spiritual power, reverence for homeland, and a belief in self-determination. Penobscot legends illuminate the cultural traits important to the Penobscot people with stories about the cultural hero, Gluskabe. Gluskabe stories illustrate that the Penobscot people value preservation of resources for future generations, hunting skills, cleverness, physical strength, bonding to place, connection to the land, spiritual power, and respect for elders. Legends provide a window to cultural beliefs. Ceremonial dances cement culture to the land and to the people living on that land. Narrative and dance traditions aid Penobscot survival through a combination of adaptation and resistance to outside forces. The Penobscot story is one facet of the Native American story.

What makes the Native American story unique in American history is the odd blend of civil rights and sovereignty that arose in response to constrictive American Indian policies in conjunction with an American tradition of treaty making. The Penobscots danced in the struggle for justice; they danced in the struggle for racial equality; they strove for economic opportunity—even as treaties and legislation rarely recognized their right to sovereignty over their own lands and people. The Penobscots consistently refused to relinquish those rights, though their efforts were often ignored.

Strategies of resistance developed and changed as a result of changing circumstances. At first, Penobscots simply removed themselves from contact with exploring Europeans. Later, they used strategies of negotiation, warfare, and alliances to restrict settlement on their lands. For instance, when settlers' cattle ate their corn, they killed them, leading to conflict with the cattle owners and creating a need for military alliances with other Abenaki communities. When an alliance with other Abenaki tribes was no longer feasible due to extended warfare and the extinction of communities, the Penobscots sought alliances with tribes to the east. All these strategies aided Penobscot survival.

Simmons, in his study of New England history and folklore, writes:

As cultural transformation and loss can be understood as consequences of Indian submersion within the larger society, cultural survival can be illuminated by attention to the ways in which Indian communities withstood these same disintegrative pressures. Indigenous cultural symbols persisted most strongly where persons of Indian descent maintained boundaries through corporate territory, political participation and internally cohesive social institutions.[2]

Today, the Penobscots maintain boundaries by retaining separate Island-based communities, using the Penobscot language, choosing subsistence activities that utilize traditional skills, retaining religious beliefs, and continuing to define themselves as an Indian nation in the face of numerous social, political, and economic changes.

Historical documents portray a mutable, unrestrained, and heterogeneous Penobscot culture. Languages spoken during the historic period include Penobscot, French, Latin, English, and Passamaquoddy-Maliseet. Racially and ethnically, the community integrated Penobscots and other related people descended from several Abenaki communities from western Maine (Norridgewock, Pigwacket, etc.), along with French and Americans of other ethnicities. Other Indian tribes represented in the community include Hurons, Mohawks, Micmacs, Maliseets, Passamaquoddies, and others. The tribe's political structure exhibited several changes, moving from a hereditary chiefdom at the beginning of the nineteenth century to an elected governor, lieutenant governor, and legislative representatives by the middle of the same century. The Penobscots later adjusted to new political realities by adopting even a biannual, alternating, two-party system of open elections.

Penobscots accepted American materials and technologies. For example, in the first part of the nineteenth century, they built bark-covered wigwams, but by the 1830s they replaced bark with wood-framed houses. However, they often used canvas tents for temporary summer residences. Many members of the community changed their residence from inland islands to the main village at Indian Island by the 1880s. Subsistence activities overlapped American culture but remained uniquely Penobscot. Hunters and gatherers became fur traders. Fur traders became river drivers and guides. Penobscot men and women transformed traditional birch-bark utensil making into basket making. In the process of building their industries, American industrialists utilized Penobscot skills in canoe building and moccasin and snowshoe manufacturing.

Penobscots often categorize themselves as "Wabanaki," a larger ethnic group that incorporated their neighbors, the Passamaquoddies and Maliseets, with whom they share some cultural traits. Penobscots also recognize cultural differences between themselves and the Passamaquoddies—their name for themselves denotes their place of residence, just as the Passamaquoddies name their community for the place for pollock fishing.

Taken as a whole, the prototypical traits of race, language, kinship, residence, and subsistence activities define Penobscots as a people in an anthropological sense. However, historical documents reveal constantly repeated themes over the past three centuries. The Penobscots wanted their lands left alone, with natural resources remaining intact. The Penobscots retained legal sovereignty over their lands, natural resources, and their people, although local white people and official representatives of the government did not always recognize these rights. The Penobscots wanted their own church and pastor, for the most part Catholic, but with some dissent in later years. The Penobscots wanted an education and schools of their own, so that they could learn to read, write, and otherwise conduct business in the American economy and culture.

The struggle for economic opportunity recurs throughout Penobscot history. At first, the effort to find new ways to make a living was coupled with a desire for education, as Penobscot leaders requested assistance in learning how to raise crops and livestock; later, they sought jobs and marketing prospects where they could use traditional knowledge and skills. In addition, the Penobscots sought justice, requesting that persons who had harmed them be prosecuted under the law. Finally, the Penobscots wanted representation and suffrage. They sent representatives to the seat of government at every legislative session with petitions from their community leaders, and they requested the right to vote.

These desires of the Penobscots contrasted sharply with what Maine historians and political leaders expected and believed about them. Constantly recurring themes in historical writings and in policy making indicate that state leaders believed the Penobscots obstructed development of the land. They believed that Penobscots would become extinct. They believed that Penobscots were strictly wards of the state—without any real rights of citizenship and without sovereignty. Many believed that Penobscots were dull and lazy and not interested in self-improvement, and that they were inferior and not worthy of citizenship. Such ignorance stems from an inability to understand or appreciate the creativity and intelligence that lived in the hearts and minds of the Indian Island people.

These attitudes have affected our understanding and analysis of the American Indian experience in Maine and the United States. Although Penobscots define themselves largely by ideal traits such as race, language, geographical location, interests, and habits, they nevertheless are and have always been Americans; as such they are and were members of a larger self-defined group, with concurrent identity, nationalism, privileges, and responsibilities. The privileges were hard earned; the work involved in earning them included serving with other American soldiers in three major wars without benefit of citizenship or suffrage.

Penobscots have long held the right to govern their own people and their own lands by virtue of the treaties negotiated between their leaders and those of the government. However, they were long kept in a state of dependence by an Indian policy that did not recognize their treaty rights. Yet they managed by virtue of a persistent petitioning of the state authorities to retain a land base and to gradually improve their own standard of living through education and industrious wage earning and basket making. The Penobscots focused their self-improvement efforts upon the education and spiritual guidance of their children. As a result, some young people were able to move on to high school and college as early as the nineteenth century. The Penobscots continue to create a community with an ethnic identity, with strong moral convictions—convictions that include American nationalism and integration into the American economy.

The state viewed the Penobscots as wards, but they did not see themselves as such. The state viewed them as an impediment to its own land-use goals. The Penobscots asked only for protection for their lands, property, and persons, and for appropriations from their own funds to run their government, provide a school and a spiritual leader, and help the poor and infirm.

The most important observation arising from the historical documents exhibits the absolutely unrelenting desire of state officials to remove sovereignty from the hands of the Indian tribal leaders and the Penobscots' persistence in resisting the state's efforts. Penobscots have a broader vision encompassing American Indian policy as a whole, based on legal precedent of great historical depth. Penobscots know that they hold ownership of the lands unless and until they sell that right by treaty. The Penobscots never sold that right entirely, though they did, under pressure, sell vast parcels of their lands to Massachusetts and Maine. This central belief in tribal sovereignty and the long-standing connection to their island territory define the community as a political and cultural entity in spite of the social and economic adaptations they have been required to make over the course of written history to the twentieth century, when,

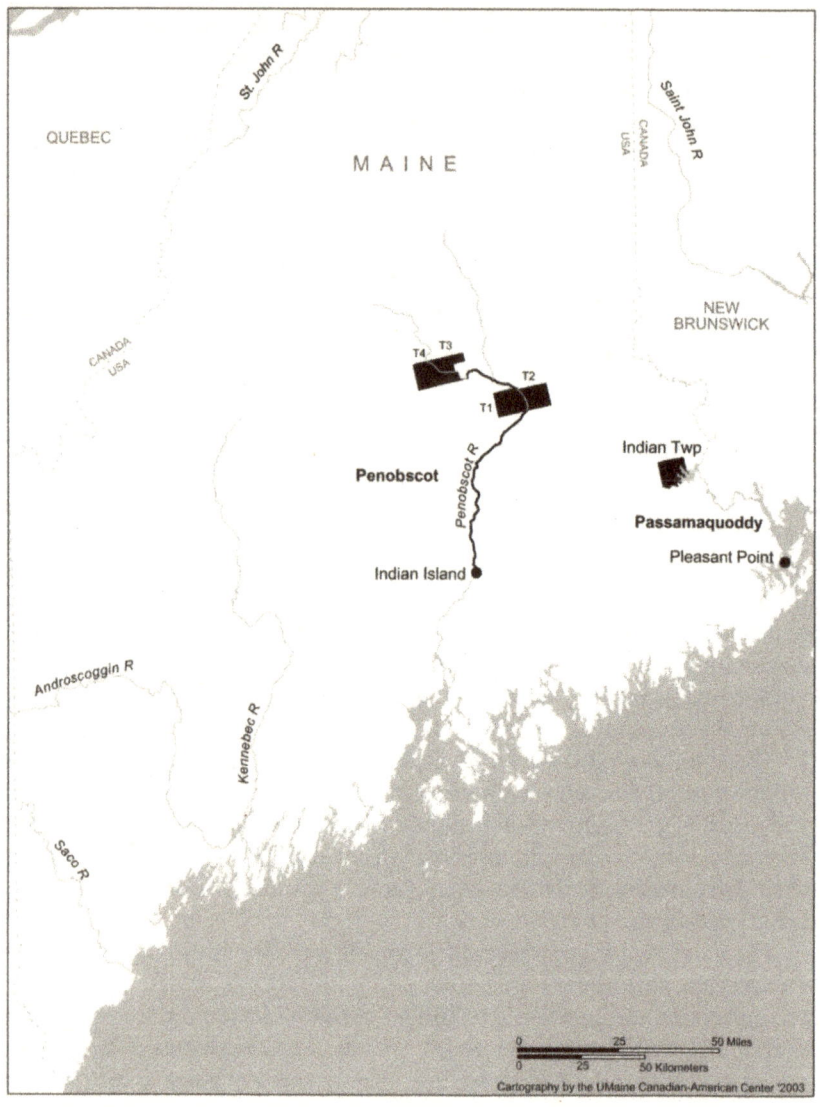

MAP 4. Post-land claims Penobscot Indian Nation land holdings. *Cartography by Michael Hermann, Canadian American Center, University of Maine.*

through the Maine Indian Claims Settlement Act of 1980, they were able to reacquire some of the lands they had previously lost.[3]

Protests and political activity were not new to Penobscot leaders in the 1970s, as the historical record illustrates. However, in the period encompassing the Great Depression and World War II, the Penobscots experienced some of the worst poverty, poor health, and hardship ever. Men and women who went to war for their country returned and were told that they could not vote and were not given jobs to support their families. They were told to engage in their own elections, that they had no voice in state and national issues, and that they were wards of the state and therefore not in need of jobs. It was the veterans and their children, the young college-age activists, who, like Gluskabe, transformed the community for the benefit of their people.

The complete in-depth story of Penobscot political activism of the twentieth century must wait for another time. Though I touched on it briefly in an earlier chapter, I will summarize here. From the 1970s to 2001, Penobscots experienced many changes, including federal recognition, housing and health improvements, success in the courts, more political clout as the result of the land claims case, and, consequently, the ability to effect change in the Maine legislature. In their political activism, the Penobscots again turned to traditions. They were aided by the Boasian tradition of American anthropology that restores and recaptures culture. They could point to the work of anthropologists such as Frank G. Speck and others who sought to restore the authentic dimension of Native American cultural identity that has endured after colonial destruction.[4] Reference to tradition helped Penobscots define themselves in terms understandable to others, especially by enlisting the aid of academics who could point to published works on their culture. Like other Native Americans in the activist movement of the 1970s, Penobscots used cultural traditions to lend weight to their land claims case by "brandishing notions of rights and entitlements as outcomes of cultural consciousness in the public arena."[5] This was a strategy that finally brought success.

Notes

Prologue (pp. 1–15)

1. Stelle U. Ogunwole, *The American Indian and Alaska Native Population 2000* (Washington, D.C.: U.S. Department of Commerce, Economics, and Statistics Administration, 2002).
2. Howard Meredith, *Modern American Indian Tribal Government and Politics* (Tsaile, Ariz.: Navajo Community College Press, 1993), 6–7.
3. Klaus Frantz, *Indian Reservations in the United States: Territory, Sovereignty, and Economic Change* (Chicago: University of Chicago Press, 1999), 99, 102, 128, 139; Meredith, 5.
4. Ward Churchill, *Struggle for the Land* (Winnipeg: Arbeiter Ring, 1999), 19–20.
5. Micaela DiLeonardo, *Exotics at Home: Anthropologies, Others, American Modernity* (Chicago: University of Chicago Press, 1998), 21.
6. Marshall Sahlins, *How "Natives" Think: About Captain Cook, for Example* (Chicago: University of Chicago Press, 1995), 12.
7. Eric Wolf, *Europe and the People without History* (Berkeley: University of California Press, 1982), 56.
8. Francis Jennings, "A Growing Partnership: Historians, Anthropologists and American Indian History," *The History Teacher* vol. 14, no. 1 (November 1980): 97.
9. Ibid.
10. William Roseberry, *Anthropologies and Histories: Essays in History, Culture and Political Economy* (New Brunswick, N.J.: Rutgers University Press, 1989), 49.
11. Sahlins, 119.
12. Vine Deloria, Jr., *Custer Died for Your Sins: An Indian Manifesto* (New York: Avon, 1970).
13. In 1970 a symposium funded by the Bureau of Indian Affairs was held at the annual meeting of the American Anthropological Association to discuss the issues raised in Deloria's book, resulting in the adoption of the AAA Code of Ethics in 1971. Thomas Biolsi and Larry J. Zimmerman, *Indians & Anthropologists: Vine Deloria Jr. and the Critique of Anthropology* (Tucson: University of Arizona Press, 1997), 4.
14. Ibid., 17.

15. Herbert T. Hoover, "Vine Deloria, Jr., in American Historiography," in Biolsi and Zimmerman, 33.
16. Elizabeth S. Grobsmith, "Growing up on Deloria: The Impact of His Work on a New Generation of Anthropologists," in Biolsi and Zimmerman, 47.
17. Vine Deloria Jr., "Anthros, Indians, and Planetary Reality," in Biolsi and Zimmerman, 213.
18. Ibid., 221.
19. Devon A. Mihesuah, *Natives and Academics: Researching and Writing about American Indians* (Lincoln: University of Nebraska Press, 1998), 2.
20. Donald Fixico, "Ethics and Responsibilities in Writing about American Indian History," in Mihesuah, 90.
21. Duane Champagne, "American Indian Studies Is for Everyone," in Mihesuah, 182.
22. Robin Fox, *The Challenge of Anthropology: Old Encounters, New Excursions* (New Brunswick, N.J.: Transaction Publishers, 1994), 14.
23. James Axtell, "A Moral History of Indian-White Relations Revisited," *The History Teacher* 16 (February 1983): 184.
24. Ibid.
25. Sahlins, 12.
26. Axtell, 101.
27. Jerry Mander, *In the Absence of the Sacred: The Failure of Technology and the Survival of the Indian Nations* (San Francisco: Sierra Club Books, 1991), 214–15. Cited in Thomas C. Parkhill, *Weaving Ourselves into the Land: Charles Godfrey Leland, "Indians," and the Study of Native American Religions* (Albany: State University of New York Press, 1997), 112.
28. Parkhill, 114.
29. Both quotes from Maine Indian Tribal State Commission, *Wabanaki: A New Dawn*, Tribal State Commission video, 1995.
30. Susan Young, "Tribe Tests of Water Led to Fine: Falsified Records Cost Champion $800,000," *Bangor Daily News*, July 24, 2000, 1.
31. Penobscot song of greeting, sung by Francis Joseph Dana of Lincoln, Maine. Cited in Natalie Curtis Burlin, *The Indians' Book* (1923; reprint, New York: Dover Publishers, 1968), 14.
32. Linda Gilbert Davenport, "Music among the Contemporary Penobscot Indians" (Master's thesis, University of Illinois, Urbana, 1977), 51.
33. Ibid.
34. Frank G. Speck, *Penobscot Man: The Life History of a Forest Tribe in Maine* (Orono: University of Maine, 1999), 270.
35. Samuel Taylor Coleridge, *Christobal*.
36. Joseph Nicolar, *The Life and Traditions of the Red Man* (Bangor: C. H. Glass, 1893).
37. Fannie Hardy Eckstorm, *Indian Place-Names of the Penobscot Valley and the Maine Coast* (Orono: University of Maine Studies, 1941); *Old John Neptune and Other Maine Indian Shamans* (Portland: The Southworth-Anthoensen Press, 1945); "The Indians of Maine," in *Maine: A History*, vol. I, ed. Louis Clinton Hatch (New York: The American Historical Society, 1919).
38. Speck, *Penobscot Man*.
39. Rev. William Hubbard, *A General History of New England from its Discovery to MDCLXXX* (Cambridge: Massachusetts Historical Society, Hillard & Metcalf, 1815).

40. James Sullivan, *The History of the District of Maine* (Boston: [s.n.] 1795, printed by I. Thomas and E. T. Andrews).

41. William D. Williamson, *The History of the State of Maine; From Its First Discovery, AD 1602, The Separation, AD 1820, inclusive* (Hallowell: Glazier, Masters & Smith, 1839).

42. William Leo Lucey, S.J., *The Catholic Church in Maine* (Francestown: Marshal Jones Co., 1957).

43. Robert Howard Lord, John E. Sexton, and Edward T. Harrington, *History of the Archdiocese of Boston in the Various Stages of Its Development, 1604–1943*, 3 vols. (New York: Sheed & Ward, 1944).

44. Colin Calloway, *Dawnland Encounters: Indians and Europeans in Northern New England* (Hanover, N.H.: University Press of New England, 1991); *The Western Abenakis of Vermont, 1600–1800: War, Migration, and the Survival of an Indian People* (Norman: University of Oklahoma Press, 1990); ed., *After King Philip's War: Presence and Persistence in Indian New England* (Hanover, N.H.: University Press of New England, 1997); *The American Revolution in Indian Country: Crisis and Diversity in Native American Communities* (Cambridge: Cambridge University Press, 1995).

45. Kenneth M. Morrison, *The Embattled Northeast: The Elusive Ideal of Alliance in Abenaki-Euramerican Relations* (Berkeley: University of California Press, 1984).

46. Neal Salisbury, *Manitou and Providence: Indians, Europeans, and the Making of New England, 1500–1643* (New York: Oxford University Press, 1982).

47. Steven F. Johnson, *Ninnuock (the People): The Algonkian People of New England* (Marlborough, Mass.: Bliss Publishing Co., 1995); Frederick Matthew Wiseman, *The Voice of the Dawn: An Autohistory of the Abenaki Nation* (Hanover, N.H.: University Press of New England, 2001).

48. Richard W. Judd, Edwin A. Churchill, and Joel W. Eastman, eds., *Maine the Pine Tree State: From Prehistory to the Present* (Orono: University of Maine Press, 1995).

49. Bunny McBride, *Molly Spotted Elk, a Penobscot in Paris* (Norman: University of Oklahoma Press, 1995), and *Women of the Dawn* (Lincoln: University of Nebraska Press, 1999).

50. Samuel de Champlain, *The Works of Samuel de Champlain*, 6 vols., ed. H. P. Biggar (Toronto: Champlain Society, 1922–36).

51. James Phinney Baxter, *Documentary History of the State of Maine* (Portland: Maine Historical Society, 1907).

52. Paul Brodeur, *Restitution: The Land Claims of the Mashpee, Passamaquoddy, and Penobscot Indians of New England* (Boston: Northeastern University Press, 1985).

1. Dancing into View: Post–World War II Political Activism (pp. 16–35)

1. James Sappier, quoted in Pamela Wood, "In Search of the 20th Century Penobscot," *Salt* (winter 1983): 51.

2. United States Congress, "An Act to Provide for the Settlement of Land Claims of Indians, Indian Nations, and Tribes and Bands of Indians in the State of Maine, Including the Passamaquoddy Tribe, the Penobscot Nation, and the

Houlton Band of Maliseet Indians, and for Other Purposes" (Washington, D.C.: Superintendent of Documents).

3. Wood, 52.
4. Ibid.
5. Ralph W. Proctor, "Report on Maine Indians: Prepared at Request of Legislative Research Committee, September, 1942." (Augusta, Maine: Legislative Research Committee, 1942). Typescript, Special Collections, Raymond F. Fogler Library, University of Maine, Orono, 9.
6. Ibid.
7. Ibid.
8. Ibid., 10.
9. Madeline Tomer Shay, tape-recorded interview. Northeast Archives #2383.
10. Maine, *A Compilation of Laws Pertaining to Indians* (Augusta: Maine Department of Indian Affairs, 1974).
11. United States Congress, "An Act to Provide for the Settlement of Land Claims."
12. Clarence Francis, quoted in Wood, 37.
13. Violet Francis, quoted in Wood, 43.
14. Montague Chamberlain, "The Penobscot Indians, a Brief Account of Their Present Condition," *Cambridge Tribune*, February 4, 1899. Chamberlain was the first to assist Penobscot boys and girls to go to Carlisle; later, other children followed.
15. Junior Pehrson, quoted in Wood, 69.
16. Michael Sockalexis, informal interview with author, August 1, 2000.
17. Andrew Akins, telephone interview with author, April 2, 2002.
18. Andrew Akins, telephone interview with author, July 31, 2000.
19. Some of the most active tribal leaders at that time were the men who had lived on the island all their lives: Mathew Sappier, Richard Sappiel, John Mitchell, Sr., Ernest Goslin, Francis "Bunny" Ranco, and others.
20. Lee-Ann Konrad with Christine Nicholas, *Artists of the Dawn: Christine Nicholas & Senabeh* (Orono: Northeast Folklore Society, 1987), 14–15.
21. "Baxter Gates Shut to Keep Occupation from Growing," *Maine Sunday Telegram*, April 18, 1976, 24A, and "Indians Want Katahdin Back," *Maine Times*, April 23, 1976, 26. "Park Rangers Seize 12 Indians," *Bangor Daily News*, April 21, 1976, 1, 2.
22. Davenport, 32.
23. John Bear Mitchell, Barry Dana, Huey, Michael Vermette, *Our Dances*, video, 1997.
24. Troy Johnson, Joane Nagel, and Duane Champagne, *American Indian Activism: Alcatraz to the Longest Walk* (Urbana: University of Illinois Press, 1997), 14.
25. Ibid., 10–11.
26. Ibid.
27. Ibid., 16.
28. Ibid., 27.
29. Vine Deloria, Jr., "The Rise of Indian Activism," in *The Social Reality of Ethnic America*, ed. R. Gomez, C. Collingham, R. Endo, and K. Jackson (Lexington, Mass.: D. C. Heath and Co., 1974), 184–85.
30. "A Traditional Indian Looks Ahead," *Wabanaki Alliance*, May 1978, 10.
31. Judith Leader, "An Ethnohistory of the Passamaquoddy Tribe" (Ph.D. diss., Boston University, 1995), 163.

32. *Bangor Daily News*, May 19, 1964, 1; May 28, 1964, 30.
33. Leader, 167.
34. Thomas N. Tureen, "Tureen Tells Story of Claims," *Wabanaki Alliance*, January 1982, 1.
35. "Under the Constitution of the United States, the power to regulate commerce with the Indian Tribes is expressly vested in Congress. By virtue of this clause, traffic or intercourse with an Indian Tribe or member of such a tribe is subject to the regulations of Congress, although it is within the limits of a State, the power of Congress being superior and paramount to the authority of any such State, within whose limits are Indian Tribes." Department of Health and Welfare, January 29, 1963, Memo from Donald F. Brown, p. 1, Maine State Archives, Maine Department of Indian Affairs Box.
36. "Passamaquoddies Go on Legal Warpath Against Commonwealth of Massachusetts," *Lewiston Journal*, March 9, 1968; "Passamaquoddies Aim: $150 Million from Bay State," *Bangor Daily News*, March 11, 1968.
37. Tureen, 1.
38. Ibid., 6.
39. Ibid.
40. United States District Court Northern Division, *The United States of America, Plaintiff, v. The State of Maine, Defendant*, Civil Action Docket no. 1966 N.D. "Justice Department Outlines Indian Case," *Bangor Daily News*, March 2, 1977, 14.
41. *Passamaquoddy v. Morton*, 528 F. 2d 370 (1st Cir 1975).
42. By legal precedent, Congress had the option of extinguishing "aboriginal title at any time." Senator William Cohen, "The Penobscot and Passamaquoddy Land Claim in Maine," *Congressional Record*, March 1, 1977.
43. Tureen, 6.
44. Ibid.
45. Ibid.
46. Ibid.
47. United States, "Maine Indian Claims Settlement Act of 1980," vol. 1, 96th Congress, Second Session, LAWS (P.L. 96-420), ch. 19, Title 25, subchapter 2, sec. 1724 and sec. 6212, U.S. Code Congressional and Administrative News, 1980.
48. "Money Arrives, Lands Bought," *Wabanaki Alliance*, May 1981, 1.
49. "The Winners," *Wabanaki Alliance*," March 1981, editorials, 2.
50. United States, "Maine Indian Claims Settlement Act of 1980," 13–14.
51. Native American Rights Fund, "Announcements," *Annual Report*, vol. 7, no. 1 (May 1981).
52. United States, U.S. Code Congressional and Administrative News, 1980, Maine Indian Claims Settlement, Federal Act, ch. 19, Title 25, subchapter 2, sec. 6212.
53. Maine Indian Tribal-State Commission web page at http://www.ptla.org/news/wabanaki/commn.htm, Fall 1996.
54. United States Census Bureau, 1990, http://www.census.gov/cdrom/lookup. The figures for the state with a total population of 1,227,928 in 1990 are 16% under high school education, 28% high school diploma, 13.5% some college, 5% associate degree, 9% bachelor's degree, and 4% graduate or professional degree. This information is not compiled for the 2000 Census.
55. Ibid. The median household income for the whole state in 1990 was $27,854.

56. Ibid.
57. Susan Hand Shetterly, "The River They Call Home," *Audubon*, July/August 2000, 81.
58. Pauleena M. MacDougall, "Grandmother, Daughter, Princess, Squaw: Native American Female Stereotypes in Historical Perspective," *Maine History* 34 (summer 1994), 37–38.
59. As related by Carol Dana to the author and in the film *Abenaki: People of the Dawn*.
60. Ibid.
61. Maine Indian Tribal-State Commission, *Wabanaki: A New Dawn*.
62. Mitchell et al., *Our Dances*.
63. Konrad with Nicholas, 18.
64. Sockalexis.
65. Mitchell et al., *Our Dances*.
66. William D. Williamson, *History of the State of Maine*, 1: 670–71. "In future ages, a Native will be viewed as a curiosity by civilized man. . . ."

2. Land, Power, and Reverence: Core Teachings That Sustain Resistance (pp. 36–53)

1. Nicolar, *Life and Traditions of the Red Man*, 9–10.
2. Ibid.
3. Henry Glassie, "Tradition," *Journal of American Folklore*, 108 (fall 1995): 396.
4. Frank G. Speck, "Penobscot Shamanism," *Memoirs of the American Anthropological Association*, vol. 6, no. 28 (Millwood, N.Y.: Kraus reprint, 1919), 258.
5. Ibid., 255.
6. Frank G. Speck "Penobscot Transformer Tales," *International Journal of American Linguistics*, vol. 1, no. 3 (New York: Douglas C. McMurtrie, 1918): 192.
7. Ibid., 192.
8. Ibid, 193.
9. Frank T. Siebert, Jr., manuscript of Penobscot tales, Siebert Papers, American Philosophical Society, Philadelphia.
10. Franz Boas, "The Eskimo of Baffin Land and Hudson Bay," *Bulletin of the American Museum of Natural History*, 15 (New York, 1901–7); "Geographical Names of the Kwakiutl Indians," *Columbia University Contributions to Anthropology*, 20 (New York, 1934); J. P. Harrington, "The Ethnogeography of the Tewa Indians" *Annual Report of the Bureau of American Ethnology*, 29 (Washington, D.C., 1916); Floyd Lounsbury, "Iroquois Place-Names in the Champlain Valley," *Report of the New York–Vermont Interstate Commission on Lake Champlain Basin*, New York: Legislative Document 9 (Albany, 1960): 21–66; Keith H. Basso " 'Stalking with Stories': Names, Places, and Moral Narratives among the Western Apache," in Edward M. Bruner and Stuart Plattner, eds., *Text, Play, and Story: The Construction and Reconstruction of Self and Society*, 1983 Proceedings of the American Ethnological Society (Washington, D.C.: The American Ethnological Society, 1984), 19–55.
11. Basso, 32.

12. See Eckstorm, *Indian Place-Names*, for many examples.
13. Speck, "Penobscot Transformer Tales," 199.
14. Ibid., 200–201.
15. Proto-Algonquian forms given to me by David Pentland, University of Manitoba.
16. Speck, "Penobscot Tales and Religious Beliefs," 6–7, and "Penobscot Shamanism," 243.
17. Eckstorm, *Old John Neptune*, 25.
18. Translations of both Speck and Siebert's informants given here. Speck, "Penobscot Shamanism," 249; Siebert, Penobscot Dictionary manuscript, author's copy, 353.
19. Speck, "Penobscot Tales and Religious Beliefs," 57.
20. Eugene Vetromile, *The Abenakis and Their History* (New York: J. B. Kirker, 1866), 62–65.
21. Speck, "Penobscot Tales and Religious Beliefs," 16.
22. In nearly every collection of Penobscot legends there is at least one about Mohawk raids.
23. McBride, *Women of the Dawn*, tells the story of these four Penobscot women.
24. "Green Corn Song." This first part is sung without accompaniment when an elderly woman representing the first mother enters the dance. It is a kind of death song honoring her for giving her life so that the people could have corn to eat. Davenport, 151.
25. Frederick Hoxie, *Parading through History: The Making of the Crow Nation in America, 1805–1935* (Cambridge: Cambridge University Press, 1995), 60. Of course, large urban centers like Cahokia did exist in North America in the past.
26. Gary B. Nash, *Red, White & Black: The Peoples of Early North America* (Upper Saddle River, N.J.: Prentice-Hall, 1992), 25; Russell Thornton, "The Demography of Colonialism," in Russell Thornton, ed., *Studying Native America: Problems and Prospects* (Madison: Wisconsin University Press, 1998), 19.
27. Perry Miller, *Errand into the Wilderness* (Cambridge, Mass.: Belknap Press, 1956), 5.
28. David B. Quinn, "The Early Cartography of Maine," in *American Beginnings: Exploration, Culture, and Cartography in the Land of Norumbega*, ed. Emerson W. Baker, Edwin A. Churchill, Richard S. D'Abate, Kristine L. Jones, Victor A. Konrad, and Harald E. L. Prins (Lincoln: University of Nebraska Press, 1994), 44.
29. David B. Quinn, Alison M. Quinn, and Susan Hillier, eds., *New American World: A Documentary History of North America to 1612*, 5 vols. (New York: Arno Press, 1979), 1:273–79.
30. Quinn, "Early Cartography of Maine," 45–46.
31. Champlain, Samuel de, *Voyages to New France, being a narrative of the many remarkable things that happened in the West Indies in the years 1599 to 1601, with an account of the manners and customs of the savages of Canada and a description of that country in the year 1603* (Ottawa: Oberon Press, 1971).
32. Samuel Eliot Morison, *The European Discovery of America* (New York: Oxford University Press, 1993), 1:309–311.
33. Henry Sweetser Burrage, *Early English and French Voyages: Chiefly from Hakluyt, 1534–1608* (New York: Barnes & Noble, 1967), 391–94, 394 n. 1.

34. Champlain, *Works*, 1:49–50.
35. Marc Lescarbot, "Nova Francia, or, The description of that part of New France which is one continent with Virginia [microform]: described in the three late voyages and plantation made by Mons. de Monts, Mons. du Pon-Gravé, and Mons. De Poutrincourt, into the countries called by the Frenchman La Cadia, lying to the southwest of Cape Breton: together with an excellent several treaty of all the commodities of the said countries, and manners of the natural inhabitants of the same," *Nova Francia* ([London?]: s.n., [1745?]), 99.
36. Champlain, *Works*, 1:88.
37. Ibid., 1:89, Lescarbot, *Nova Francia*, 99.
38. Champlain, *Works*, 1:105.
39. Ibid., 108.
40. Ibid.
41. Ibid., 111–13.
42. Ibid., 403–14.
43. Frank T. Siebert, Jr., "The Identity of the Tarratines, with an Etymology," *Studies in Linguistics*, 23 (1973): 69–76. (Pring called the Micmacs Tarentyns, a Basque word that historians have used incorrectly to designate any number of tribes, including the Penobscots, but should apply only to the Micmacs.)
44. Lescarbot, *Nova Francia*, 101.
45. William D. Williamson, *History of the State of Maine*, 1:215.
46. We know from archaeological evidence that there were numerous small villages along the coast that no longer existed after this time. See David Sanger, "An analysis of Seasonal Transhumance Models for Pre-European State of Maine," *Review of Archeology* 17 (spring 1996): 54–58.
47. Lewis Spence, *Myth and Ritual in Dance, Game, and Rhyme* (London: Watts and Co., 1947).
48. Glassie, 405.
49. Ibid.

3. Facing the Future: The Seventeenth Century (pp. 54–67)

1. Glassie, 396.
2. Henry F. Dobyns, *Their Number Become Thinned: Native American Population Dynamics in Eastern North America* (Knoxville: University of Tennessee Press in cooperation with the Newberry Library Center for the History of the American Indian, 1983), 10.
3. W. H. McNeill, *Plagues and Peoples: A Natural History of Infectious Diseases* (New York: Anchor Press/Doubleday, 1976), 177.
4. Ibid., 186, 190.
5. Ibid., 202.
6. Ann F. Ramenofsky, *Vectors of Death: The Archeology of European Contact* (Albuquerque: University of New Mexico Press, 1987), 98–100.
7. Dobyns, 10.
8. Ramenofsky, 100, 173.
9. Ibid., 174.
10. Speck, *Penobscot Man*, 16.
11. Sanger, 54–58.

12. Bruce Bourque, "Aboriginal Settlement and Subsistence on the Maine Coast," *Man in the Northeast* 6 (1973), 3–20.
13. R. Thwaites, Lettre du P. Biard, in *Travels and Explorations of the Jesuit Missionaries in New France* (Cleveland: Burrows Brothers, 1896), cited in Sanger, 54.
14. Samuel De Champlain, *Les Voyages Du Sieur de Champlain Xaintongeois, Capitaine ordinaire pour le Roy al marine* (Paris: Iaean Berjon's shop, M.DC.XIII); Champlain, *Works*, 292, 321.
15. A period from about A.D. 1300 to 1700 in which the temperatures of the Northern Hemisphere were colder than normal.
16. Letter from Father Biard to Reverend Father Christopher Baltazar, Provincial of France, at Paris, Reuben Gold Thwaites, ed., *The Jesuit Relations and Allied Documents: Travels and Explorations of the Jesuit Missionaries in New France, 1610–1791* (New York: Pageant Book Co., 1959), vol. 1: *Acadia*, 169, 177.
17. Ibid., 1:169.
18. Letter from Port Royal Acadia to General of Society of Jesus, by Rev. Pierre Biard, 1611, in ibid., 1:257.
19. Letter from Port Royal Acadia to General of Society of Jesus, by Rev. Pierre Biard, 1611, in ibid., 2:75.
20. Bruce G. Trigger, *Natives and Newcomers: Canada's "Heroic Age" Reconsidered* (Kingston and Montreal: McGill-Queen's University Press, 1985), 246.
21. Letter from Port Royal Acadia to General of Society of Jesus, by Rev. Pierre Biard, in Thwaites, ed., *Jesuit Relations* 2:89.
22. Hubbard, *General History of New England*, 161.
23. Ibid.
24. Ibid.
25. A type of small, wooden boat introduced to the region by Basque fishermen.
26. Speck, "Penobscot Transformer Tales," 192.
27. Letter of Sebastian Rasles, in Thwaites, ed., *Jesuit Relations*, 67:133.
28. Letter from Father Sebastian Rasles, 12 Oct. 1723, in ibid., 67:137.
29. Sullivan, 282.
30. See Morrison, *Embattled Northeast*; David Lynn Ghere, "Abenaki Factionalism, Emigration and Social Continuity: Indian Society in Northern New England, 1725 to 1765" (Ph.D. diss., University of Maine, Orono, 1988); Calloway, *Dawnland Encounters*.
31. Ronald O. MacFarlane, "The Massachusetts Bay Truckhouses in Diplomacy with the Indians," *New England Quarterly* 11 (March 1938): 48–65; and Massachusetts Council, "Resolution Concerning trade with the Eastern Indians" (October 14, 1727), Massachusetts Archives, 31:149.
32. Burlin, 7–8.
33. Eckstorm, "Indians of Maine," 46–47.
34. Father Louis P. Thury to Minister, January–February 1699, Bibliotheque de St. Sulpican, Montreal (copies in Public Archives of Canada).
35. Champlain, *Works*, 321.
36. Sullivan, 160.
37. Hubbard, *General History of New England*, 629.

38. Charles II of England ceded part of the District of Maine to France in the Treaty of Breda. Sullivan, 158.
39. Gorham Munson, "St. Castin: A Legend Revised," *Dalhousie Review*, vol. 45, no. 3 (1965): 348.
40. Ibid., 359; Sullivan; John E. Godfrey, "Jean Vincent, Baron De Saint Castin," *Collections of the Maine Historical Society* (Bath: Maine Historical Society, 1876), 1st series, 7:41–71; and "Castine The Younger," *Collections of the Maine Historical Society* (Bath: Maine Historical Society, 1876) 1st series, 7:75–92.
41. Godfrey, "Castine the Younger," 7:76.
42. Eckstorm, "Indians of Maine," 46–47.
43. Gabriel Druillettes, in Thwaite, ed., *Jesuit Relations*, 36:79.
44. William D. Williamson, *History of the State of Maine*, 575.

4. War Dance: Shifting Strategies in the Dance of Resistance (pp. 68–92)

1. "War Dance," Burlin, 8.
2. Letter from Father ****, Missionary to the Abenakis St. Francois, October 21, 1757, in Thwaites, ed., *Jesuit Relations* 71:95–101.
3. Ibid.
4. Calloway, *Western Abenakis of Vermont*, 89.
5. By Abenaki, I am referring to the peoples of Maine who were not specifically living on the Penobscot River. These included the Norridgewock or Caniba of the Kennebec, the Pigwackets of Fryburg and the Sokokis near the Saco, the people of the Androscoggin River, and the Wawenocks near the St. George River. After numerous wars wiped out their villages, some of these people later joined the Penobscots; others went to Canadian villages, while some remained in small family groups near their old villages.
6. This strongly supports the idea that the Jesuits had no role in inciting the war in spite of English fears. See Morrison, *Embattled Northeast*, 158.
7. Calloway, *Western Abenakis of Vermont*, 79.
8. Leo Bonfanti, *Biographies and Legends of the New England Indians*, New England Historical Series (Wakefield, Mass.: Pride Publications, 1970), 5:24.
9. William Hubbard, *The history of the Indian wars in New England, from the first settlement to the termination of the war with King Philip in 1677* (New York: B. Franklin, 1971), reprint of the 1865 ed. first published in 1677 *A narrative of the troubles with the Indians in New England* (page citations are to the reprint edition), 410; William D. Williamson, *History of the State of Maine*, 547.
10. William D. Williamson, *History of the State of Maine*, 517. See also Speck, *Penobscot Man*, 230–36, for a discussion of Penobscot kinship system and its political ramifications.
11. Hubbard, *The history of the Indian wars in New England*, 669–670.
12. William Hubbard, *A narrative of the troubles with the Indians in New England, from the first planting thereof in the year 1607 to this present year 1677. But chiefly of the late troubles in the two last years, 1675. and 1676. To which is added a discourse about the warre with the Pequods in the year 1637* (Boston: Printed by John Foster, 1677), microfilm: Ann Arbor, Mich., University Microfilms [n.d.], 1 reel (American culture series, reel 7.76) 2:149–50.

NOTES   213

13. Calloway, ed., *After King Philip's War*, 4.
14. Raymond J. DeMallie, "Kinship: The Foundation for Native American Society," in Thornton, ed., 321–328.
15. William D. Williamson, *History of the State of Maine*, 519; Frank T. Siebert, Jr., "First Maine Indian War: Incident at Machias," in *Actes du Quatorzieme Congres Des Algonquinistes*, ed. William Cowan (Ottawa: Carleton University, 1983), 137–58.
16. Morrison, *Embattled Northeast*, 112; Province and Court Records of Maine, February 21, 1683, 3:190.
17. William D. Williamson, *History of the State of Maine*, 588, 594.
18. Ibid., 575–76.
19. Ibid.
20. Ibid.
21. Ibid., 614–15.
22. Ibid.
23. Massachusetts archives 1622–1799 (Boston: Commonwealth of Massachusetts, Archives Division), 1977 reels; microfilm M3821. 1–326, Raymond H. Fogler Library, University of Maine, Orono, 30:464–71.
24. William D. Williamson, *History of the State of Maine*, 643.
25. Ibid., 646.
26. Ibid., 648.
27. Frank T. Siebert, Jr., "Wenemouet, Wenongonet," in *Dictionary of Canadian Biography* 2:664.
28. Ibid., 665.
29. Baxter, *Documentary History of the State of Maine* (hereafter *DHSM*), 23:204, 206.
30. *DHSM*, 23:5.
31. *DHSM*, 11:149.
32. *DHSM*, 23:32, 37.
33. Siebert, "Wenemouet, Wenongonet," 2:664.
34. Ibid.
35. Father Gaulin au Tremblay, October 24, 1701, in Casgrain, H. R. (Henri Raymond), *Les Sulpiciens et les prêtres des Missions-étrangères en Acadie (1676–1762)*, (Québec, Pruneau & Kironac, 1897), 234ff.; cf. Arch. Col., B 22 3 fol. 154, Note du Ministre, Villieu au Ministre, October 20, 1700, *Collection de Manuscripts contenant lettres, Memoires, et autres documents historiques relatifs a la Nouvelle-France* (hereafter, *Coll. de Mss.*), 4 vols. (Quebec: Legislature de Quebec, 1883–85), 2:337, and Lord, Sexton, and Harrington, 1:81.
36. Thomas Church, "The Old French and Indian Wars, from 1689 to 1704," in Benjamin Church, *The History of the Great Indian War of 1675 and 1676, Commonly Called Philip's War*, ed. Samuel G. Drake (Hartford, 1851), 283, reprinted in John Romeyn Brodhead, *Documents Relative to the Colonial History of the State of New York* (Albany: Weed, Parsons and Co., 1937), 9:762 (citation is from reprinted edition).
37. Samuel Penhallow, *The History of the Wars of New-England with the Eastern Indians, or A narrative of their continued perfidy and cruelty, from the 10th of August, 1703, to the peace renewed 13th of July, 1713. And from the 25th of July, 1722, to their submission 15th December, 1725, which was ratified August 5th, 1726* (Cincinnati: Reprinted for Wm. Dodge by J. Harpel, 1859), 14–133.

38. Benjamin Church, *The History of the Eastern Expeditions of 1689, 1690, 1692, 1696, and 1704 Against the Indians and the French*, ed. Henry M. Dexter (Boston, 1867), 99–120.

39. A conference was held with five Eastern Indians January 11–13, 1714. James Phinney Baxter, the Baxter manuscripts (Portland: Maine Historical Society, 1889–1916): Collections of the Maine Historical Society, 2nd series (hereafter Bax. Mss.). Documents relating to the early history of Maine gathered "from the archives of Massachusetts, the Office of the public records in London, and the Bureau of marine and colonies in Paris," 23:52.

40. Massachusetts Council, in Library of Congress Records of the States of the United States. Microfilm. December 27, 1714 (hereafter RSUS); Everett Kimball, *The Public Life of Joseph Dudley, a study of the colonial policy of the Stuarts in New England, 1660–1715*. New York: Longmans Green and Col., 1911, 132.

41. Vaudreuil to Minister, October 31, 1718, *Coll. de Mss.*, 3:31–32.

42. Massachusetts Archives, 51:302ff: Massachusetts Council Records, January 7, February 18, 1718/19.

43. A Journal of Commissioners at Portsmouth, July 13, 1713, Bax. Mss., 23:49; Treaty of Eastern Indians, July 11, 1713, Bax. Mss., 23:39, 40.

44. Cited in James E. Falkowski, *Indian Law/Race Law: A Five-Hundred-Year History* (New York: Praeger, 1992), 30.

45. Brodhead, 9:879–80; Vaudreuil au Ministre, November 14, 1713, Archives de Colonies, Ottowa; Public Archives of Canada, C11A, 34, 49.

46. *DHSM*, 24:244–45; Robert Earle Moody, "The Maine Frontier, 1607–1763" (Ph.D. diss., Yale University, 1978), 361–62; Charles Knowles Bolton, *Scotch-Irish Pioneers in Ulster and America* (Baltimore: Genealogical Publishing, 1981), 215–38; William Willis, ed., *Journals of the Reverend Thomas Smith and the Rev. Samuel Deane, Pastors of the First Church in Portland* (Portland: Joseph Bailey, 1849), 87n.

47. "Georgetown on Arrowsick Island August 9th, 1717," in "Indian Treaties," *Collections of the Maine Historical Society* (Portland: Maine Historical Society, 1898), 1st ser., vol. 3, 361–75.

48. David Ghere, "Diplomacy and War on the Maine Frontier," in *Maine the Pine Tree State: From Prehistory to the Present*, ed. Richard W. Judd, Edwin A. Churchill, and Joel W. Eastman (Orono: University of Maine Press, 1995), 129.

49. Governor Dummer to Governor Vaudreuil, January 19, 1724/25 Massachusetts Archives, 52:106–9. Published in William B. Trask, ed., *Letters of Colonel Thomas Westbrook and Others Relative to Indian Affairs in Maine, 1722–1726* (Boston, 1901), 88–91.

50. Massachusetts Council Records, July 25, 1721; October 19, 1721; February 9, 1721/22; February 19, 1721/22.

51. Massachusetts Archives, 21:106–8, Declaration dated July 25, 1722.

52. Kenneth M. Morrison, "Sebastien Rasles and Norridgewock, 1724: The Eckstorm Conspiracy Thesis Reconsidered," *Maine Historical Society Quarterly* 14 (1974): 76–97; Fannie H. Eckstorm, "The Attack on Norridgewock, 1724," *New England Quarterly* 7 (1934): 541–78; and Penhallow, 104, 111.

53. *Dictionary of Canadian Biography*, 2:665.

54. Ibid., 665–66.

55. *DHSM*, 10:362, 365.

56. David Ghere discussed the nature of the eighteenth-century Abenaki po-

litical factions in his Ph.D. dissertation, "Abenaki Factionalism, Emigration and Social Continuity."

57. Indians' Letter, January 28, 1726, Bax. Mss., 23:208–10.
58. *DHSM*, 10:389–90.
59. Ibid., 394, 401, 403–5.
60. Penhallow, 123–27; "Conference with the Eastern Indians, at the Ratification of the Peace, Held at Falmouth in Casco-Bay, in July and August, 1726, *Collections of the Maine Historical Society* 3:377–405; Ghere, "Abenaki Factionalism, Emigration and Social Continuity," 173. Ghere calls the negotiators the conciliatory faction of the Penobscot tribe.
61. *DHSM*, 23:204.
62. Ibid., 10:95, 403–5; *Dictionary of Canadian Biography* 2:664.
63. Morrison, *Embattled Northeast*, 185–90.
64. Ibid.
65. David Ghere, "The 'Disappearance' of the Abenaki in Western Maine: Political Organization and Ethnocentric Assumptions," in *After King Philip's War: Presence and Persistence in Indian New England*, ed. Colin Calloway (Hanover, N.H.: University Press of New England, 1997), 77.
66. Samuel Purchas, "Description of Mawooshen," in *Hakluytus posthumus, or, Purchas his Pilgrimes: contayning a history of the world in sea voyages and lande travells by Englishmen and others* (Glasgow: J. MacLehose and Sons, 1905–7). Purchas enumerates fifteen villages with 2,490 men, so a population of about 10,000 persons seems reasonable, if his figures are accurate.
67. *DHSM*, 23:189.
68. Ibid., 209–10.
69. Ibid., 217.
70. Jabez Bradbury to Governor, June 18, 1744, Bax. Mss., 290–91; John Oulton to Shirley, August 8, 1744, in Edmund Bailey O'Callaghan, *The Documentary History of the State of New York* (Albany: Weed, Parsons and Co., 1850–51), 9:1107.
71. Shirley to Bradbury, July 22, 1745, and Bradbury to Shirley, July 29, 1745, in William Shirley, *Correspondence of William Shirley*, 1:253–54; 261; reprinted in *Journal of the Massachusetts House of Representatives*, August 23, 1745.
72. Joseph L. Peyser, ed., *On the Eve of the Conquest: The Chevalier de Raymond's Critique of New France in 1754* (East Lansing: Michigan State University Press, 1997), 60.
73. Ibid., 74.
74. *DHSM*, 23:418.
75. Ibid., 426–27.
76. Loron, letter from Fort Richmond, February 11, 1742, in ibid., 285.
77. Ibid.
78. Ibid.
79. Ibid., 289.
80. Ibid., 24:22–23.
81. Ibid., 34.
82. Ibid., 36–37, 46.
83. Ibid., 41, 57.
84. Ibid., 62, 63.
85. Hugh Finlay's Journal, September 1773–June, 1774; Fannie Hardy Eckstorm papers, Special Collections, Raymond H. Fogler Library, University of

Maine, Orono, box 611, f88; Indian Conference August 14, 1765, Bax. Mss., 24:126–28; and J. W. Hanson, *History of the Old Towns of Norridgewock and Canaan* (Boston: The Author, 1849), 88–91.

86. Also, the Penobscots suffered from an epidemic of smallpox, which they contracted from goods they had received from Canada. Bradbury at Ft. Georges to Gov. Phipps February 1757, Massachusetts Archives, 33:761.

87. Ghere, "Diplomacy and War on the Maine Frontier, 1678–1759," in *Maine the Pine Tree State*, ed. Judd, Churchill, and Eastman, 138–39.

88. *Collections of the Maine Historical Society*, 5:370.

89. Governor Pownall's Certificate, May 23, 1759, Province of Massachusetts Bay—Penobscot Dominions of Great Britain Possession Confirmed by Thomas Pownall, Governor, *DHSM*, 23:337–38.

90. *DHSM*, 23:368.

91. John Howard Ahlin, *Maine Rubicon: Downeast Settlements during the American Revolution* (Calais, Maine: Calais Advertiser, 1966), 4. Ahlin cites Governor Hutchinson, who referred to the Down East region as "an asylum for debtors and criminals." Hutchinson to Hillsborough, Boston, November 11, 1769, Massachusetts Archives, 25:39.

92. *DHSM*, 24:7.

93. Ghere, "Abenaki Factionalism, Emigration and Social Continuity," 6.

5. Liberties and Lands: Disappointment in the Promise of the New Nation (pp. 93–106)

1. Eric Foner, *The Story of American Freedom* (New York: W. W. Norton & Co., 1998), 51.
2. Ibid., 78.
3. William D. Williamson, *History of the State of Maine*, 41.
4. *DHSM*, 24:254.
5. Massachusetts Provincial Congress to Eastern Indians, Watertown, May 15, 1775, Massachusetts Archives, 193:194; Massachusetts Resolves, June 15, Massachusetts Archives, 144:313.
6. Chief Orono: Paper read before the Bangor Historical Society, August 6, 1929, Eckstorm papers, box 611, f74. Eckstorm cites a number of historical sources on Chief Orono in this paper including Williamson.
7. Bax. Mss., 14:123–24.
8. Letter of Honorable Enoch Freeman to Massachusetts Provincial Congress, Falmouth, May 5, 1775, ibid., 14:245.
9. Ibid., vol. 14.
10. Ahlin, 135.
11. Kenneth Roberts, ed., *March to Quebec: Journals of the Members of Arnold's Expedition* (New York: Doubleday, 1953).
12. "Colonel Arnold's Journal of his expedition to Canada, 52 (see also n. 2); "Captain Henry Dearborn Journal of the Quebec Expedition," 135; "Journal of Captain Simeon Thayer's March Through the Wilderness To Quebec," 254; "John Joseph Henry," 313–15; "Dr. Senter," 203. All in ibid.
13. "Dr. Senter," ibid., 203.
14. Ibid.

15. Kenneth Roberts believed it was Montresor's map. See Roberts, introduction, ibid.
16. "Journal of Arnold," ibid., 61
17. Roberts, 315.
18. "John Joseph Henry," ibid., 344.
19. Calloway, *American Revolution in Indian Country*, 12.
20. Indian Conference, August 22, 1763, Bax. Mss., 116–23. Governor Bernard promised the Penobscots that the Fort Pownall soldiers would not be allowed to hunt beaver and other furbearers, only deer and moose near the fort.
21. Massachusets Resolve, October 16, 1775, Massachusetts Archives, 207:14.
22. Massachusetts Resolves, October 13 and 16, 1775, Massachusetts Archives, 207:13, 144:33. Massachusetts Resolves, October 14, 1775, Massachusetts Archives, 207:15.
23. Penobscot Indians to John Lane, November 22, 1775, Massachusetts Archives, 194:378; Massachusetts Resolves, November 9, 1776, Massachusetts Archives, 211:49.
24. "Bangor Revolutionary Heroes," by Isabelle Graham Eaton, newspaper clipping of unknown provenance in Eckstorm papers, box 618, f10.
25. Letter from Thomas Fletcher to Council, August 16, 1776, Bax. Mss., 24:367.
26. Massachusetts General Court Committee Report, September 7, 1776, Massachusetts Archives, 144:364; 195:294. Only ten Micmacs and Maliseets went to New York to join Washington.
27. Ahlin, 72.
28. Frederick Kidder, *Military Operations in Eastern Maine and Nova Scotia during the Revolution* (Albany: Joel Munsell, 1867), 126.
29. Kidder, 126, 129, 130; Massachusetts Archives, 198:197, 144:212.
30. Massachusetts Archives, 144:221, and Colonel Josiah Brewer to Artemus Ward, Penobscot, May 27, 1777, Massachusetts Archives, 197:96.
31. Allan to Massachusetts General Court, September 25, 1777, Massachusetts Archives, 144:221.
32. Kidder, 126.
33. Ibid., 203–8.
34. Ibid.
35. Letter of John Allan in a report to Council, October 8, 1778, Bax. Mss., 16:101.
36. In the House of Representatives, March 9, 1778, Petition of Andrew Gilman, *DHSM*, 15:380–81, 386–87, 408–9. Charles H. Lagerbom, "Jonathan Lowder's Truckhouse: The History and Archæology of a Colonial Trading Post on the Maine Frontier During the American Revolutionary War" (master's thesis, University of Maine, Orono, 1991), 59; see also Lagerbom's n. 39.
37. Letter from John Lowder, May 21, 1777, Massachusetts Archives, 197:147.
38. John E. Cayford, *The Penobscot Expedition* (Orrington, Maine: C & H Publishing Co., 1976), 2.
39. John Calef, ed., *The Siege of Penobscot: Containing a Journal of the Proceedings of His Majesty's Forces against the Rebels in July 1779* (New York: New York Times, 1971), 295.

40. Massachusetts Archives, 37:145. See also Kidder, 285, for a list of Penobscot soldiers and families.
41. Massachusetts Provincial Congress to Eastern Indians, Watertown, May 15, 1775, Massachusetts Archives, 193:194, Massachusetts Resolves, June 15, Massachusetts Archives, 144:313.
42. Letter of John Allan about Penobscots in Kidder, 235.
43. In Council, September 10, 1779, and Resolve in the House of Representatives, September 27, 1779, *DHSM*, 17:121, 247–248. Brewer was dismissed in October 1782 amid reports of embezzlement and scandal. Lagerbom, n. 41, 76.
44. James Phinney Baxter, ed., *DHSM*, vol. 9: Bax. Mss. (Portland: LeFavor-Tower Co., 1914) 1, 2. The Penobscot men included Orono, his grandson, son of the late chief French Mitchell, Chief Attean, and two members of the Penobscot council, 8.
45. Ibid., 7.
46. Ibid., 19:9. In Senate, October 31, 1780, Jedediah Preble, chairman. Resolves as above passed November 6, 1780, 15–16.
47. June 22, 1781, Petition of Juniper Berthiaume, Petition of Josiah Brewer, Resolve passed June 27, 1781, ibid., 291–93.
48. Petition of Andrew Gilman, June 26, 1781, Resolve passed July 2, 1781, ibid., 297–98.
49. Ibid.
50. "Complaint of Juniper Berthiaume," written at Winslow, November 20, 1781, ibid., 373.
51. Ibid., 20:10.
52. Resolve June 22, 1782," ibid., 46–47.
53. Memorial of Eastern Indians to Governor Hancock, Boston, August 27, 1782. Resolve, October 17, 1782. Ibid., 81, 82.
54. June 4, 1783, Resolve, ibid., 232–33.
55. Ibid., 261, 315, 385.
56. Joseph Williamson, "The British Occupation of Penobscot During the Revolution," *Maine Historical Society*, 2nd series (Portland, 1890), 398.
57. Massachusetts Provincial Congress to Eastern Indians, Watertown, May 15, 1775, Massachusetts Archives, 193:194; Massachusetts Resolves, June 15, Massachusetts Archives, 144:313.

6. Dancing in Place: Retaining a Land Base (pp. 107–24)

1. Penobscot barter dance song and narrative from Burlin, 7–8.
2. The idea of civilization originated among Protestant missionaries who believed that non-Christians lived outside of the civilized world. See, for example, Society for the Propagation of the Gospel, *Sermon* (Boston: Nathaniel Wills, 1814).
3. Callahan H. North, "Henry Knox, His Part in the American Revolution, 1775 to 1784" (Ph.D. diss., New York University, 1956), 322.
4. Ibid.
5. Reginald Horsman, *Expansion and American Indian Policy, 1783–1812* (East Lansing: Michigan University Press, 1967); Francis Paul Prucha, *American Indian Policy in the Formative Years: The Indian Trade and Intercourse Acts, 1790–1834* (Cambridge, Mass.: Harvard University Press, 1962).

6. Alan Taylor, *Liberty Men and Great Proprietors* (Chapel Hill: University of North Carolina Press, 1990).
7. Ibid.
8. North, 228.
9. "Governor's address in re: Indians" October 4, 1786, *DHSM* 21:236–37.
10. B. Lincoln, Thomas Rice, Rufus Putnam, Penobscot River, August 30, 1786, ibid., 239–41.
11. Ibid., 247–48.
12. Deed recorded in Hancock County Registry of Deeds, Ellsworth, book 4:70.
13. Recorded May 3, 1809, ibid., book 27:6.
14. Eckstorm, "The Indians of Maine," 1:63.
15. "Major Treat, a great trader with the Indians at Penobscot supposes the number of Indians on this river must have exceeded 700 souls." William D. Williamson, *History of the State of Maine*, 2:372. The term governor came to Penobscot leaders with English; previously they called themselves sagamores.
16. Ibid., 373.
17. Such as Genesis 1:28, Psalms 115:16.
18. Salisbury, 177.
19. W. H. Prescott, *The Conquest of Mexico*, 2 vols. (New York: Dutton, 1843).
20. Lewis Henry Morgan, *League of the Ho-de-no-sau-nee, or Iroquois* (Rochester: Sage, 1851), cited in Trigger, 10.
21. Frances Parkman, *The Conspiracy of Pontiac and the Indian War after the Conquest of Canada* (Toronto: George Morang, 1851), and *The Jesuits in North America in the Seventeenth Century* (Boston: Little, Brown & Co., 1927).
22. Trigger, 17.
23. McKenney to Elias Cornelius, July 26, 1817, Office of Indian Trade, Letters Sent, RG 75, National Archives, vol. D, 375, cited in Herman J. Viola, *Thomas L. McKenney: Architect of America's Early Indian Policy, 1816–1830* (Chicago: Sage Books, 1974), 24.
24. William L. Barney, *The Passage of the Republic* (Lexington, Mass.: D.C. Heath and Co., 1987), 2.
25. Miller, 5.
26. Lord, Sexton, and Harrington, 1:331–34.
27. John Godfrey's ms., 1:101, "Extracts from Daniel Little's Journal," Maine Historical Society Manuscript Collections, Portland. The original journal is cited elsewhere as being in the Archives of the First Congregational Parish of Kennebunk, Maine.
28. J. O. Plessis, *Journal des Visites Pastorales*, ed. Tetu (Quebec, 1903), 138, cited in Lord, Sexton, and Harrington, 448.
29. Quebec Dioc. Arch., N.B. IV, 1, cited in ibid., 448–49.
30. Ibid.,1:447–77.
31. Washington to Bishop Carroll, April 10, 1792, in *The writings of George Washington* ed. Worthington Chauncey Ford (New York: G. P. Putnam's Sons, 1889–[93]) 12:257.
32. "Bishop of Quebec to Father Ciquart, June 24, 1794" Quebec Dioc. Arch., cited in Lord, Sexton, and Harrington, 1:519.
33. Father Cheverus to Bishop Carroll, January 26, 1797; Father Matignon

to Bishop Carroll, February 24, 1797, Baltimore Dioc. Arch., 2 M 9, 5 G 8, cited in ibid., 519.

34. Bishop Matignon to Penobscots and Passamaquoddies, Boston, July 22, 1797, Portland Dioc. Arch., cited in ibid., 529.

35. Lucey, 23.

36. June 7, 1798, Baltimore Dioc. Arch., 2 N 13, cited in Lord, Sexton, and Harrington.

37. Father Cheverus to Father Matignon, Penobscot, June 30, 1798, Baltimore Dioc. Arch., cited in ibid., 531–32.

38. *Massachusetts Acts and Resolves*, 1798–99 (ed. of 1897), 217.

39. Father Romagne to Bishop Carroll, Passamaquoddy, January 25, 1800, Baltimore Dioc. Arch., 7 E 6. The interpreter he mentions is Orono, who died the following year at the advanced age of 113. *Columbian Centinel*, March 21, 1801, cited in Lord, Sexton, and Harrington, 1:590.

40. Massachusetts Council Records, June 14, 1799, June 18, 1800, and June 9, 1801; also Father Cheverus to Bishop Carroll, March 10, 1801, and Father Matignon to the Bishop, March 16, 1801, Baltimore Dioc. Arch., cited in ibid., 590.

41. Father Cheverus to Bishop Carroll, May 26, 1804; Father Matignon to Bishop Carroll, June 18, 1804, cited in ibid., 592.

42. *The Indian Prayer Book, compiled and arranged for the benefit of the Penobscot and Passamaquoddy Tribes* (Boston: H. L. Devereux, 1834), cited in ibid., 591.

43. According to Lord, Sexton, and Harrington, Romagne inoculated more than 150 Passamaquoddies and Penobscots in the following year. I assume this was for smallpox. The implication is that he performed the inoculations himself. Father Matignon to Bishop Carroll, June 18, 1804, Baltimore Dioc. Arch., cited in ibid., 592. Vaccination using cowpox was first successfully performed by Edward Jenner in 1796 and soon was practiced in America.

44. John Blake papers, 1810–21, Bangor Historical Society.

45. Bishop Cheverus to Archbishop Carroll, October 23, 1814, Baltimore Dioc. Arch., cited in Lord, Sexton, and Harrington, 1:662.

46. Bishop Cheverus to Bishop Plessis, August 26, 1818, Quebec Dioc. Arch., cited in ibid., 684.

47. *Massachusetts Acts and Resolves*, January 22, 1819.

48. Frank G. Speck, "Characteristics of Social Life," in *Penobscot Man*, 203–9.

49. See especially "Tales of Gluskabe the Deceiver" in Speck, "Penobscot Transformer Tales," 189–200.

50. Instructions to Moses Greenleaf to survey 8000 acres of Land to Thomas Johnson and others, January 29, 1815, also letter dated February 15, 1815, Massachusetts Archives.

51. Joseph Treat, "Journal and Plans of Surveys, 1820," manuscript, Executive Council papers, Maine State Archives.

52. *Resolves of the General Court of the Commonwealth of Massachusetts* (Boston: Russell, Cuther & Co., 1816), chap. 176.

53. William D. Williamson, *History of the State of Maine*, 2:669.

54. *Resolves*, chap. 120, 424–29. Concerning the nine townships of land on the Penobscot River, June 13, 1817, and p. 507, February 13, 1818.

55. *Resolves*, chap. 270, 710, "Resolve in favor of agent of Penobscot Indians," February 20, 1819.

NOTES   221

56. *Resolves*, chapter 272, 711, "Resolve relative to Treaty with Penobscot Indians," February 20, 1819.
57. "Report of John Blake, Esq. Agent to the Penobscot Indians, to his Excellency the Governor for the year 1811." Letter dated December 30, 1811, at Orrington, in Blake papers in Bangor Historical Society Collections.
58. Letter From William Jenks to General Blake, dated September 12, 1811, at Bangor, Blake papers.
59. Letter in Blake papers.
60. These aspects of resistance will be discussed in the following chapters.
61. Interview with Theodore Mitchell by the author, Northeast Archives 2387:011. Mitchell is speaking about the 1920s, when the local chapter of the KKK used to sneak over the river to Indian Island and burn crosses at night, but the quote relates to earlier times as well.
62. William D. Williamson, *History of Maine*, 2:669.

7. Bible, Primer, Hoe, and Plow: Resistance through Religion, Education, and Subsistence (pp. 125–49)

1. "Green Corn Song," in Davenport, 166.
2. Nicolar, *Life and Tradition of the Red Man*, 64.
3. Report of January 22, 1818, *American State Papers: Indian Affairs*, IA, 2:150–51.
4. Francis Paul Prucha, *The Great Father: The United States Goernment and the American Indians* (Lincoln: University of Nebraska Press, 1984), 1:136. Bernard W. Sheehan, *Seeds of Extinction: Jeffersonian Philanthropy and the American Indian* (Chapel Hill: University of North Carolina Press, 1973), 1. Jefferson's ideas reflect a linear model of stages of society from savagery to civilization. See Ronald L. Meek, *Social Science and the Ignoble Savage* (Cambridge: Cambridge University Press, 1976), and Lewis Henry Morgan, *Ancient Society; or, Researches in the Lines of Human Progress from Savagery through Barbarism to Civilization* (New York: Henry Holt & Co., 1877).
5. Robert F. Berkhofer, Jr., *The White Man's Indian: Images of the American Indian from Columbus to the Present* (New York: Knopf, 1978); Prucha, *American Indian Policy in the Formative Years*; Ronald N. Satz, *American Indian Policy in the Jacksonian Era* (Lincoln: University of Nebraska Press, 1975), 1–63.
6. *Resolves*, chap. 3, January 19, 1821. The first time the Penobscots sent six representatives. They were Captain John Neptune, Captain Peal Molly, Captain Luey, Captain Peal Tomer, Captain Joseph, and Captain Solomon. Transportation, room, and board in the amount of $125 was paid for them.
7. Women did not hold this office until after World War II.
8. *Resolves of the Maine Legislature* (Portland: Francis Douglas, 1820), chap. 16, June 20, 1820.
9. Ibid. (Portland: Thomas Dodd, 1821), chap. 10, February 9, 1821.
10. Ibid., chap. 175, 766–68, March 5, 1821.
11. *Acts*, chap. 323, 1071, February 23, 1826, in *Resolves of the Legislature of the State of Maine* (Augusta, Maine: Smith & Robinson, Printers to the State, 1820–1839).
12. *Statutes at Large* 3 (1789–1976): 516–17.
13. Lord, *The History of the Archdiocese of Boston* 2:74.

14. *Public Laws of Maine*, chap. 20, 29, 1821.
15. "Indians in Maine," *Christian Mirror*, January 24, 1823.
16. Society for the Propagation of the Gospel (SPG), *Sermon*.
17. SPG, *Sermon*, November 5, 1829 (Boston: Putnam and Hunt, 1829).
18. Letter of J. P. Warren of the *Christian Mirror* to the editor of the *Whig and Courier* written at Portland, April 10, 1883.
19. "The Journals of John Edwards Godfrey," 275–77. The journal that Josiah Brewer kept while teaching at Indian Island was later given to the Bangor Historical Society. It burned in the fire of 1911 in the Bangor Public Library. A copy made by John E. Godfrey has not come to light.
20. "Wayfarer's Notes: The Bangor Theological Seminary," *Sprague's Journal of Maine History*, vol. 1, no. 2, July 1913, 68–72.
21. *Resolves of the Legislature of the State of Maine*, chap. 17, 489, February 13, 1826.
22. Daniel Pike to Samuel Call, Indian Agent, April 5, 1824, National Archives.
23. *Public Laws*, chap. 392, 1159.
24. "Indian Agent Report," *Documents of the Legislature*, Senate no. 45, 3, 1852.
25. Ibid.
26. J. C. Knowlton, E. Douglass, and J. A. Blanchard, superintending school committee of Old Town, report, Thirty-Seventh Legislature no. 1, Office of the Secretary of State, Augusta, 1858, *Documents of the Legislature*, pp. 3–4. Smallpox continued to plague Penobscots throughout most of the nineteenth century due to poor or nonexistent health care.
27. Vetromile arrived in June 1854, serving first at Indian Island as assistant pastor to John Bapst in the Maine missions and later at Pleasant Point to about 1880.
28. Knowlton, Douglas, and Blanchard, report, 5.
29. *Resolves of the State of Maine*, March 1859.
30. Ibid., 6.
31. James A. Purinton, *Reports of the Indian Agents of the State of Maine* (Augusta: Stevens & Sayward, 1861), 7.
32. Ibid.
33. *Public Laws*, 1862.
34. George F. Dillingham, *Report of the Agent of the Penobscot Tribe of Indians*, Senate no. 23 (Augusta: Stevens & Sayward, 1865), 3.
35. Ibid.
36. Dillingham, *Report* (1866), 3.
37. Dillingham, *Report* (1878), 5, 6.
38. Joseph Nicolar, "Report of Superintendent of Farming," Old Town, Maine, December 22, 1879, in ibid., 8–9. Nicolar later published a book, *The Life and Traditions of the Red Man*.
39. Charles A. Bailey, Indian Agent's Report to the Honorable Governor and Council of Maine (Augusta: Sprague & Son, 1880).
40. Charles A. Bailey, *Report of the Agent of the Penobscot Tribe of Indians for the year 1881* (Augusta: Sprague & Son, 1882), 6.
41. Bailey, *Report . . . 1882* (1883), 6.
42. John H. Stowe, *Report of the Agent of the Penobscot Tribe of Indians for the year 1888* (Augusta: Burleigh & Flynt, 1889), 5.

43. Ibid., 6–7.
44. Stowe, *Report . . . 1890* (1891), 6–7.
45. Ibid.
46. Stowe, *Report . . . 1891* (1892), 6–7.
47. Stowe, *Report . . . 1893* (1894), 5.
48. Ibid., 9.
49. Ibid.
50. Ibid.
51. Chamberlain, "The Penobscot Indians." Chamberlain was so impressed that he supplied the Penobscot school with a library of books.
52. George H. Hunt, "Penobscot Indian Report," December 29, 1899, Indian Affairs, Maine State Archives, Augusta, 7.
53. George H. Hunt, "Agent's Report, Penobscot Indians," December 30, 1902, No. 803. In Council, the Standing Committee on Indian Affairs, Maine State Archives, Augusta, 4–5.
54. No author given, Penobscot Indians Agent of ——— Annual Report, December 13, 1906, 3.
55. D. Lyman Wormwood, superintendent of schools, to George H. Hunt, appended to "Penobscot Indians, Report of Agent, 31 December, 1909."
56. Executive Council papers, box 19, f41.
57. Ibid.
58. James B. Vickery, Richard W. Judd, and Sheila McDonald, "Maine Agriculture, 1783–1861," in Judd et al., 246–52.
59. Joseph Treat, "Journal of Plans of Surveys," 33, manuscript written in 1820. Maine State Archives, Augusta.
60. Signed at Orson Island December 29, 1835, by Governor John Attean, Lieutenant Governor John Neptune, and thirty-eight men of the tribe. Legislative Graveyard (LGY), 1835, box 101, f2, Maine State Archives, Augusta.
61. LGY, box 125, f12. Order of the House, January 30, 1839. And box 167–85, chap. 85, 1839.
62. LGY, 1836, box 101, f2.
63. Typescript report on Indian Affairs prepared about 1934 from Council Report Warrants in the Registers of the Council, 1838, Maine State Library, Augusta.
64. "Report of the Indian Agent to the Legislature," in *Documents of the Legislature* (Augusta: William T. Johnson, 1852), 4.
65. *Resolve of the Maine Legislature*, February 23, 1866.
66. Purinton, *Reports . . . 1860*, 6–8.
67. Samuel Call, "Report to Governor and Council," Council Reports nos. 468, 479, Maine State Archives, Augusta.
68. At this time there were three villages on the Penobscot River: Indian Island, Olamon Island, and Mattanawcook Island. However, individual families also lived on some of the other islands above Old Town.
69. Executive Council report, box 48, f49, June 25, 1835. "The agent has caused eight acres to be cleared for a public farm and is waiting for the means to erect buildings."
70. LGY, box 102, f2, January, 1836. Their request seems to have gone unheeded.
71. Purinton, *Reports . . . 1860*, 6–8.
72. Purinton, *Reports . . . 1861*, 6–8.

73. Richard W. Judd, "Maine's Lumber Industry," in Judd et al., 265.

74. Goodall, Steven Lincoln, *Board of Agriculture*, Annual Report of the Secretary of the Maine Board of Agriculture (Augusta: Stevens & Sayward, Printers for the State, 1856–1877), 110–11.

75. Petition to Governor Smith and the Executive Council from John Neptune, Lieutenant Governor, and Joseph Socabasin, delegate. Part 5 of the petition reads: "White men are cutting timber and grass on the islands in the river. Their cattle and sheep are eating the Indian's plants. . . . [We pray] if anybody's creatures be found upon an island doing any damage or injury, they may be treated and their owners prosecuted, just as if we were white men. . . . Bad men and their cattle do us much evil." Executive Council papers, box 36, f29, 1831.

76. Sam'l W. Hoskins and Joseph Nicolar, *Reports of the Agent and the Superintendent of Farming of the Penobscot Tribe of Indians* (Augusta: Sprague, Owen & Nash, 1879), 10.

77. Dillingham, *Report* (1869), 5.

78. Dillingham, *Report* (1876), 5.

79. Hoskins and Nicolar, 6.

80. Bailey, *Report* (1880), 7.

81. Bailey, *Report* (1881–87); Stowe, *Report* (1888–89).

82. George H. Hunt, *Report of the Indian Agent of the Penobscot Tribe of Indians* (Augusta: Burleigh & Flynt, 1894), 7.

83. George H. Hunt, "Penobscot Indians, Report of Agent, 1900," Indian Affairs, Maine State Archives, Augusta.

8. Spirit of a Nation: Retaining Political Sovereignty (pp. 150–64)

1. Lewis Henry Morgan, *League of the Iroquois* (New York: Corinth Books, 1962), 249–51.

2. Ward Churchill, "The Tragedy and the Travesty: The Subversion of Indigenous Sovereignty in North America," in *Contemporary Native American Political Issues*, ed. Troy R. Johnson (Walnut Creek, Calif.: AltaMira Press, 1999), 19.

3. Ibid., 20.

4. Maine inherited treaty obligations from Massachusetts and interpreted its role as guardian of the tribe's interests.

5. "Report of Samuel Call, Indian Agent," Executive Council papers for 1827, box 2, f28.

6. Signed at Old Town, November 14, 1827, by Captain Francis Lolar, Jo Lion, Captain Peol Molly, Captain Etienne, Captain Francis Sappiel, and Captain Peol Mitchell. Council Reports no. 908, 1828.

7. Bangor, January 22, 1828, Executive Council papers, box 22, f9.

8. *Legislative Acts*, chap. 392, February 19, 1828.

9. I have found no other references to the Indian Court and do not know how long it was in session or when it first met.

10. The resolves also included thanks from the tribe to Bishop Fenwick for sending the tribe a religious instructor and adviser, and to Reverend Mr. Barber (the priest). Also, the council wished that the Indians accompanying the priest on his journey to Passamaquoddy be supplied with provisions paid for from the tribal funds. Executive Council papers, box 25, f33. John Etienne, Governor and

Joseph Marie signed the letter dated June 24, 1828. Francis Sappiel and his four brothers and Peol Molly were opposed.

11. Ghere, "Abenaki Factionalism, Emigration and Social Continuity."

12. Dean Snow, "Eastern Abenaki," in *Handbook of North American Indians*, vol. 15: *Northeast*, ed. Bruce Trigger (Washington, D.C.: Smithsonian Institution, 1978), 145.

13. Probably the grandfather of Civil War hero Colonel Joshua L. Chamberlain of Brewer.

14. January 22, 1829, Executive Council papers, box 22, f9.

15. February 14, 1829, ibid.

16. Virgil H. Barber, Portland, Maine, March 2, 1830, ibid., box 31, f45.

17. Report on the Memorial of Virgil H. Barber, ibid., box 32 f45.

18. Ibid., box 33, f48. Letter dated March 25, 1830.

19. Ibid., report no. 17, January 25, 1831, box 26, f26.

20. Ibid.

21. Alfred G. Hempstead, *The Penobscot Boom and the Development of the West Branch of the Penobscot River for Log Driving*, University of Maine Studies, 2nd series, no. 18 (Orono: University of Maine Press, 1931; privately reprinted, n.p., 1975), 23.

22. Ibid., 110, and Edward D. Ives et al., *Argyle Boom, Northeast Folklore* 17 (Orono: Northeast Folklore Society, 1976).

23. A boom is a construction in the river used to sort logs during log drives. It consists of logs and rafts of logs chained together. See Hempstead.

24. Petition brought by delegates John Neptune and Joseph Sockbasin, January 25, 1831, Executive Council papers, box 36, f29.

25. *Resolves* 26–28, 1929; 31–14, 1831; 28–37, 1830; LGY 86–87, 1834; and *Resolves of the Legislature of the State of Maine*, 1838.

26. Executive Council papers.

27. Ibid., report no. 268, December 30, 1839. Signed by Governor Thomas Sockalexis and Lieutenant Governor Attean Orson (New Party); Executive Council papers, report no. 68. Letter dated January 15, 1842, at Old Town, signed by Governor John Attean, Lieutenant Governor John Neptune, and councillors (Old Party).

28. Letter To the Rev. B. Fenwick, Bishop of Boston, Mass., Old Town Indians, June 14, 1836. Photocopy of letter at St. Ann's Church, Indian Island.

29. LGY, box 109, f37, January session, 1837.

30. Ibid., box 111, f8.

31. ibid., box 125, f12.

32. *Legislative Laws*, box 167, chap. 85.

33. For a discussion of the assimilation policy, see Henry Eugene Fritz, *The Movement for Indian Assimilation, 1860–1890* (Philadelphia: University of Pennsylvania, 1963).

34. *Public Laws*, 1839.

35. Executive Council papers, report no. 268, December 30, 1839. Signed by Governor Thomas Sockalexis, Lieutenant Governor Attean Orson and others.

36. Ibid., report no. 68, letter dated January 15, 1842, at Old Town, signed by John Attean, John Neptune, and councillors.

37. Hartly Crawford to His Excelly John Fairfield, January 13, 1843, in ibid., report no. 106. The United States followed earlier practices established by the British and other Europeans to present silver medals to chiefs and warriors as

tokens of friendship and as signs of allegiance and loyalty on the part of those who accepted them. See Francis Paul Prucha, *Indian Peace Medals in American History* (Madison: State Historical Society of Wisconsin, 1971).

38. Executive Council papers, report no. 106, January 1843. Signed by Representative Solomon Swassin and others.
39. Ibid., report no. 30, February 5, 1844.
40. Ibid., reports no. 190, letters 3 and 4, February 1843.
41. Ibid.
42. Ibid., report no. 30, letter, January 28, 1844.
43. Ibid., report no. 6, letter, January 1, 1845, at Old Town.
44. Ibid., report no. 227, 1846.
45. Ibid., report no. 55, petition, June 7, 1848.
46. Proctor, 82–86. *Murch v. Tomer*, 21 Maine, 537. Opinion of Court as drawn up by C. J. Whitman. U.S. Constitution, 15th Amendment, and U.S. Congress Act of June 2, 1924 (43 Stat. 253).
47. Although earlier in the century priests advocated on behalf of Penobscots with the state to obtain appropriations for the church and school, it was not until 1878 that the Catholic Church was able to exert such influence again with the establishment of the Sisters of Mercy.
48. Purinton, *Reports* (1860), 7.
49. This according to Glenn Starbird, former tribal genealogist who investigated the matter. Other sources for Penobscot Civil War veterans are Maine State Archives, United States 1890 census, and National Archives in Washington.
50. *Public Laws*, 1867.
51. Dillingham, *Reports* (1874), 6–7. Letters and petitions in LGY, 1875, box 621, "Indefinitely Postponed."
52. LGY, 1875, box 621, "Indefinitely Postponed."
53. Frank Speck suggested that the tribe had developed a moiety system, and this may have accounted for what later became political factions and parties. It bears further consideration. Speck, *Penobscot Man*, 234–36.

9. Paddling Song: Traditional Skills as a Tool of Resistance (pp. 165–82)

1. Andrew Dana, "Paddling Song," in Davenport, 162.
2. Ibid., 183.
3. Ronald L. Trosper, "Traditional American Indian Economic Development Policy," in *Contemporary Native American Political Issues*, ed. Troy R. Johnson, 140–43.
4. Calvin Martin, *Keepers of the Game: Indian-Animal Relationships and the Fur Trade* (Berkeley: University of California Press, 1978), 40.
5. Speck, *Penobscot Man*, 7.
6. Victor R. Fuchs, *The Economics of the Fur Industry* (New York: Columbia University Press, 1957), 17.
7. Ibid., 117.
8. Ibid., 120.
9. Ibid., 4.
10. Dillingham, *Reports* (1866), 6.

11. Hoskins & Nicholar, "Reports of the Indian Agents of the State of Maine, 1879," (Augusta: Stevens & Sayward), 6.

12. Edward D. Ives, *George Magoon and the Down East Game War* (Urbana: University of Illinois Press, 1988), 61–94.

13. Harold Adam Innis, *The Fur Trade in Canada: An Introduction to Canadian Economic History* (New Haven: Yale University Press, 1930), 320.

14. "Account Book of Jonathan T. Hardy with Penobscot Indians, 1850–1856," Eckstorm papers, box 614, f67; "Indian Pawn Papers 1837–1850," ibid., box 616, f66–74; various papers concerning accounts of fur business in Maine, ibid., box 613, f73–77.

15. "Walter Manly Hardy Journal," portions typed by his daughter Fannie, original destroyed by her, ibid., box 614, f73, 121.

16. "Account Book of Jonathan T. Hardy," ibid., box 614, f67.

17. "Act Relating to the Separation of Maine from Massachusetts Proper by the General Court of Massachusetts, June 19, 1819. Sec. 1 Art. 5, Indians of Maine," *DHSM*, vol. 8, 1902. Also "Treaty with the Penobscot Tribe of Indians, by the Commonwealth of Massachusetts, June 29, 1818," Maine *DHSM*, vol. 8, 1902. General John Blake, agent for Massachusetts, 1810–21, reported on his distribution of these goods in his annual report to the governor. "The Blake Papers": photocopies of originals owned by the Bangor Historical Society.

18. A pawn was a bit of silver, either a religious medal or a medal given by federal or state officials to a tribal leader. Some of the Indians held silver pawns that they had received from the government and that they frequently used to secure debts for necessities at the trading post. "Indian Pawn Papers," typescript with comments by Fannie Hardy Eckstorm, Eckstorm papers, box 616, f66–74.

19. "Account Book of Jonathan T. Hardy," Eckstorm papers, box 14, f67.

20. Ibid.

21. Letter, JTH to M., dated Boston, December 26, 1863, ibid., box 613, f73.

22. *Loup cervier*, French for "wildcat."

23. Eckstorm papers, box 614, f67–71.

24. Ibid., f67. Note that records for all months' expenditures were not included in this notebook; 1845 figures are fall hunt expenses, while 1846–48 are spring hunt expenses. Totals: Sept.–Dec. 1845, $238.54; Jan.–June 1846, $1,775.41; Jan.–April 1847, $482.09; Jan.–May 1848, $418.03.

25. Local lumber business statistics indicate a growing business: 1833, 25,906,000 ft. logs rafted; 1843, 70,896,000 ft. logs rafted; 1853, 161,564,000 ft. rafted. In David Norton, *Sketches of the Town of Old Town From its earliest settlement to 1879* (Bangor: S. G. Robinson, 1881), 25.

26. Innis, 320.

27. "Account Book of Jonathan T. Hardy," Eckstorm papers, box 614, f67.

28. These figures gleaned from ibid.

29. Some of the frequently occurring trappers' names in the Hardy account books include Jacob Fish of Lincoln, Parker Stevens, Metcalf, Rufus Hodgkins, Pomroy, Severance, Ayer, O'Maley, McAllister, Sylvester, Harriman, Cook of Canaan, Thompson at the Bend, Edwin O. Shorey, J. Parkin & Co., George Foster, B. Penny, Lunt & Leighton, B. J. Stinson of Deer Isle, Jos. Libby, Peter Powers, Charles Rawles, and a number of others including unnamed peddlers and "strangers."

30. The Hardy journals, Eckstorm papers, box 614, f73.

31. Eugene Vetromile, *Indian Good Book* (New York: E. Dunigan & Bro., 1856). Vetromile's knowledge of the Penobscot language was minimal, but he often took a stab at it anyway. This book was largely compiled from the notes of two earlier missionaries, Romagne and Demillier, "The Indian Prayer Book," September 17, 1841 (in Maine Historical Society collections, Eugene Vetromille's papers, Manuscript Collections no. 114).

32. Walter Manly Hardy, "Fall Fur Hunt in Maine," parts 1–6, *Forest and Stream* 54 (January–June 1910), vol. 54, no. 1, 728–31; 2: 768–70; 3: 808–11; 4: 848–51; 5: 888–90; 6: 928–29.

33. Ibid. Old Jonathan was Manly's father.

34. Ibid., 44.

35. Fannie Hardy Eckstorm to Frank Speck, dated at Brewer, March 7, 1941, Eckstorm papers, box 612, f37.

36. The Hardy journals, ibid., box 614, f73.

37. Eckstorm, *Penobscot Man*.

38. Hempstead, 30–32. A drive boss oversaw the entire operation that brought logs from the woods of interior Maine down a major river to sorting booms where they were sorted before being carried to lumber mills.

39. David C. Smith, *A History of Lumbering in Maine, 1861–1960*, University of Maine Studies no. 93 (Orono: University of Maine Press, 1972), 78.

40. Eckstorm, *Penobscot Man*, 236.

41. Ibid., 258.

42. Smith, 82.

43. Purinton, *Report* (1861), 6.

44. Dillingham, *Report* (1866), 6.

45. Hoskins and Nicolar, 6.

46. Bailey, *Report* (1883), 5.

47. Bailey, *Report* (1885), 6. This was not Joseph Attean, governor of the Penobscot tribe in 1862, but he, too, died on a river drive in 1870. See Eckstorm, *Penobscot Man*, 63–146.

48. Bailey, *Report* (1887), 7.

49. Ibid.

50. Hunt, *Report* (1895), 10.

51. Ira E. Pinkham, n.p. "Report for year ending Dec. 1, 1919," 4, Maine State Archives, Augusta.

52. These are located in the Special Collections of the Raymond H. Folger Library at the University of Maine. The original collection included a Penobscot Lumbering Association box containing papers, correspondence, books, and checkbooks not catalogued. A second file contained records kept for the operations of the Penobscot boom, including two notebooks for lumber and logs rafted on the river in the 1850s—two volumes, 28 items. Third, there were ledgers that included records of accounts, time and payroll, inventories, log agents' reports, insurance papers, and letter books—320 volumes, 1854–1916 (according to Ives, *Argyle Boom*, 133).

53. Penobscot Lumbering Association Ledgers, July, August 1906, September 1908, September 1909.

54. A beat was a group of joints. A joint was a group of logs with the same mark that were fastened together by chains. Ives, *Argyle Boom*, 38–39.

55. Ibid., 38.

56. Ibid., 29–37.

57. Tape-recorded interview with Roy Dana, Sr., at his home on Indian Island, December 1, 1992. Northeast Archives #2384, transcript, 100.
58. Ives, *Argyle Boom*, 46; Northeast Archives #792, 204.
59. Hunt, *Report* (1894), 7.
60. Hunt, *Report* (1907), 4.
61. Joel W. Eastman and Paul E. Rivard, "Transportation and Manufacturing," in *Maine the Pine Tree State*, ed. Richard Judd et al.
62. Gerald E. Morris, *The Maine Bicentennial Atlas and Historical Survey* (Portland: The Maine Historical Society, 1976), 16.
63. Nathan Lowrey, "Tales of the Northern Maine Woods: The History and Traditions of the Maine Guide," in *Motor Camps and Maine Guides*, *Northeast Folklore* Volume 28, part 2 (Orono: The Northeast Folklore Society, 1989), 73–74.
64. Joseph Treat, "Journal of Plans of Surveys" (1820), Executive Council Records, Maine State Archives, Augusta, 14.
65. "Joseph Treat to John Neptune," handwritten receipt by Joseph Treat signed by John Neptune in his own hand, dated November 23, 1820, Executive Council papers, box 1, f40, 1820.
66. Charles T. Jackson, *Reports on Geology of Maine* (Augusta: Maine Geological Survey, 1837).
67. Henry David Thoreau, *The Maine Woods* (Boston: Ticknor and Fields, 1864; reprint, Thomas Y. Crowell Co., 1966), 12–13.
68. Ibid., 117.
69. One example of a Yankee folk song sung in Abenaki was collected by Frank T. Siebert and sung by Andrew Dana. A copy of the song can be found in the collections of the Penobscot Primer Project, created by Richard Garrett with the assistance of Carol Dana, Barry Dana, Madeline Shay, and Frank Siebert. Hudson Museum, University of Maine, Orono.
70. Thoreau, 152.
71. Ibid., 153.
72. Ibid., 206.
73. Ibid., 207.
74. Ibid., 209.
75. Ibid., 233.
76. Ibid., 241.
77. The Hardy journals, Eckstorm papers, box 614, f73.
78. *Laws of Maine*, 1897, chap. 262.
79. LGY, 1897, "Leave to Withdraw." (No index.)
80. Ibid., 1902, "Leave to Withdraw, Mitchell Attean et al."
81. Tape-recorded interview by author with Roy Dana, Sr..
82. "Extract of a letter from a friend Down East," addressed "to Friend Gibson," dated at Bangor, December 6, 1845. In *The True Workingman* (Lynn, Mass.), December 27, 1845.
83. Boston, Rhode Island, and various summer spots in Maine were visited by Penobscots selling baskets at midcentury. See Joyce Butler, *Spirits in the Wood* (Portland: Maine Historical Society, 1997), 2–4.
84. Discussion of Mary Neptune in "Appendix, Joseph Nicolar's Place Names" in Eckstorm, *Indian Place-Names of the Maine Coast*, 237–38.
85. Eckstorm, *Old John Neptune*, 26.
86. Dillingham, *Report* (1877), 7.

87. Dillingham, *Report* (1879), 6.

88. George H. Hunt, n.p., "Report of the Indian Agent of the Penobscot Tribe of Indians," Old Town, Maine, December 19, 1911, Maine State Archives, Augusta.

89. Pinkham.

10. Birches and Baskets: Commodification of Culture and Economic Resistance (pp. 183–95)

1. Nicolar, *Life and Traditions of the Red Man*, 32.

2. Sawdust was put down on the icy path across the river to prevent the ice from melting too quickly.

3. Wooden Canoe Heritage Association, Ltd., "Old Town Canoes," reprint of 1910 catalogue of the Old Town Canoe Company, "Canoes First Made by Indians," 3.

4. Ibid., 5.

5. Jerry Stelmok and Rollin Thurlow, *The Wood and Canvas Canoe: A Complete Guide to Its History, Construction, Restoration, and Maintenance* (Gardiner: The Harpswell Press, 1987), 17.

6. Ibid., 19–20.

7. Ibid., 21.

8. Ibid., 30.

9. Ibid., 24, 26–27.

10. Ibid., 17–33

11. Wooden Canoe Heritage Association, 3.

12. Matthew W. Stirling, "American's First Settlers, the Indians," *National Geographic*, November 1937, 565.

13. Wooden Canoe Heritage Association, 5.

14. Robert F. Grady, "A Visit with Henry Mitchell, American Indian Canoe Maker at His Home," American Life Histories: Manuscripts from the Federal Writer's Project, 1936–1940. http://memory.loc.gov/ammem/wpaintro/wpahome.html

15. Penobscots, living on reservation land, did not pay property tax. As a result, they were not allowed to vote in Maine, though by federal law they had received that right during the previous decade.

16. Carter Jones Meyer and Diana Royer, ed., *Selling the Indian: Commercializing and Appropriating American Indian Cultures* (Tucson: University of Arizona Press, 2001), xii.

17. Erik Trump, "'The Idea of Help': White Women Reformers and the Commercialization of Native American Women's Arts," in ibid., 160.

18. Ruth B. Phillips, *Trading Identities: The Souvenir in Native North American Art from the Northeast, 1700–1900* (Seattle: University of Washington Press, 1998), 3.

19. S. Elizabeth Bird, "Savage Desires: The Gendered Construction of the American Indian in the Popular Media," in Meyer and Royer, eds., *Selling the Indian*, 62–98.

20. Phillips, 10.

21. Trump, 160.

22. Phillips, 4.

23. John Glossian, Penobscot, 1848, cited in Butler, 2.
24. Theodore Mitchell and Madeline Shay, tape-recorded interviews.
25. Phillips, 10.
26. Eckstorm, *Handicrafts*, 24.
27. Joan Lester, "We Didn't Make Fancy Baskets Until We Were Discovered: Fancy-Basket Making in Maine," in Ann McMullen and Russell G. Handsman, eds., *A Key Into the Language of Woodsplint Baskets* (Washington, Conn.: American Indian Archaeological Institute, 1987), 53.
28. John H. Stowe, Indian Agent Report (Augusta: Burleigh & Flynt, 1889), 7.
29. Lester, 53, and Frank G. Speck, "Eastern Algonkian Block Stamp Decoration: A New World Original or an Acculturated Art," *Archeological Society of New Jersey, Research Series* 1 (Trenton, N.J., 1947), 22.
30. Theodore Mitchell, tape-recorded interview.
31. Pauleena MacDougall, "Native American Industry: Basket Weaving among the Wabanaki," in *American Indian Studies: An Interdisciplinary Approach to Contemporary Issues*, ed. Dane Morrison (New York: Peter Lang Publishing, 1997), 167–92.
32. Pauleena MacDougall, "Weaving a Tradition: Women Basket Makers in Penobscot Culture," in Marli Weiner, ed., *Of Place and Gender: Women in Maine History* (Orono: University of Maine Press, 2003).
33. *The Hill-Top*, vol. 27, no. 9 (1922), 4.
34. Phillips, 14.
35. Ibid., 67.
36. Ibid., 196.
37. Federal Writers' Project, Works Progress Administration, *Maine: A Guide "Down East,"* American Guide Series (Boston: Houghton Mifflin Co., 1937).
38. Federal Writers' Project, 295–96.
39. Grady.
40. Theodore Mitchell, tape-recorded interview.
41. Madeline Shay, tape-recorded interview.

Epilogue: The Role of Tradition in the Story of a People (pp. 196–201)

1. Richard M. Dorson, "Preface," in *Handbook of American Folklore*, ed. Richard M. Dorson (Bloomington: Indiana University Press, 1983), x.
2. William S. Simmons, *Spirit of the New England Tribes: Indian History and Folklore* (Hanover, N.H.: University Press of New England, 1986), 257–58.
3. United States, "Maine Indian Claims Settlement Act of 1980," vol. 1, 96th Congress, Second Session, LAWS (P.L. 96-420), ch. 19, Title 25, subchapter 2, sec. 1724 and sec. 6212, U.S. Code Congressional and Administrative News, 1980.
4. Regina Bendix, *In Search of Authenticity: The Formation of Folklore Studies* (Madison: University of Wisconsin Press, 1997), 212.
5. Simon J. Bronner, *Following Tradition: Folklore in the Discourse of American Culture* (Logan: Utah State Press, 1998), 480–81.

Bibliography

Books and Articles

Ahlin, John Howard. *Maine Rubicon: Downeast Settlements during the American Revolution.* Calais, Maine: Calais Advertiser, 1966.
Akins, Andrew. Telephone interviews with author, April 2, 2002, and July 31, 2000.
Axtell, James. "A Moral History of Indian-White Relations Revisited." *The History Teacher* 16 (February 1983): 184.
Bailey, Charles A. *Report of the Agent of the Penobscot Tribe of Indians.* Augusta: Sprague & Son, 1881–1888.
Bangor Daily News, May 19 and 28, 1964.
Barney, William L. *The Passage of the Republic.* Lexington, Mass.: D.C. Heath and Co., 1987.
Baxter, James Phinney, ed. The Baxter manuscripts, Portland: Maine Historical Society, 1889–1916: *Collections of the Maine Historical Society,* 2nd series, vols. 1–9. Documents relating to the early history of Maine gathered "from the archives of Massachusetts, the Office of the public records in London, and the Bureau of marine and colonies in Paris." Portland: LeFavor-Tower Co., 1914.
Bendix, Regina. *In Search of Authenticity: The Formation of Folklore Studies.* Madison: University of Wisconsin Press, 1997.
Berkhofer, Robert F., Jr. *The White Man's Indian: Images of the American Indian from Columbus to the Present.* New York: Knopf, 1978.
Biolsi, Thomas, and Larry J. Zimmerman. *Indians & Anthropologists: Vine Deloria Jr. and the Critique of Anthropology.* Tucson: University of Arizona Press, 1997.
Boas, Franz. "The Eskimo of Baffin Land and Hudson Bay." *Bulletin of the American Museum of Natural History* 15. New York, 1901–7.
———. "Geographical Names of the Kwakiutl Indians." *Columbia University Contributions to Anthropology* 20. New York, 1934.
Bolton, Charles Knowles. *Scotch-Irish Pioneers in Ulster and America.* Baltimore: Genealogical Publishing, 1981.
Bonfanti, Leo. *Biographies and Legends of the New England Indians.* New England Historical Series, 24. Wakefield, Mass.: Pride Publications, 1970.

Bourque, Bruce. "Aboriginal Settlement and Subsistence on the Maine Coast." *Man in the Northeast* 6 (1973): 3–20.
Brodeur, Paul. *Restitution: The Land Claims of the Mashpee, Passamaquoddy, and Penobscot Indians of New England*. Boston: Northeastern University Press, 1985.
Brodhead, John Romeyn. *Documents Relative to the Colonial History of the State of New York*, vol. 9. Albany: Weed, Parsons and Co., 1853–87.
Bronner, Simon J. *Following Tradition: Folklore in the Discourse of American Culture*. Logan: Utah State University Press, 1998.
Bruner, Edward M., and Stuart Plattner, eds. *Text, Play, and Story: The Construction and Reconstruction of Self and Society*. 1983 Proceedings of the American Ethnological Society. Washington, D.C.: American Ethnological Society, 1984.
Burlin, Natalie Curtis. *The Indians' Book*. 1923; reprint, New York: Dover Publishers, 1968.
Burrage, Henry Sweetser. *Early English and French Voyages: Chiefly from Hakluyt, 1534–1608*. New York : Barnes & Noble, 1967.
Butler, Joyce. *Spirits in the Wood*. Portland: Maine Historical Society, 1997.
Calef, John, ed. *The Siege of Penobscot: Containing a Journal of the Proceedings of His Majesty's Forces against the Rebels in July 1779*. New York: New York Times, 1971.
Calloway, Colin. *The American Revolution in Indian Country: Crisis and Diversity in Native American communities*. Cambridge: Cambridge University Press, 1995.
———. *Dawnland Encounters: Indians and Europeans in Northern New England*. Hanover, N.H.: University Press of New England, 1991.
———. *The Western Abenakis of Vermont, 1600–1800: War, Migration, and the Survival of an Indian People*. Norman: University of Oklahoma Press, 1990.
———, ed. *After King Philip's War: Presence and Persistence in Indian New England*. Hanover, N.H.: University Press of New England, 1997.
Cartwright, Steve. "Money Arrives, Lands Bought." *Wabanaki Alliance*, May 1981, 1.
———. "The winners." *Wabanaki Alliance*, March 1981, editorials, 2.
———. "A Traditional Indian Looks Ahead." *Wabanaki Alliance*, May 1978.
Casgrain, H. R. (Henri Raymond). *Les sulpiciens et les prêtres de Missions-étrangères en Acadie (1676–1762)*. Québec: Pruneau & Kironac, 1897.
Cayford, John E. *The Penobscot Expedition*. Orrington, Maine: C & H Publishing Co., 1976.
Chamberlain, Montague. "The Penobscot Indians, a Brief Account of Their Present Condition." *Cambridge Tribune*, February 4, 1899.
Champagne, Duane. "American Indian Studies Is for Everyone." In *Natives and Academics: Researching and Writing about American Indians*, ed. Devon Mihesuah. Lincoln: University of Nebraska Press, 1998.
Champlain, Samuel de. *The Works of Samuel de Champlain*. 6 vols., ed. H. P. Biggar. Toronto: Champlain Society, 1922–36.
Church, Benjamin. *The History of the Eastern Expeditions of 1689, 1690, 1692, 1696, and 1704 Against the Indians and the French*, ed. Henry M. Dexter. Boston, 1867.
Church, Thomas. "The Old French and Indian Wars, from 1689 to 1704." In Benjamin Church, *The History of the Great Indian War of 1675 and 1676, Commonly Called Philip's War*, ed. Samuel G. Drake (Hartford, 1851), 283.

Reprinted in Brodhead, *Documents Relative to the Colonial History of New York*, 9:762. (Citation is from reprinted edition.)
Churchill, Ward. *Struggle for the Land*. Winnipeg: Arbeiter Ring, 1999.
Cohen, Senator William. "The Penobscot and Passamaquoddy Land Claim in Maine." *Congressional Record*, March 1, 1977.
Columbian Centinel, March 21, 1801.
Dana, Roy, Sr. Tape-recorded interview. Northeast Archives #2384. Maine Folklife Center, University of Maine, Orono.
Davenport, Linda Gilbert. "Music among the Contemporary Penobscot Indians." Master's thesis, University of Illinois, Urbana, 1977.
Deloria, Vine, Jr. "Anthros, Indians, and Planetary Reality." In *Indians & Anthropologists: Vine Deloria Jr. and the Critique of Anthropology*, ed. Thomas Biolsi and Larry J. Zimmerman. Tucson: University of Arizona Press, 1997.
———. *Custer Died for Your Sins: An Indian Manifesto*. New York: Avon, 1970.
———. "The Rise of Indian Activism." In *The Social Reality of Ethnic America*, ed. R. Gomez, C. Collingham, R. Endo, and K. Jackson. Lexington, Mass.: D. C. Heath and Co., 1974.
DeMallie, Raymond J. "Kinship: The Foundation for Native American Society." In *Studying Native America: Problems and Prospects*, ed. Russell Thornton. Madison: University of Wisconsin Press, 1998.
DiLeonardo, Micaela. *Exotics at Home: Anthropologies, Others, American Modernity*. Chicago: University of Chicago Press, 1998.
Dillingham, George F. *Report of the Agent of the Penobscot Tribe of Indians*. Senate no 23. Augusta: Stevens & Sayward, 1865–79.
Dobyns, Henry F. *Their Number Become Thinned: Native American Population Dynamics in Eastern North America*. Knoxville: University of Tennessee Press in cooperation with the Newberry Library Center for the History of the American Indian, 1983.
Dorson, Richard M. "Preface." In *Handbook of American Folklore*, ed. Richard M. Dorson. Bloomington: Indiana University Press, 1983.
Eckstorm, Fannie H. "The Attack on Norridgewock, 1724." *New England Quarterly* 7 (1934): 541–78.
———. *The Handicrafts of the Modern Indians of Maine*. Bar Harbor: Lafayette National Park Museum, 1932; reprint, Robert Abbe Museum, 1980.
———. *Indian Place-Names of the Penobscot Valley and the Maine Coast*. Orono: University of Maine Studies, 1941.
———. "The Indians of Maine." In *Maine: A History*, vol. 1, ed. Louis Clinton Hatch. New York: The American Historical Society, 1919.
———. *Old John Neptune and Other Maine Indian Shamans*. Portland: The Southworth-Anthoensen Press, 1945.
———. *The Penobscot Man*. New York: Houghton Mifflin, 1904; reprint, New Hampshire Publishing Co., 1972.
Falkowski, James E. *Indian Law/Race Law: A Five-Hundred-Year History*. New York: Praeger, 1992.
Federal Writers' Project, Works Progress Administration. *Maine: A Guide "Down East."* American Guide Series. Boston: Houghton Mifflin Co., 1937.
Fixico, Donald. "Ethics and Responsibilities in Writing about American Indian History." In *Natives and Academics: Researching and Writing about American Indians*, ed. Devon A. Mihesuah. Lincoln: University of Nebraska Press, 1998.

Foner, Eric. *The Story of American Freedom.* New York: W. W. Norton & Co., 1998.
Ford, Worthington Chauncey, ed. *The writings of George Washington.* New York: G. P. Putnam's Sons, 1889–[93].
Fox, Robin. *The Challenge of Anthropology: Old Encounters, New Excursions.* New Brunswick, N.J.: Transaction Publishers, 1994.
Frantz, Klaus. *Indian Reservations in the United States: Territory, Sovereignty, and Economic Change.* Chicago: University of Chicago Press, 1999.
Fritz, Henry Eugene. *The Movement for Indian Assimilation, 1860–1890.* Philadelphia: University of Pennsylvania Press, 1963.
Fuchs, Victor R. *The Economics of the Fur Industry.* New York: Columbia University Press, 1957.
Ghere, David Lynn. "Abenaki Factionalism, Emigration and Social Continuity: Indian Society in Northern New England, 1725 to 1765." Ph.D. diss., University of Maine, Orono, 1988.
———. "Diplomacy and War on the Maine Frontier." In *Maine the Pine Tree State: From Prehistory to the Present,* ed. Richard W. Judd, Edwin A. Churchill, and Joel W. Eastman. Orono: University of Maine Press, 1995.
———. "The 'Disappearance' of the Abenaki in Western Maine: Political Organization and Ethnocentric Assumptions." In *After King Philip's War: Presence and Persistence in Indian New England,* ed. Colin Calloway. Hanover, N.H.: University Press of New England, 1997.
Glassie, Henry. "Tradition." *Journal of American Folklore* 108 (fall 1995): 430.
Godfrey, John E. "Castine The Younger." *Collections of the Maine Historical Society.* Bath: Maine Historical Society, 1876, 1st series, vol. 7.
———. "Jean Vincent, Baron De Saint Castin." *Collections of the Maine Historical Society.* Bath: Maine Historical Society, 1876, 1st series, vol. 7.
Grady, Robert F. "A Visit with Henry Mitchell, American Indian Canoe Maker at His Home." American Life Histories: Manuscripts from the Federal Writer's Project, 1936–1940. http://memory.loc.gov/ammem/wpaintro/wpahome.html
Grobsmith, Elizabeth S. "Growing up on Deloria: The Impact of His Work on a New Generation of Anthropologists." In *Indians & Anthropologists: Vine Deloria Jr. and the Critique of Anthropology,* ed. Thomas Biolsi and Larry J. Zimmerman. Tucson: University of Arizona Press, 1997.
Hanson, J. W. *History of the Old Towns of Norridgewock and Canaan.* Boston: The Author, 1849.
Hardy, Walter Manly. "Fall Fur Hunt in Maine," parts 1–6. *Forest and Stream* 54 (January–June, 1910), vol. 54, no. 1, 728–31; 2: 768–70; 3: 808–11; 4: 848–51; 5: 888–90; 6: 928–29.
Harrington, J. P. "The Ethnogeography of the Tewa Indians." *Annual Report of the Bureau of American Ethnology* 29. Washington, D.C., 1916.
Hatch, Louis Clinton. *Maine: A History.* New York: The American Historical Society, 1919.
Hempstead, Alfred G. *The Penobscot Boom and the Development of the West Branch of the Penobscot River for Log Driving.* University of Maine Studies, 2nd series, no. 18. Orono, Maine: The University Press, 1931; privately reprinted, n.p., 1975.
The Hill-Top, vol. 27, no. 9 (1922).
Hoover, Herbert T. "Vine Deloria, Jr., in American Historiography." In *Indians & Anthropologists: Vine Deloria Jr. and the Critique of Anthropology,* ed.

Thomas Biolsi and Larry J. Zimmerman. Tucson: University of Arizona Press, 1997.

Horsman, Reginald. *Expansion and American Indian Policy, 1783–1812*. East Lansing: Michigan University Press, 1967.

Hoskins, Sam'l W., and Joseph Nicolar. *Reports of the Agent and the Superintendent of Farming of the Penobscot Tribe of Indians*. Augusta: Sprague, Owen & Nash, 1879.

Hoxie, Frederick. *Parading through History: The Making of the Crow Nation in America, 1805–1935*. Cambridge: Cambridge University Press, 1995.

Hubbard, Rev. William. *A General History of New England From its Discovery to MDCLXXX*. Cambridge, Mass.: Hillard & Metcalf, 1815.

———. *The history of the Indian wars in New England, from the first settlement to the termination of the war with King Philip in 1677*. New York: B. Franklin, 1971. Reprint of the 1865 ed. first published in 1677 as *A narrative of the troubles with the Indians in New England*.

———. *A narrative of the troubles with the Indians in New England, from the first planting thereof in the year 1607 to this present year 1677. But chiefly of the late troubles in the two last years, 1675 and 1676. To which is added a discourse about the warre with the Pequods in the year 1637*. Boston: Printed by John Foster, 1677; microfilm: Ann Arbor, Mich., University Microfilms [n.d.], 1 reel. American culture series, reel 7.76.

The Indian Prayer Book, compiled and arranged for the benefit of the Penobscot and Passamaquoddy Tribes. Boston: H. L. Devereux, 1834.

"Indians in Maine." *Christian Mirror*, January 24, 1823.

Innis, Harold Adam. *The Fur Trade in Canada: An Introduction to Canadian Economic History*. New Haven: Yale University Press, 1930.

Ives, Edward D. *George Magoon and the Down East Game War*. Urbana: University of Illinois Press, 1988.

Ives, Edward D., et al. *Argyle Boom*. Northeast Folklore 17. Orono: Northeast Folklore Society, 1976.

Jackson, Charles T. *Reports on Geology of Maine*. Augusta: Maine Geological Survey, 1837.

Jennings, Francis. "A Growing Partnership: Historians, Anthropologists and American Indian History." *The History Teacher*, vol. 14, no. 1 (November 1980).

Johnson, Steven F. *Ninnuock (the People): The Algonkian People of New England*. Marlborough, Mass.: Bliss Publishing Co., 1995.

Johnson, Troy Joane Nagel, and Duane Champagne. *American Indian Activism: Alcatraz to the Longest Walk*. Urbana: University of Illinois Press, 1997.

Judd, Richard W., Edwin A. Churchill, and Joel W. Eastman, eds., *Maine the Pine Tree State: From Prehistory to the Present*. Orono: University of Maine Press, 1995.

"Justice Department Outlines Indian Case." *Bangor Daily News*, March 2, 1977.

Kidder, Frederick. *Military Operations in Eastern Maine and Nova Scotia during the Revolution*. Albany: Joel Munsell, 1867.

Konrad, Lee-Ann, with Christine Nicholas. *Artists of the Dawn: Christine Nicholas & Senabeh*. Orono: Northeast Folklore Society, 1987.

Leader, Judith. "An Ethnohistory of the Passamaquoddy Tribe." Ph.D. diss., Boston University, 1995.

Lescarbot, Marc. *Histoire de la Nouvelle-France / par Marc Lescarbot*. Suivie des Muses de la Nouvelle-France [microform]. Paris: Librairie Tross, 1866.

Lord, Robert Howard, John E. Sexton, and Edward T. Harrington. *History of the Archdiocese of Boston in the Various Stages of its Development, 1604–1943.* 3 vols. New York: Sheed & Ward, 1944.

Lounsbury, Floyd. "Iroquois Place-Names in the Champlain Valley." *Report of the New York–Vermont Interstate Commission on Lake Champlain Basin.* New York: Legislative Document 9. Albany, 1960.

Lowrey, Nathan. "Tales of the Northern Maine Woods: The History and Traditions of the Maine Guide." In *Motor Camps and Maine Guides, Northeast Folklore* Volume 28, part 2. Orono: The Northeast Folklore Society, 1989.

Lucey, William Leo, S.J. *The Catholic Church in Maine.* Francestown, N.H.: Marshal Jones Co., 1957.

MacDougall, Pauleena M. "Grandmother, Daughter, Princess, Squaw: Native American Female Stereotypes in Historical Perspective." *Maine History* 34 (summer 1994): 37–38.

———. "Native American Industry: Basket Weaving among the Wabanaki." In *American Indian Studies: An Interdisciplinary Approach to Contemporary Issues,* ed. Dane Morrison. New York: Peter Lang Publishing, 1997.

———. "Weaving a Tradition: Women Basket Makers in Penobscot Culture." In *Of Place and Gender: Women in Maine History,* ed. Marli Weiner. Orono: University of Maine Press, 2003.

MacFarlane, Ronald O. "The Massachusetts Bay Truckhouses in Diplomacy with the Indians." *New England Quarterly* 11 (March 1938).

Maine Indian Tribal-State Commission. *Wabanaki: A New Dawn.* Tribal State Commission video, 1995.

Maine Indian Tribal-State Commission. "Pine Tree Legal Assistance." http://janus.state.me.us/legis/statutes30/title30sec6212.html. February 18, 1999.

———. *A Compilation of Laws Pertaining to Indians.* Augusta: Maine Department of Indian Affairs, 1974.

Maine, State of. Acts and resolves passed by the . . . Legislature of the state of Maine. Augusta: Stevens & Sayward, 1840–1965.

———. Legislature. Legislative Research Committee. *Public laws of Maine.* Augusta [s.n.], 1820–39.

———. *Resolve of the Maine Legislature,* February 23, 1866. Portland: Francis Douglas, 1820.

———. *Resolves of the Legislature of the State of Maine.* Augusta: Smith and Robinson, Printers to the State, 1820–39.

———. *Resolves of the State of Maine,* chapter 17, 489, February 13, 1826; March 1859.

Maine Historical Society. *Documentary History of the State of Maine.* Portland: Bailey and Noyes, 1869–1916. 24 v. Collections of the Maine historical society. Second series. I. A history of the discovery of Maine, by J. G. Kohl. 1869. II. A discourse on western planting, written . . . 1584, by R. Hakluyt . . . Preface and an introduction, by L. Woods . . . ed. . . . by C. Deane. 1877. III. The Trelawny papers. ed. . . . by J. P. Baxter. 1884. IV–VI. The Baxter manuscripts. [v. 1–3] ed. by J. P. Baxter. 1889–1900. VII–VIII. The Farnham papers . . . comp. by Mary F. Farnham. 1901–02. IX–XXIV. The Baxter manuscripts. [v. 4–19] ed. by J. P. Baxter. 1907–16.

Mander, Jerry. *In the Absence of the Sacred: The Failure of Technology and the Survival of the Indian Nations.* San Francisco: Sierra Club Books, 1991.

Martin, Calvin. *Keepers of the Game: Indian-Animal Relationships and the Fur Trade.* Berkeley: University of California Press, 1978.
Massachusetts, State of. *Massachusetts Resolves,* June 15, Mass. Archives 144: 313. In *Resolves of the General Court of the Commonwealth of Massachusetts.* Boston: Russell, Cuther & Co., 1816.
McBride, Bunny. *Molly Spotted Elk, a Penobscot in Paris.* Norman: University of Oklahoma Press, 1995.
———. *Women of the Dawn.* Lincoln: University of Nebraska Press, 1999.
McMullen, Ann, and Russell G. Handsman, eds. *A Key into the Language of Woodsplint Baskets.* Washington, Conn.: American Indian Archaeological Institute, 1987.
McNeill, W. H. *Plagues and Peoples: A Natural History of Infectious Diseases.* New York: Anchor Press/Doubleday, 1976.
Meek, Ronald L. *Social Science and the Ignoble Savage.* Cambridge: Cambridge University Press, 1976.
Meredith, Howard. *Modern American Indian Tribal Government and Politics.* Tsaile, Ariz.: Navajo Community College Press, 1993.
Meyer, Carter Jones, and Diana Royer, eds. *Selling the Indian: Commercializing and Appropriating American Indian Cultures.* Tucson: University of Arizona Press, 2001.
Mihesuah, Devon A. *Natives and Academics: Researching and Writing about American Indians.* Lincoln: University of Nebraska Press, 1998.
Miller, Perry. *Errand into the Wilderness.* Cambridge, Mass.: Belknap Press, 1956.
Mitchell, John Bear, Barry Dana, Huey, and Michael Vermette, producers. *Our Dances.* Video, Indian Island School, 1997.
Mitchell, Theodore. Tape-recorded interview. Northeast Archives #2387. Maine Folklife Center, University of Maine, Orono.
Moody, Robert Earle. "The Maine Frontier, 1607–1763." Ph.D. diss., Yale University, 1978.
Morgan, Lewis Henry. *Ancient Society; or, Researches in the Lines of Human Progress from Savagery through Barbarism to Civilization.* New York: Henry Holt & Co., 1877.
———. *League of the Ho-de-no-sau-nee, or Iroquois.* Rochester: Sage, 1851.
———. *League of the Iroquois.* New York: Corinth Books, 1962.
Morris, Gerald E. *The Maine Bicentennial Atlas and Historical Survey.* Portland: The Maine Historical Society, 1976.
Morrison, Kenneth M. *The Embattled Northeast: The Elusive Ideal of Alliance in Abenaki-Euramerican Relations.* Berkeley: University of California Press, 1984.
———. "Sebastien Rasles and Norridgewock, 1724: The Eckstorm Conspiracy Thesis Reconsidered." *Maine Historical Society Quarterly* 14 (1974).
Munson, Gorham. "St. Castin: A Legend Revised." *Dalhousie Review,* vol. 45, no. 3 (1965).
Murch v. Tomer, 21 Maine, 537. Opinion of court as drawn up by C. J. Whitman. U.S. Constitution, 15th Amendment and U.S. Congress, Act of June 2, 1924 (43 Stat. 253).
Nash, Gary B. *Red, White & Black: The Peoples of Early North America.* Englewood Cliffs, N.J.: Prentice-Hall, 1992.

Native American Rights Fund. "Announcements." *Annual Report*, vol. 7, no. 1 (May 1981). Boulder, Colo.: Native American Rights Fund. http://www.narf.org/pubs/index.html

Nicolar, Joseph. *The Life and Traditions of the Red Man*. Bangor: C. H. Glass, 1893.

———. "Report of Superintendent of Farming," Oldtown, Maine, December 22, 1879. In George F. Dillingham, *Report of the Agent of the Penobscot Tribe of Indians*. Augusta: Stevens & Sayward, 1879.

North, Callahan H. "Henry Knox, His Part in the American Revolutions, 1775 to 1784." Ph.D. diss., New York University, 1956.

Norton, David. *Sketches of the Town of Old Town From its Earliest Settlement to 1897*. Bangor: S. G. Robinson, 1881.

O'Callaghan, Edmund Bailey. *The Documentary History of the State of New York*. Albany: Weed, Parsons and Co., 1850–51.

Ogunwole, Stelle U. *The American Indian and Alaska Native Population 2000*. Washington, D.C.: U.S. Department of Commerce, Economics, and Statistics Administration, 2002.

Parkhill, Thomas C. *Weaving Ourselves into the Land: Charles Godfrey Leland, "Indians," and the Study of Native American Religions*. Albany: State University of New York Press, 1997.

Parkman, Frances. *The Conspiracy of Pontiac and the Indian War after the Conquest of Canada*. Toronto: George Morang, 1851.

———. *The Jesuits in North America in the Seventeenth Century*. Boston: Little, Brown & Co., 1927.

"Passamaquoddies Aim: $150 Million from Bay State." *Bangor Daily News*, March 11, 1968.

"Passamaquoddies Go on Legal Warpath against Commonwealth of Massachusetts." *Lewiston Journal*, March 9, 1968.

Penhallow, Samuel. *The History of the Wars of New-England with the Eastern Indians, or A narrative of their continued perfidy and cruelty, from the 10th of August, 1703, to the peace renewed 13th of July, 1713. And from the 25th of July, 1722, to their submission 15th December, 1725, which was ratified August 5th, 1726*. Cincinnati: Reprinted for Wm. Dodge by J. Harpel, 1859.

Peyser, Joseph L., ed., *On the Eve of the Conquest: The Chevalier de Raymond's Critique of New France in 1754*. East Lansing: Michigan State University Press, 1997.

Phillips, Ruth B. *Trading Identities: The Souvenir in Native North American Art from the Northeast, 1700–1900*. Seattle: University of Washington Press, 1998.

Pinkham, Ira E. "Report of the Indian Agent of the Penobscot Tribe of Indians," Old Town, Maine, December 12, 1919. Maine State Archives, Augusta.

Prescott, W. H. *The Conquest of Mexico*. 2 vols. New York: Dutton, 1843.

Prucha, Francis Paul. *American Indian Policy in the Formative Years: The Indian Trade and Intercourse Acts, 1780–1834*. Cambridge, Mass.: Harvard University Press, 1962.

———. *The Great Father: The United States Government and the American Indians*. 2 vols. Lincoln: University of Nebraska Press, 1984.

———. *Indian Peace Medals in American History*. Madison: State Historical Society of Wisconsin, 1971.

Purchas, Samuel. "Description of Mawooshen." In *Hakluytus posthumus, or*

Purchas his Pilgrimages: contayning a history of the world in sea voyages and lande travells by Englishmen and others. Glasgow: J. MacLehose and Sons, 1905–7.
Purinton, James A. *Reports of the Indian Agents of the State of Maine.* Augusta: Stevens & Sayward, 1860–61.
Quinn, David B. "The Early Cartography of Maine." In *American Beginnings: Exploration, Culture, and Cartography in the Land of Norumbega,* ed. Emerson W. Baker, Edwin A. Churchill, Richard S. D'Abate, Kristine L. Jones, Victor A. Konrad, and Harald E. L. Prins. Lincoln: University of Nebraska Press, 1994.
Quinn, David B., Alison M. Quinn, and Susan Hillier, eds. *New American World: A Documentary History of North America to 1612.* 5 vols. New York: Arno Press, 1979.
Ramenofsky, Ann F. *Vectors of Death: The Archeology of European Contact.* Albuquerque: University of New Mexico Press, 1987.
Roberts, Kenneth, ed. *March to Quebec: Journals of the Members of Arnold's Expedition.* New York: Doubleday, 1953.
Roseberry, William. *Anthropologies and Histories: Essays in History, Culture and Political Economy.* New Brunswick, N.J.: Rutgers University Press, 1989.
Sahlins, Marshall. *How "Natives" Think: About Captain Cook, for Example.* Chicago: University of Chicago Press, 1995.
Salisbury, Neal. *Manitou and Providence: Indians, Europeans, and the Making of New England, 1500–1643.* New York: Oxford University Press, 1982.
Sanger, David. "An Analysis of Seasonal Transhumance Models for Pre-European State of Maine." *Review of Archeology* 17 (spring 1996).
Satz, Ronald N. *American Indian Policy in the Jacksonian Era.* Lincoln: University of Nebraska Press, 1975.
Shay, Madeline. Penobscot Primer Project, created by Richard Garrett with the assistance of Carol Dana, Barry Dana, and Frank Siebert. Hudson Museum, University of Maine, Orono.
Shay, Madeline Tomer. Tape-recorded interview. Northeast Archives #2383. Maine Folklife Center, University of Maine, Orono, 1985.
Sheehan, Bernard W. *Seeds of Extinction: Jeffersonian Philanthropy and the American Indian.* Chapel Hill: University of North Carolina Press, 1973.
Shetterly, Susan Hand. "The River They Call Home." *Audubon,* July/August 2000.
Shirley, William. *Correspondence of William Shirley* 1:253–54; 261; reprinted in *Journal of the Massachusetts House of Representatives,* August 23, 1745.
Siebert, Frank T., Jr. "First Maine Indian War: Incident at Machias." In *Actes du Quatorzieme Congres des Algonquinistes,* ed. William Cowan. Ottawa: Carleton University, 1983.
———. "The Identity of the Tarratines, with an Etymology." *Studies in Linguistics* 23 (1973).
———. "Wenemouet, Wenongonet." In *Dictionary of Canadian Biography* 2:664.
Simmons, William S. *Spirit of the New England Tribes: Indian History and Folklore.* Hanover, N.H.: University Press of New England, 1986.
Smith, David C. *A History of Lumbering in Maine, 1861–1960.* University of Maine Studies no. 93. Orono: University of Maine Press, 1972.
Snow, Dean. "Eastern Abenaki." In *Handbook of North American Indians,* vol.

15: *Northeast*, ed. Bruce Trigger. Washington, D.C.: Smithsonian Institution, 1978.
Society for the Propagation of the Gospel. *Sermon.* Boston: Nathaniel Willis, 1814.
———. *Sermon*, November 5, 1829. Boston: Putnam and Hunt, 1829.
Sockalexis, Michael. Informal interview with author, August 1, 2000.
Speck, Frank G. "Eastern Algonkian Block Stamp Decoration: A New World Original or an Acculturated Art." *Archeological Society of New Jersey, Research Series* 1. Trenton, N.J., 1947.
———. *Penobscot Man: The Life History of a Forest Tribe in Maine.* Orono: University of Maine Press, 1999.
———. "Penobscot Tales and Religious Beliefs." *The Journal of American Folk-Lore* 48, no. 187 (January–March 1935):1–107.
———. "Penobscot Shamanism." In *Memoirs of the American Anthropological Association*, vol. 6, no. 28. Millwood, N.Y.: Kraus reprint, 1919.
———. "Penobscot Transformer Tales." *International Journal of American Linguistics*, vol. 1, no. 3. New York: Douglas C. McMurtrie, 1918.
Spence, Lewis. *Myth and Ritual in Dance, Game, and Rhyme.* London: Watts and Co., 1947.
Sprague's Journal of Maine History, vol. 1, no. 2, (July 1913).
Stelmok, Jerry, and Rollin Thurlow. *The Wood and Canvas Canoe: A Complete Guide to Its History, Construction, Restoration, and Maintenance.* Gardiner: The Harpswell Press, 1987.
Stirling, Matthew W. "America's First Settlers, the Indians." *National Geographic*, November 1937, 565.
Stowe, John H. *Reports of the Agent of the Penobscot Tribe of Indians for the Years 1888–1894.* Augusta: Burleigh & Flynt, 1894.
Sullivan, James. *The History of the District of Maine.* Boston: [s.n.] 1795. Printed by I. Thomas and E. T. Andrews.
Taylor, Alan. *Liberty Men and Great Proprietors.* Chapel Hill: University of North Carolina Press, 1990.
Thoreau, Henry David. *The Maine Woods.* Boston: Ticknor and Fields, 1864; reprint, Thomas Y. Crowell Co., 1966.
Thornton, Russell, ed. *Studying Native America: Problems and Prospects.* Madison: Wisconsin University Press, 1998.
Thwaites, Reuben Gold. "Lettre du P. Biard." In *Travels and Explorations of the Jesuit Missionaries in New France.* Cleveland: Burrows Brothers, 1896.
———, ed. *The Jesuit Relations and Allied Documents: Travels and Explorations of the Jesuit Missionaries in New France, 1610–1791.* New York: Pageant Book Co., 1959.
Trask, William B., ed. *Letters of Colonel Thomas Westbrook and Others Relative to Indian Affairs in Maine, 1722–1726.* Boston, 1901.
Trigger, Bruce G. *Natives and Newcomers: Canada's "Heroic Age" Reconsidered.* Kingston and Montreal: McGill-Queen's University Press, 1985.
The True Workingman (Lynn, Mass.), December 27, 1845.
United States. "Maine Indian Claims Settlement Act of 1980," vol. 1, 96th Congress, Second Session, LAWS (P.L. 96-420), ch. 19, Title 25, subchapter 2, sec. 1724 and sec. 6212, U.S. Code Congressional and Administrative News, 1980.
———. U.S. Code Congressional and Administrative News, 1980, Maine Indian Claims Settlement, Federal Act, ch. 19, Title 25, subchapter 2, sec. 6212.

———. Report of January 22, 1818, *American State Papers: Indian Affairs*, Indian Affairs, 2:150–51.
United States Congress. "An Act to Provide for the Settlement of Land Claims of Indians, Indian Nations, and Tribes and Bands of Indians in the State of Maine, Including the Passamaquoddy Tribe, the Penobscot Nation, and the Houlton Band of Maliseet Indians, and for Other Purposes." Washington, D.C.: Superintendent of Documents, 1980.
United States District Court Northern Division. *The United States of America, Plaintiff, v. The State of Maine, Defendant.* Civil Action Docket no. 1966 N.D.
Vetromile, Eugene. *The Abenakis and Their History.* New York: J. B. Kirker, 1866.
———. *Indian Good Book.* New York: E. Dunigan & Brother, 1856.
Viola, Herman J. *Thomas L. McKenney: Architect of America's Early Indian Policy, 1816–1830.* Chicago: Sage Books, 1974.
United States Census Bureau, 1990, http://www.census.gov/cdrom/lookup
Whig and Courier, April 10, 1883.
Williamson, Joseph. "The British Occupation of Penobscot During the Revolution." *Maine Historical Society*, 2nd series. Portland, 1890.
Williamson, William D. "History of Penobscot County." In *Collections of the Maine Historical Society.*
———. *The History of the State of Maine; From Its First Discovery, AD 1602, The Separation, AD 1820, inclusive.* Hallowell: Glazier, Masters & Smith, 1839.
Willis, William, ed. *Journals of the Reverend Thomas Smith and the Rev. Samuel Deane, Pastors of the First Church in Portland.* Portland: Joseph Bailey, 1849.
Wiseman, Frederick Matthew. *The Voice of the Dawn: An Autohistory of the Abenaki Nation.* Hanover, N.H.: University Press of New England, 2001.
Wolf, Eric. *Europe and the People without History.* Berkeley: University of California Press, 1982.
Wood, Pamela. "In Search of the 20th Century Penobscot." *Salt* (winter 1983).
Wooden Canoe Heritage Association, Ltd. "Old Town Canoes." Reprint of 1910 catalogue of the Old Town Canoe Company. "Canoes First Made by Indians."
Wormwood, D. Lyman, superintendent of schools, to George H. Hunt, appended to "Penobscot Indians, Report of Agent to Indian Affairs," December 31, 1909. Executive Council papers, Maine State Archives.
Young, Susan. "Tribe Tests of Water Led to Fine: Falsified Records Cost Champion $800,000." *Bangor Daily News*, July 24, 2000, 1.

Manuscript Sources

Blake, Papers of General John, Indian Agent for Massachusetts, 1811–1821. Photocopy. Bangor Museum and Center for History, Bangor, Maine.
Collection de Manuscripts contenant lettres, Memoires, et autres documents historiques relatifs a la Nouvelle-France. 4 vols. Quebec: Legislature de Quebec, 1883–85.
Eckstorm, Fannie Hardy. Papers. Special Collections. Raymond H. Fogler Library, University of Maine, Orono.
Executive Council papers, 1820–49. 48 boxes. Maine State Archives, Augusta.
Executive Council Reports no. 908, 1828. Maine State Archives, Augusta.

Hunt, George H. Report of the Indian Agent of the Penobscot Tribe of Indians, 1899–1906. Indian Affairs, Maine State Archives, Augusta, Maine.
"The Journals of John Edwards Godfrey." Special Collections. Raymond H. Fogler Library, University of Maine, Orono.
Lagerbom, Charles H. "Jonathan Lowder's Truckhouse: the history and archæology of a colonial trading post on the Maine frontier during the American Revolutionary War." Master's thesis, University of Maine, Orono, 1991.
Legislative Graveyard, 1835–1902. Maine State Archives, Augusta.
Letter to the Rev. B. Fenwick, Bishop of Boston, Mass. Old Town Indians, June 14, 1836. Photocopy at St. Ann's Church, Indian Island.
Massachusetts Archives, 1622–1799. Boston: Commonwealth of Massachusetts, Archives Division. 1977 reels. Microfilm M3821 1–326. Raymond H. Fogler Library, University of Maine, Orono.
Massachusetts Council Records, July 25, 1721; October 19, 1721; February 9, 1721/22; February 19, 1721/22; Massachusetts Council, "Resolution Concerning trade with the Eastern Indians," October 14, 1727. Raymond H. Fogler Library, University of Maine, Orono.
Penobscot Lumbering Association Ledgers. 2 vols., 28 items. Special Collections. Raymond H. Fogler Library, University of Maine, Orono.
Proctor, Ralph W. "Report on Maine Indians: Prepared for the Legislative Research Committee, September 1942." Typescript. Augusta, Maine: Legislative Research Committee, 1942. Special Collections, Raymond F. Fogler Library, University of Maine, Orono.
Siebert, Frank T., Jr. Manuscript of Penobscot tales. Siebert Papers, American Philosophical Society, Philadelphia.
Siebert, Frank T., Jr. Penobscot Dictionary. Ms. Papers of Frank T. Siebert, American Philosophical Society Library, Philadelphia, Pennsylvania.
Treat, Joseph. "Journal and Plans of Surveys, 1820." Manuscript. Executive Council Records, Maine State Archives, Augusta.
United States Census Bureau. 1890 Census, National Archives, Washington, D.C. Maine State Archives, Augusta.
Vetromille, Eugene. Papers. Manuscript Collections no. 114. Maine Historical Society, Portland.

Index

Abenakis: early contact of, with Europeans, 49–51; epidemics, 58; in colonial era wars, 71, 72–3, 78, 79, 80, 81–2, 84, 85, 86
accommodationists: defined, 4
activists, 201
agents: complaints to state about, 152, 153–4, 155–6, 160–1; intra-tribal conflicts over, 151–2, 161
agriculture, 141–2; as basis of assimilation, 114, 122; corn cultivation, 57–8; failure of, 146, 147–8; priests encourage, 63–4; state assistance for, 142–5, 148
Akins, Andrew: as reform leader, 22–23
Akwesasne Notes, 25
Alcatraz: occupation of, 24, 25
alliances, Penobscot: with Abenakis, 71, 72–3, 84, 86, 197; with French, 69, 72, 85, 86; with Micmacs, 74; with Passamaquoddies and Maliseets, 90, 99–100
American Indian Movement (AIM): 23, 24, 25
Arnold, Benedict: fails to rely on Penobscots, 97–8
assimilation: as American Indian policy, 93–4; 107, 108–9, 112, 198; resisted by Penobscots, 150, 195. *See also* agriculture
Attean, John, 112; death on river drive, 176; and intra-tribal factions, 152, 154, 158, 160

Attean, Joseph: described by Thoreau, 178–9
Axtell, James: on politics of Native American studies, 7–8

Bank, Dennis: and AIM, 26
Banks, John, 32, 33
barter dance game and ceremony. *See* dancing; trade and trading posts
baskets and basket making, 181; Calais co-op, 23; during Depression era, 19; more lucrative than farming, 145, 149; for tourist trade, 188–92, 198. *See also* Maine Indian Basketmakers Alliance
Basso, Keith: on place names, 38
Baxter State Park: occupation of, 23
Berthiaume, Juniper: as priest for Penobscots, 115
Bessabez (Beshabes): death of, 50, 52; encounters with European explorers, 47, 48–9; and Micmac-Abenaki war, 49, 50, 51
Boas, Franz, 3; on place names, 38
Bourque, Bruce, 157
Brewer, Josiah: serves in Revolutionary War, 99, 101, 102; as truckmaster for Penobscots, 104, 105

Call, Samuel: as agent for Penobscots, 151–2
Calloway, Colin: on importance of trade, 99; Indians as the frontier, 72; war as ecological disaster, 70

canoes: birch-bark, 183–4; canvas replaces bark, 184–5; Old Town Canoe Company, 184, 185–7
Carlisle Indian School: as secondary school for Indians, 21, 139
Carter, Jimmy: and Indian Land Claims, 29
Castin. *See* St. Castin, Jean-Vincent d'Abbadie de
Catholicism: adopted by Penobscots, 54, 59; Penobscot retention of, 34–5, 114–16, 118, 119, 149, 198; and traditional culture, 119. *See also* education; Jesuits; Sisters of Mercy
Chamberlain, Joshua Samuel: as agent for Penobscots, 153–4, 155
Champagne, Duane: on politics of Native American studies, 7
Champlain, Samuel de, 57; encounters Penobscots, 47: on early Penobscot wars, 50–1
Cheverus, John: as priest for Penobscots, 116–17
Church, Benjamin: leads British assaults on French and Penobscots, 74
civil rights and voting rights: lack of, 18, 19; and taxes, 187
Civil War: Penobscot participation in, 162–3
Cox, Archibald: and Indian Land Claims, 28–9
cultural revival: after Lands Claim settlement, 33–4. *See also* Penobscot traditional culture
culture: anthropological definition of, 3
Curtis, Kenneth, 28

Dana, Albert C., 29
Dana, Barry: and cultural revival, 23, 24, 34; and Mount Katahdin run, 33
Dana, Carol: and cultural revival, 33
Dana, Roy: and guides, 181; on river drives, 175
dancing: barter dance, 107; green corn dance, 43; as metaphor for Penobscot history, 12; traditional, 10–11; war dance, 68–9
Dawes Severalty Act (1887), 159

Deloria, Vine, Jr.: on Alcatraz occupation, 25; critique of non-native scholarship, 4–6
DeMallie, Raymond J., 71
Dillingham, George: on fur trade, 167
discrimination. *See* education, and discrimination in public schools; racism and discrimination
diseases and epidemics, 52, 75, 77; population losses due to, 55–8, 84; social and cultural changes as result of, 59
Dobyns, Henry F., 55, 56

Eckstorm, Fannie Hardy, 172; on Chief Orono, 95; on Indian guides, 180; on Indian river drivers, 173
education, 126; and discrimination in public schools, 21; Indian Island school, 130–2; literacy levels, 133, 134, 140; Mattanawcook Island school, 132, 137, 138; Olamon Island school, 133, 137, 138, 139–40; Protestant mission schools, 128–30; Sisters of Mercy as teachers, 135–8; state support for, 130–1, 133, 134, 135, 136, 137, 140. *See also* Carlisle Indian School; Sisters of Mercy
environmental issues: continuing disputes involving, 32; in Gluskabe tales, 37–8; and Maine Indian Tribal-State Commission, 30. *See also* Penobscot traditional culture, reverence for land in
Euro-Americans: initial contact with Penobscots, 46–53; world views of, contrasted with Indians, 45–6, 80–1

firearms: as essential for hunting, 71; impact of, on Indian wars, 51–2
Fixico, Donald, 6, 7
Fox, Robin: on politics of Native American studies, 7
Francis, Roland "Senabeh": influence on traditionalists, 23
Francis, Violet: on Indian Island bridge, 21
French, the. *See* alliances, Penobscot, with French

Gellers, Donald: and Passamaquoddy suit (1968), 27
Ghere, David, 88; on tribal factions, 153
Glassie, Henry: on dynamics of tradition, 52-3
Gluskabe, 35; and traditional Penobscot culture, 36-8, 119-20, 196
Great Depression: impact on Penobscots, 192-5
guides and guiding, 171; and conflicts with game laws, 180; Penobscots employed as, 148; use of traditional skills in, 176-81
guns. *See* firearms
Gunter, William B.: and Indian Land Claims, 29

Hardy, Jonathan: and fur trade, 167-71
Hardy, Walter "Manly": and fur trade, 168, 171-2
Harrington, J. P., 38
Hathaway, William, 28
Hayford, Arvida: as agent for Penobscots, 160-1
Hoskins, Samuel W.: on fur trade, 167-8
Houlton Band of Maliseets: and Indian Land Claims settlemet, 29
hunting: firearms as essential for, 71; and fur trade in nineteenth century, 165, 166-72. *See also* trade and trading posts
Hussey, Samuel: as agent for Penobscots, 154-6

Indian Island: bridge to mainland, 21; mid-twentieth century conditions, 18-19; school, 21, 130-2; village destroyed (1723), 82
Indian policy, American: philosophic basis of, 112-14, 126-8
Indian rights movement: precursors of, 22, 24-5

Jennings, Francis: on ethnohistory, 4
Jesuits: as advocates for Penobscots, 69, 71-2, 77-8, 79-80, 104, 105. *See also* Catholicism

Kennedy, Ernest: on river drives, 176
Ketchum, Louis: as guide, 197-80
King George's War, 85
King Philip's War, 70-3
King William's War, 73-4
kinship: as basis of alliances, 50, 55, 64-5, 71, 72, 91
Knox, Henry: negotiates for Penobscot land, 110; and Nonintercourse Act (1790), 28
Korean War: as catalyst for political action, 18
Kyros, Peter, 28

LaDuke, Winona: cited, 1
land. *See* Penobscot lands
land allotments: and intra-tribal factions, 159
language: cultural significance of, 38-9; Penobscots learn English and French, 63; retention of, 197
Lauverjat, Etienne: as advocate for Penobscots, 79-80
linguistics, 16
Lolar, Jake, 9
Longley, James: leads opposition to Indian Land Claims, 28
Loron. *See* Saguarum, Loron
Loundsbury, Floyd, 38
Lowder, Jonathan: serves in Revolutionary War, 101; as truckmaster, 99-100, 103-4
lumbering: creates market for hides, 169-70; by Penobscots as assertion of sovereignty, 155; on Penobscot lands, 141, 142; river drives, 173-6; and shore leases, 147, 155-6, 160; as source of employment, 145-6

Madockawando: as leader, 73, 74-5
Maine Central Railroad: and tourist business, 178
Maine Indian Basketmakers Alliance, 34. *See also* baskets and basket making
Maine Indian Land Claims, 18; settlement of (1980), 9, 29-30; roots of, 26-7; and Tom Tureen, 27, 28-29;

Maine Indian Land Claims *(continued)* status of tribes after settlement of, 30–2
Maine Indian Land Claims Act (1980), 201
Maine Indian Tribal-State Commission: established, 30
Maine State Indian policy, 126–8
Maliseets: and war with Abenakis (1607–1615), 50–1. *See also* Houlton Band of Maliseets
Massachusetts Bay Colony: armed conflicts with, 82–4, 89; Penobscot negotiations with, 81–2, 86–8, 94–5, 103–4; and 1786 treaty, 27–8; trading abuses by, 78–9, 86–8
McKenney, Thomas L.: and American Indian policy, 114
McNeill, W. H., 55
Means, Russell: and AIM, 26
Micmacs: alliance with Penobscots, 74; early trade with Europeans, 49; and war with Abenakis (1607–1615), 49, 50, 51
Mihesuah, Devon: on research standards, 6
Mitchell, Dana, 9; and cultural revival, 33
Mitchell, Henry: on taxation, 193–4; on working at Old Town Canoe, 186–7
Mitchell, Theodore: on basket trade, 191, 193
Mohawks: as enemies of Abenakis, 42, 64, 66
Morgan, Lewis Henry: racist assumptions in writings of, 113
Muscongus Patent: and expansion of settlements on Penobscot land, 89
Muskie, Edmund S., 28

National Indian Youth Council, 24
Native Americans: current status of, 1–2; early studies of, 3–4; Indian critiques of non-native scholarship, 4–8; stereotypes of, 9; struggles between traditionalists and accommodationists, 4
negotiation, 196–7

Neptune, John: as guide, 178
Neptune, Lewis: as guide to Henry David Thoreau, 178
Neptune, Stanley, 23; and cultural revival, 33, 34
Newell, Wayne: and cultural revival, 34
Nicolar, Joseph: and Gluskabe tales, 36, 37
Nixon, Richard: and Indian Land Claims suit, 28
Nonintercourse Act (1790): as basis of land claims suit (1968), 27, 28

Old Town Canoe Company: founding of, 185–6; Penobscots employed by, 186–7
Orono, Joseph: family background, 95; negotiates with Massachusetts, 94–5, 103–4; rejects attempts to take land, 110, 111

pan-Indian culture, 4
Parkhill, Thomas: on stereotypes of Native American, 8
Parkman, Francis: racist assumptions in writings of, 113
Passamaquoddies: gain federal status, 23; and Maine Indian Land Claims case, 9, 27, 29–30; in Revolutionary War, 90, 99–100, 101
Paul, Erlene: as reform leader, 22
Pehrson, Walter, 23
Pehrson, Junior: on schooling, 21
Pemaquid: fought over by French and English, 72, 73, 74, 75
Penobscot lands: islands retained, 120–4; lost to state, 157, 158–9. *See also* settlements, expansion of, into Penobscot territory
Penobscots: gain federal status, 23; historiography, 13–14; Indian Island, 14; retreat to Canada, 78, 88–9
Penobscot traditional culture, 46–53; and Catholicism, 119; Grandmother Woodchuck tales, 37–8; Green Corn Mother, 43–4; heroes in, 41–2; reverence for land in, 120–1. *See also* Gluskabe

Penobscot tribal government, 197; election of chiefs, 160, 161, 163, 165; intra-tribal factions, 152-3, 157-8, 160-2. *See also* agents; Massachusetts Bay colony, Penobscot negotiations with; Orono, Joseph; Revolutionary War, negotiations with Massachusetts for support during; Saguarun, Loron; Wambemando; Wenemouet; Wenongonet
Phillips, Ruth: on Indian arts, 189, 190
Polis, Joseph: as guide to Thoreau, 179
Pownall, Thomas: captures Chief Loron, 89; claims Penobscot land by right of conquest, 111
Prescott, William H.: racist assumptions in writings of, 113
Proctor, Ralph: on pre-World War II conditions on Indian Island, 18-19
Protestantism: and agrarian ideal, 114; and missions to Penobscots, 115
Pə̀mole, 41-2

Queen Anne's War, 78-9
Quinn, David, 47

racism and discrimination, 194; in historical writings, 113; in Old Town schools, 21
Ramenofsky, Ann F., 56
Ranco, Nick: on river drives, 175
Rasles, Sabastian: as advocate for Abenakis, 74, 82
religion: *See* Catholicism; education, Protestant mission school; Jesuits; Sisters of Mercy
Revolutionary War: and Benedict Arnold's expedition, 97-8; Maliseet and Passamaquoddy participation in, 99-100, 101; negotiations with Massachusetts for support during, 94-5, 96-7, 99-100, 105; Penobscot expedition, 103; Penobscot participation in, 95-7, 98, 100, 101, 103
river drives. *See* lumbering
Romagne, James Rene: as priest for Penobscots, 117-18, 119. *See also* Catholicism; Jesuits

Roman Catholic Church. *See* Catholicism
Roseberry, William: on ethnohistory, 4

Saguarum, Loron, 83; and peace and trade negotiations, 85, 86, 87; taken prisoner by Massachusetts, 89
Sahlins, Marshall: on culture, 3, 8
Sanger, David, 57
Sapiel, Aselema "Sammy": and "Longest Walk," 26
Sapiel, Francis C. "Bobcat": speaks with Carter about Land Claims, 29
Sapiel, Nicholas: as reform leader, 22
Sapier, James, 18; on religion, 34; as reform leader, 22
Secord, Theresa: and cultural revival, 33, 34
settlements: expansion of, into Penobscot territory, 69, 72, 73, 79-80, 81-2, 89-90, 111
severalty. *See* land allotments
Shad Island: lost, 136; regained, 122
shamanism, 23
Shay, Madeline: on making baskets 34, 195
Sisters of Mercy: as teachers in Penobscot schools, 21, 135-8
smallpox. *See* diseases and epidemics
Smith, Margaret Chase, 28
Sockabasin, Allen J., 29
Sockabasin, Louise, 26
Sockalexis, Michael (Ranco): and cultural revival, 33, 35; as reform leader, 22
sovereignty, 199; conflicts with state over, 153, 154, 155
Speck, Frank G., 57, 201; and Gluskabe tales, 36, 37; on dancing, 11;
Spence, Lewis: on persistence of Native religions, 52
spirituality: as source of power and strength, 40-1
squaw: elimination of in Maine place names, 32, 33
State of Maine v. Dana: implications of, for Land Claims case, 29
St. Castin, Anselm d'Abbadie de, 66, 77; captured in Dummer's War, 82

St. Castin, Jean-Vincent d'Abbadie de: close relations of, with Penobscots, 64–6, 71; marries Madockawando's daughter, 72; and Pemaquid tranding post, 72–3, 74
Stevens, John: as leader of Passamaquoddy activism, 27

Thom, Melvin: and Indian rights, 24
Thoreau, Henry David: on Indian guides, 178–9
tourist trade: baskets for, 188–92; summer pageant, 195
trade and trading posts: and exploitation of Indians, 77, 78–9, 86–8; Penobscot dependence on, 61–2, 71, 91, 98–9; problems with, during Revolutionary War, 96–7, 99–100, 101–2, 103–5. *See also* agents
traditionalists: defined, 4; and radical politics, 23–4
Trafton, Mark Samuel: as agent for Penobscots, 156
treaties, 196: of 1786 rejected by Penobscots, 110–11; of 1794 and land claims case, 26–7; of 1794 leaves Penobscots with only islands, 112; of 1796, 28
Trosper, Ronald: on Native American traditions, 165
Trump, Erik: on appeal of Indian arts and crafts, 188

Tureen, Thomas: enlists Cox, 28–9; takes over Passamaquoddy suit (1968), 27

United States Indian Land Claims Commission (1946), 3

Voeglin, Erminie Wheeler, 3

Wabanaki Federation: founded, 23
Waldo Patent, 109–10
Wambemando, 88
wars: Dummer's war, 82–4; King Phillip's War, 70–3; King Williams's War, 73–4; among Maine tribes, 49; Queen Anne's War, 78–9. *See also* Civil War; Revolutionary War; World War II
Washington, George, 27
Wenemouet: and end of Abenaki alliance, 84, 86; and peace negotiations, 82–3
Wenongonet: as Penobscot chief, 75, 77
Williamson, William D., 35, 51; on Revolutionary War in Maine, 94, 95
Wilson, Richard: opposed by AIM, 26
Wolf, Eric: on culture, 3
women: as basket makers, 154, 181; as farmers, 142; and guiding, 180; in Penobscot oral tradition, 37–8, 42–4
World War II: as catalyst for political action, 18–20